Unleashing Kids' Potential

What Parents, Grandparents, and Teachers Need to Know

By

KAREN A. WALDRON, PH.D.

ROBERT D. REED PUBLISHERS • SAN FRANCISCO, CA

Robert D. Reed Publishers
750 La Playa Street, Suite 647
San Francisco, CA 94121
Phone: 650/994-6570 • Fax: -6579
E-mail: 4bobreed@msn.com
Website: www.rdrpublishers.com

Text Designer: Marilyn Yasmine Nadel
Book Cover: Julia A. Gaskill at Graphics Plus

ISBN 1-885003-89-7
Library of Congress Card Number: 2001088125
Produced and Printed in the United States of America

To my parents, John and Mary Powers,
who gave me a loving home with strong direction
and delightful humor,

And to my brother, Kevin John Powers, whose close
friendship I will always cherish.

Table of Contents

Acknowledgments

So many thanks to my wonderful professional readers and personal friends, who put aside their own work to assure this manuscript's accuracy and readability. Laura M. Allen, Ph.D., Laura Martin Labatt, M.A., and Cheryl R. Hamilton, Ph.D. have given me invaluable input through their wise insights. I am in their debt for so many hours spent.

My husband, Michael J. Kutchins, continues to be a delightful friend, reader, and computer expert throughout my writing projects. His humor and good-natured reflections combine experience and common sense in an uncommon way. He keeps me honest while having fun.

Joy McQueen, a poignant writer herself, reviewed each of the major stories in this book for their sensitivity and meaningfulness. Her comments made the difference between reading about a child's experience and experiencing a child.

Trinity University continues to afford me time to be creative. What a wonderful job: to teach bright students, visit schools weekly, and reflect and write about my experiences. I am grateful for these fine opportunities.

This book includes countless stories and anecdotes about children at risk of failure, whose families and teachers help them reach a marvelous potential. I thank each of them for the lessons they have taught me and for enabling me to share their stories with others.

Preface

*There is always a moment in childhood when the
door opens and lets the future in.*

Graham Greene

It's harder to raise children today, but it's more exciting. The
same evening news contains stories of teens building homes
in Latin America and shooting one another in urban America.
We read about the amazing possibilities of the computer, but
worry about children's addiction to computer-based games
and chat rooms. Parents and teachers together observe some
children enter the school building eagerly each morning,
while others drag their backpacks slowly behind them.

Rarely have so many extended family members cared and
become involved. From grandparents to stepparents, the community of adults raising our children is truly a village. The core
of their concern is love and the desire to help each child be
Special, be a *Winner*. I wrote this book about unleashing children's potential, because I believe that all children can win in
life by becoming happy, successful, and fulfilled. But they
can't do it alone.

As a teacher and family counselor, for years I observed how
some children overcame terribly difficult situations. Ranging
from hurried families where parents had little time to share,
to mean-spirited divorces, poverty or illness, these children
not only coped, but flourished. Why? If we understood how
they reached their potential despite adversity, couldn't we

help all children go beyond today's culture of drugs and violence?

The research and stories about children who overcame tremendous odds is fascinating. They all share one thing: An adult who cared, most often a parent or teacher. And if other adults can turn around the life of a child who is failing at school or has a disability, what wonderful hints they can give us for supporting our own children.

As a parent, I feel that nothing else I've done personally or professionally really matters if my children don't turn out well. Looking about at the love and concern on other parents' faces, I know I'm not alone. We're serious about raising children today. Indeed, there's a pressured realization that failure is not an option. Yet, it's understandable that parents have trouble visualizing future doctors or teachers in their children who spend money carelessly, won't clean up the kitchen or even complete tomorrow's homework. In this book, I explore the best ways to get in touch with children and teens, build their esteem, and help them take responsibility for their present and future behaviors.

When a child has a problem such as a learning disability or a naturally withdrawn personality, I consider how the popular theory of *Multiple Intelligences* can help us find otherwise hidden talents. Without a violin or piano, Mozart would never have been as great. Without a soccer field or a summer science program, a child may never develop a natural skill. I've learned that alienated children rarely reach their potential, but may instead act outwardly or inwardly in violence or substance abuse. I discuss ways to keep these lonely children out of trouble by moving them from withdrawal and isolation back into school and community activities.

I'm troubled by today's *civility crisis*, where children are increasingly aggressive and negative toward parents and teachers. Since today's rude children are tomorrow's rude adults, it will be difficult to reach a high potential without developing strong, positive social skills. Not surprisingly, research on children who overcome daily problems emphasizes their sense of optimism and ability to work with others. I explore how adults can transform children's behaviors from rudeness to kindness, making life more enjoyable at home and school while establishing future social patterns.

Each child, home, and classroom has a story to tell. My favorite part of writing this book has been to share these stories with you. In our personal conversation, brilliant Pulitzer Prize Winner Doris Kearns Goodwin tells her own story, one of overcoming her mother's illness and death to achieve a fantastic potential. We learn how Bob and Eileen Monetti not only dealt with their son's death over Lockerbie, Scotland, in the explosion of Pan Am 103, but went on to change the lives of many others. But most of the stories include the more common struggles of families feeling overwhelmed by today's pressures or of teachers working with parents to give children a wholesome childhood. They share one thing in common: All of them want today's children to be happy, to avoid the land mines around them, such as substances and violence, and to take charge of the journey from successful childhood to successful adulthood.

From Risk to Resilience

A Conversation with Doris Kearns Goodwin

S he slept in the *Winston Churchill* Bedroom of the White House. She was the first woman journalist to ever enter the Boston Red Sox locker room. As assistant to Lyndon Baines Johnson during his final years as President, Doris Kearns Goodwin completed writing his memoirs and moved on to create works probing the psychological character of the Presidency. A renowned historian, she was awarded the Pulitzer Prize in 1995 for *No Ordinary Time*, a brilliant analysis of Franklin and Eleanor Roosevelt.

In *Wait Till Next Year*, her book about growing up as a Brooklyn Dodgers fan in a city impassioned with baseball, she reveals her other side, one not reported in her Harvard Ph.D. studies or insights as a popular news commentator. The youngest of three sisters, Doris recounts a difficult, but loving, childhood. She knew her mother only as an invalid, bound to the house with a heart badly damaged by rheumatic fever. In her early thirties, her mother had the weakened arteries of a seventy-year old. Doris became obsessed with having her mother recite stories of her own youth before the illness. She believed that remembrances of healthier times would allow her mother's mind to control her body and keep the heart condition from worsening. Despite these fervent efforts, when Doris was 15, her mother died.

Even with tragedy in their home, Doris' parents had managed to create a sense of family resilience, one that would allow their children not only to cope with daily crises, but also to gain self-confidence and carry stability and competence into adulthood. When I interviewed Doris Kearns Goodwin about her childhood and the factors lending her strength, she reflected candidly on the many people who shaped her as she developed a wonderful enthusiasm and excitement for life.

What did your family do to help you to cope with your mother's illness?

"I think watching my father deal with my mother's illness was probably the most important model. If he had been laid low by it, if he had been depressed by it, if he had really made it seem as if our lives were constricted by it, then I'm sure that the children would have taken their signal from him. But somehow, the most important person in her life, her husband, was able to still have vitality, excitement, and a love of life, and be able to never make us feel that he was constricted by her.

"Here was a man who was so social, as I later learned when he got married the second time. He loved to go out to dinner, loved to go to plays, travel to Europe, all these things that he had never done when he was married to my mother because she couldn't. And yet, never once did he make us feel that he was being prevented from things he wanted to do. *It seemed like he made the things that they were able to do the things that he thought he loved.* So, they would have a card game on Friday nights and they would listen to the ball games together.

"He made it feel like it was more fun to just be home. On the weekends, you could listen to a game or go to the beach or do whatever was possible around the house. He would have all sorts of projects—painting or wallpapering, so that in a certain sense ... what he did was shape what made him happy by what was possible."

It must have been really difficult for your mother to want to do things with her children, but be physically unable. How did she handle this?

"She didn't have the same type of resilient temperament that my father did. Especially by the time I came along she must have been worn down in part by the illness which had gotten much more severe. She was pretty healthy during the childhood of my older sisters, so they remember a somewhat more active mother than I knew.

"... There were times as a child when I remember feeling sad that I couldn't have a lot of kids over to my house. You always wanted to have the kind of house where the kids felt welcomed, but we had to be quiet—not that she would be sleeping, because she really did not sleep that much. But, you just somehow knew that she couldn't be disturbed. The house had become such an important security domain for her that having a lot of people run through it would have been troubling.

"The interesting thing is sometimes later in life you are able to make up for the things that you missed when you were young. When my sons were growing up in Concord, we lived on the main street of the town and our house became the place where everybody came. It was probably not a coincidence. I'm not sure I did it consciously, but all of our boys' friends would call it *The Clubhouse* because everyone wanted to gather there. There were times when I would come home and my kids wouldn't even be there. There would be a dozen kids just waiting for the other kids to come in. And the door was never locked. We had a pool table and a jukebox and a huge room they could all come into."

In addition to your parents, were there others in your life who supported you?

"We had a real neighborhood so that there was a sense in which there were other adults, and children, who were a part of your everyday life. For example, even if my mother were in the hospital, I knew that the mother of the girl who lived next door to me would take care of me when I came home. So, you could feel loved by a larger number of people than a nuclear family might have allowed.

"Not only just the parents of my friends, but the owners of those stores—you know, the people who worked in those stores around the corner—became really just as close to you as your parents' friends and your own friends did. ... There was a sense as you walked in your small world of being affirmed all the time by the neighbors who knew you, who respected you, who teased you, who really were part of your daily life.

"The extension of that were teachers at school. You walked to the elementary school nearby. I always loved school, so that meant probably being a good student and getting the reinforcement of teachers. I always talked too much, so on my report cards would always be "Talks too much in class." But aside from that, I did well. There was a sense of feeling, a sense of wonderful teachers who made you feel special.

"We had that group of our own friends and we always did get along really well. I guess for some reason I didn't feel a sense of worry about how I was being accepted by the other kids.... I just always felt I was liked by them, by my peers in the classes.

"I think part of that is if you go into a room imagining that people will like you, and if you are open and not caught up in your own worries and are interested in them, it almost becomes full circle that it works out that way. Obviously, that confidence has to come from the home and from the temperament to begin with. But once it's there, it is the greatest gift you can have. When you move into larger and larger circles, each one requires your starting all over again socially. But you bring the confidence that it worked out pretty well in the last setting."

In gaining this confidence, how important was your positive temperament in comparison with the influence of parents who taught you how to deal with adversity?

"The temperament gives you a certain kind of stance toward the world. But if the world continually knocks that away from you, the world being parents or friends or the environment or poverty, or whatever it is, without reinforcement, then it's almost like the fire needed to keep burning isn't given any sustenance. Think of that positive temperament someone is given as part of their makeup: It is a gift, there is no question. But it can be diminished or squandered or lost if the environmental factors don't allow that fire to keep burning....

"I think it was the luck of growing up with a father who reinforced it, with a mother who I always felt loved me even though she was so ill. She could really concentrate on me because I was the only child left at home. My sisters were older, and because she wasn't dividing her attention between a social life or a professional life, she was always there when I got home. She was the one who would rehearse the catechism questions or my school stuff with me.

"There was always a sense that both parents were deeply caring about how well I did when I went to school. And then, growing up in a stable environment where there wasn't divorce at the time and there wasn't violence. It was a time when childhood was something that we could all enjoy."

Chapter 1

It's Harder to Raise Children Today

Children are like wet cement.
Whatever falls on them makes an impression.

Haim Ginott

Somehow, tomatoes were redder in 1950. They were bigger, firmer, and thicker then, as they bubbled in marinara sauce, their strong aroma wafting out windows as we played potsy on fractured Brooklyn sidewalks. Even today, smelling that rich red sauce takes me home.

Mothers visited on stoops, eyes never wandering from their charges or from cars speeding down busy streets. Roller-skating was for adventuresome, older boys, shoving the younger ruthlessly as they stumbled across the cracks. During races, girls were relegated to a safety zone to skip rope. *A...my name is Alice and I come from Alabama. My husband's name is Alfred and we grow apples...* When boredom intervened, the pace accelerated, pairs skipped together and coordinated gales of hysterical laughter as they collapsed on the sidewalk.

Fathers crowded in cramped living rooms, their radios blaring Dodger games out on humid streets. Campanella was news. Mantle was Lucifer. Hopes shattered for pennants, they nodded bitterly and murmured *Wait 'til next year*, agonizing over unforeseeable injuries and errant ref calls. Budgets rarely allowed trips to Ebbetts Field, but in their pounding hearts they were the best of fans.

Weekdays my father drove a beer truck, making deliveries to Brooklyn and Jersey stores and bars. Always looking for more work, he awaited flu season each winter. "I don't wish drivers sick," he would say with a twinkle, "but just a short bout to help us all."

On good weeks, my brother took me to the Sunday matinee at the Kismet Theater. Wearing 3-D glasses, we screamed as knives flew at us from the screen or as tigers charged with mouths open. Later, Kevin announced that it really "hadn't been that scary." Just illusions. When I was old enough to understand, he would explain.

I remember Lafayette and DeKalb Avenues for their sounds. The accents, the languages, the animation. There was Benny Rosen, his colorful Yiddish words introducing *yenta* and *chudspah* into my childhood vocabulary. My father's pinochle partner, he taught me to add on the back of old envelopes.

"If I'm her teacher, she might throw a few points my way," with a smile. "Anyhow, it can't hurt."

Al was ebony black with a laugh that my mother said stopped traffic. If it did, people in those cars were smiling. He dropped in for precious minutes, shared a joke or story, and ran off next door to tell it again. His own laughter and the pungent trail of huge cigars followed him down the block.

But it was in my friends' homes that the sounds of Brooklyn erupted. Petsi's mother was huge, surrounded by endless scores of children, fighting or laughing or both. She snatched me into her huge lap and stuffed hot-pastried meats in my mouth. Through Petsi's translation, in rapid Spanish she spoke of her family in Puerto Rico. Tears flowing freely, her body heaved with emotion. Then she grabbed my short curls, hugged me powerfully, and dropped me back to the floor, replacements climbing skillfully into her lap. That tiny, hot apartment engendered the purest kind of love.

The Bendoskys were solemn, struggling with the language their children already mastered. Preferring silence to embarrassment, they spoke little, but their eyes communicated volumes. At first, a Polish fear of police and crowds encouraged their suspicion of neighborhood activities. But the loud warmth of Italian, Irish, and Puerto Rican women worked its magic. Mr. Bendosky became a maddened Dodgers fan, pounding tables and jeering fiercely in Polish when a bunt went foul or a pop-fly ended the game. Gradually, his wife took turns with my mother walking their sons to St. John's school each day.

But the heart of the neighborhood was Aunt Rosie's kitchen. Here, sounds and smells blended. Evenings, neighbors converged as well, drawn as much by Rosie's warmth as Uncle Mike's homemade red wine. The men listened to games in that kitchen, shouting in accents so familiar that their children outside could follow the Dodgers based on their fathers' cheers or moans.

The loftiest of three tiny apartments, there was a balcony overrun seasonally with tomato plants. While their combined output might be consumed by a few days of her sauces, Aunt Rosie plucked their yield singularly, adding each to store-bought goods as a cherished gem, a polished diamond. Often I was allowed to choose and wash the ripest, which she then sliced artfully and placed in the already bubbling sauce.

"This is a good one," she said each time. It always was.

Aunt Rosie had no children, so she cherished me along with the countless nieces and nephews racing through her home. But of these, Nancy was her favorite, beautiful with dark ringlets and huge brown eyes. Nancy was also my best friend.

Her carefree body danced constantly, hands clapping and feet racing. Delighted with movement, she laughed loudly and easily. Yet she was enraged by a trapped butterfly or moved to tears when her baby cousin cried. While mothers visited on shaded stoops, we whispered about the older girls, their hair and clothes. But mostly, we ran and played potsy, jumping into each numbered square balanced on one foot. Nancy's nimbleness and speed won the games, but even the toughest of boys cheered her on. Her arm around my shoulder, she giggled us home, her curls bouncing.

We shared those evenings with others, but were inseparable all day, especially in Aunt Rosie's kitchen. At lunchtime, while mothers walked older children to and from school, we brought our dolls and sat them in chairs for her feast, chastening them to mind their manners. As we fussed with their petticoats and posture, Aunt Rosie sang in soft Italian and cut the thick dough on her small pastry-maker. She coached us in the words to those songs, our imperfect Italian sounds mimicking her own nostalgic tone.

Ninna, nanna, ninna ooh,
questo bimbo a chi lo do?
se lo do all'uomo nero
se lo tiene un anno intero
se lo do alla Befana
se lo tiene una settimana
sel lo do all sua mamma
se lo coccola e se lo nanna.

My mother shook her head smilingly later in the day as I sang loudly to my dolls in broken Italian.

"So much for Danny Boy."

Sauce and pasta shaped our days. Aunt Rosie produced remarkable noodles at whim. Large, flat manicotti were her specialty, although I loved the bows she pinched so quickly. All covered with marinara. Meatball dimensions also changed daily, ranging from small to huge. That was the only other surprise.

Until Polio.

I heard my parents whispering in the evening, strangely uncommunicative. Within weeks, the sounds of laughter left our Brooklyn streets as we self-quarantined in cloistered apartments. No more roller-skating or stoop-talk. Especially the youngest not allowed outside. Small groups of mothers gathered and dispelled hastily, seeking news and comfort.

For a brief time, older children continued at school. But the epidemic spread. Early, Kevin complained of aching joints, of pain in his legs. Weeping and angry, my mother refused to take him to the doctor.

"That's where the infantile paralysis spreads," she insisted to my distraught father. Although Kevin's aches gradually subsided, it was the last time he went to school for months. Soon neighborhood parks were closed. The radio told us pools would not open in summer, that we were not to drink from public fountains. It didn't matter. None of us went outside anymore.

My heart longed for the sounds, for Benny to play pinochle again, for Al's evening laughter. I missed Rudy, the Good Humor Man, who would stop his truck and chat patiently as we compared chocolate cones with ice cream sandwiches. But mostly I yearned for those noon hours Nancy and I lived in

Aunt Rosie's kitchen. It was a suspended time, waiting for life to return in the same way. But it never did.

One evening, a surprising knock on our door. Aunt Rosie stood there, tears streaming endlessly down her face.

"Nancy has it. They took her to the hospital."

Days passed into weeks as she improved. Then worsened. New words: *Meningitis. Paralysis. Fear.*

"How much does it hurt?" I asked.

"A lot," my mother responded shakily. "But she's in the hospital and they'll make it hurt less."

"Will she die?"

"Only if God wants to take her now."

"But she can't dance anymore, Mom. If God took her, he'd want to see her dance."

The deaths mounted. My mother turned off the radio.

Nancy's fever finally passed and her pain was controlled. She came home. But more months dragged by before the epidemic subsided and I could see her.

Belying a terribly weakened state, her smile was ebullient. Even her voice beamed. She sat in a big chair in Aunt Rosie's kitchen, surrounded by neighbors and plates of food. Standing back shyly, I observed her diminished size and awkwardly bowed legs.

"What're those?" I asked, pointing.

"Hot packs. They help my legs feel better."

"Can you walk?"

A head shake.

"Why not?"

A shrug.

"Can you play?"

Another shrug.

"I'm ready to go home," I told my mother.

"No. We'll stay awhile."

Every night we stayed awhile, until Nancy's eyelids drooped and families filtered back into quiet streets. I don't know how many people were packed in that kitchen. Al entertained adults with his stories, while Petsi's mother scurried after wandering children. Mrs. Bendosky brought kielbasa and Uncle Mike poured his red wine freely. Aunt Rosie hovered over Nancy, pausing only to stir the next day's sauce.

The day her braces were fit, solemnity gripped the visitors as we persuaded her to stand.

"They hurt," she complained. "Take them off."

No one listened.

Mr. Bendosky patted her hair. In his new English, he slowly pronounced, "It is good to walk." His wife only nodded.

Al added, "There's a story of a child who learned to dance again, after she never thought she could. I wonder if that child is you."

"Meatballs for everybody when she stands," Aunt Rosie pronounced.

We cheered, shouted, cajoled. Amidst her protests, Uncle Mike swung Nancy's awkward legs from the recliner to the floor. He and my father pulled her sagging body to an arch, supporting her arms and slight weight as she struggled to push herself back onto the chair.

They forced her upright. No ninth-inning homer ever received wilder ovations from a louder, more enthused crowd.

Long seconds passed. The frown of pain relaxed as her broad smile returned slowly.

Aunt Rosie's face swam with tears as neighbors hugged each other. Losing themselves to the moment, they spoke Italian, Spanish, and Polish in unison. Nancy's silver-covered legs quivered under the weight of their love.

Parents carried sleeping children home late that night, all semblance of time ignored. Crossing streets, they shouted to each other, lingering for last-minute conversations. The sounds had returned to our neighborhood.

I've been in this world a good while longer now. Years have passed and neighbors moved on. But in my life, the purest melting pot I have ever known was that night in Aunt Rosie's kitchen.

Adults Helping Each Other

Like the vines growing outside her window, Aunt Rosie seemed so strong to a child. Until her family was threatened, she appeared able to handle anything. But the adults knew better. Perhaps it was their own neediness that helped them understand that even strength has its limits. Most of my father's work came when others "called in sick." After hours of waiting, many days he came home with no paycheck. Yet others respected him for his work ethic. The Bendoskys spoke little English and originally distrusted everyone. Neighbors understood this as a natural reaction from fears for family in Poland. Al was the only African-American. Instead of focusing on race, families relished his delightful company. My Irish-Catholic father's best friend was Jewish. Even today I use those wonderful Yiddish expressions and remember the math facts I wrote on the back of envelopes, recording their pinochle scores.

No one was resilient all the time or without the help of others. Nor did they expect to be. From this neighborhood, I learned that we all help each other be strong. And when we're in need, others will be there. Despite low income and job pressures, those small apartment buildings were the best of worlds, people helping each other survive during adversity. Love and caring permeated Aunt Rosie's kitchen, regardless of racial and ethnic differences. Perhaps adults worked together more willingly when children were ill. Or maybe shared activities, such as walking children to school or following sports, helped them focus on the commonality of daily lives. Whatever the joy or calamity, they were there for each other and felt safer in an unpredictable world.

Brooklyn, or any large city, appears an unlikely village, but it doesn't have to be. Neighborhoods can become families. We hear a good deal about the "extended family," where we embrace individuals close to us into our daily personal lives. I believe that today's world requires us to move toward an *expanded family*. This concept takes us back to the traditional neighborhood of Aunt Rosie's kitchen, of adults taking responsibility for supporting each other and all related children through good and bad times.

To handle adversity, children need even more help than adults. Especially with today's widespread drugs and gangs, it's so easy for them to become unsuspecting victims, responding impulsively to social situations and ruining their lives. Raised by an expanded family that directs them around life's land mines, they can become strong and well-adjusted. But it rarely happens without adult input.

In their research on situations that foster strength in children, Emmy Werner and Ruth Smith described the significance of people outside the immediate home. They discussed how learning to trust both family and non-family members provides emotional support, rewards children's growth in competence, and promotes their self-esteem. It's good to be loved by your parents, but it's even better to be loved by more people. And if they're there to answer your questions, to lift you up physically and emotionally when you fall down, you learn to model on their behaviors in your own adulthood.

But when the neighborhood can't help, the family must make it alone.

Parents Helping Children

Unhappy with the school's requirement that we teachers visit every student's home, I grumbled on the way to Crystal's apartment that Saturday morning. Physically frightened, I moved through tenement housing, with cracked glass windows and expletives bursting from inside apartments. How intimidating a home for a thirteen-year old child. No wonder she often seemed quiet and subdued in class, afraid to take risks even to answer a question.

That morning turned out to be one of the most revealing of my career. Crystal's slim, immaculately-dressed mother greeted me warmly at the door. Calling for Crystal to join us, she took my hand and led me inside the tiny apartment to the kitchen. Light beamed through shiny windows. No cracks here. Brightly colored fabrics and blankets covered the few pieces of furniture. The kitchen was cleanly-scrubbed, with uncluttered counter-tops, and an open back door to welcome outdoor warmth. Using a paper napkin to wipe off the already-gleaming black chair, she invited me to sit.

She smiled as she saw me staring at kitchen and living-room walls, covered with schoolwork. Even spelling tests that I had graded so casually had a place of honor.

"We want Crystal to know she can grow up to be something. That's why we're glad you came today. We told her that school's her only way out of this here neighborhood, that you care enough about her to come visit." Guilt.

Crystal talked nonstop over delicious cake. With her mother's encouragement, she pulled out library books, stories of girls who climbed out of poverty or adversity and into success. She read for us, delightfully contrasting the voices of each character. I had never seen her so animated or involved.

A startle of loud thuds ascending the back stairs. Crystal's father stumbled in, disheveled and clumsy, a big smile on his face. Reeking of alcohol, he leaned on the counter and greeted me as an old friend.

"If I'd 'a had teachers like you, I would'a stayed in school."

"Daddy, you promised!" With a wail, she ran to her room.

Crystal's mother wearily shook her head and coaxed her husband into the bedroom to sleep. She returned alone and lowered herself slowly into the kitchen chair.

"He don' mean nothin' bad. He works all night and stops with his friends on the way home. It'll kill Crystal he embarrassed her in front of you. She won't be back out here."

But she was in school on Monday and we talked. About parents who love their children and work hard to raise them. About Crystal's responsibility to reciprocate by staying out of trouble to make them proud.

Discussing her father's drunkenness, Crystal contemplated, "I know he loves me. He always tells me. He just gets tired and relaxes too much with his friends. Says it's like smoking, tough to quit. So I should never start on cigarettes and especially alcohol. That way I'll never embarrass my own children." She concluded with a shrug, "He means well. He just drinks too much." Behind that small desk, the child was already sounding like her wise mother.

The Crystals of the world continue to amaze and delight me. Without the expanded family of the neighborhood to support them, these children overcome extreme stress to take charge of their lives and become well-adjusted adults. In my work as a teacher and a counselor of at-risk children, I am often puzzled by their remarkable sustenance and strength-of-character from a young age. Why do some "make it" despite adversity and go on to have pleasurable, fulfilling lives, while others quit early, overcome by seemingly insurmountable circumstances?

Importantly, what lessons can they teach us? In an uncertain, often overwhelming world, how can we use their experiences to improve the quality of life of *all* children? And what do their parents have to tell us? Despite her impoverished situation, Crystal's mother has rich knowledge.

We tend to be in awe of those special children who seem so much stronger, better than the rest of us at handling severe problems. In the 1970's, E.J. Anthony explored this notion of invulnerability, theorizing that some children simply are tougher than others, that they will surpass all expectations despite frequent and severe exposure to stress. He used the analogy of three dolls—one made of glass, one of plastic, and one of steel—to illustrate children's varied response to problems. The glass doll shatters from the blow of a hammer, while the plastic doll is permanently and badly scarred. But the steel doll emits only a slight metallic sound despite repeated blows, appearing to be indestructible.

At first, this easy explanation of inborn strength was broadly popular. Based on natural toughness, the child would make it or not. Despite anything adults did to help, the ability to endure stress seemed to vary within each individual.

I didn't see this in my work with children like Crystal. She wasn't naturally strong. She lacked the invincibility of E.J. Anthony's steel doll. Indeed, she might even have been the glass one. At times her temperament seemed ready to shatter quickly from blows of adversity, except for her mother's strength and both parents' love. Exposure to poverty, alcohol, and dreadful neighborhood role models had less impact than did support and direction at home.

The last time I saw Crystal, she was giggling with a group of girls as they planned their move into high school. Healthy, funny, and bright, their staccato comments diverged nonstop from choice of math and foreign language to boys. I have no doubt she's moved out of poverty by now. With her mother behind her, she couldn't miss.

Survival Stress

There are many possible stresses in a child's life, often resulting in anxiety, depression, and withdrawal or aggression. As in Crystal's daily world, the consequences of poverty can be overwhelming unless other factors are present to lessen their impact. When you're poor, options are more limited. Currently, one American child in four lacks health insurance to cover doctor's visits and prescriptions. The impact is far-reaching. For example, incidents of untreated otitis media, middle-ear infections, abound among economically disadvantaged children, resulting in hearing losses from accumulated scar tissue. When the children attend school, they have difficulty learning phonics, immediately lessening their ability to read. These obstacles continue to accumulate in their young lives. Sadly, readily-available antibiotics that could cure infections and prevent later learning problems are beyond the financial reach of many families.

All too often, indigent neighborhoods provide few role models to guide youth out of poverty. When gangs are rampant, there may be limited opportunities to choose alternatives that lead to a more fulfilling adult life. Many children of poverty lack options. When school doesn't meet their needs, they attend infrequently, growing further behind and becoming disengaged from the academic process. By legal age, they quit at the promise of earning money on the street or in minimum-wage jobs. The cycle continues.

Poverty by itself is not enough to cause low grades or a lack of interest in education. Crystal's parents knew that school was her chance for a better life, and their belief became hers. Literacy became a minimum, not a maximum, goal. As psychologist David Elkind notes, *Children's success in school is far more related to the attitude of their parents toward education than to the family's financial status.* Yet, the two are often closely related. When parents are angry at the educational system that failed them personally, they pass these negative sentiments on to their children. Why should a child try to achieve high grades or suffer through evening homework if there's no reward? And when parents of any economic status complain about the teacher, the child mimics their comments, externalizes blame for low achievement, and has excuses for lack of personal effort.

Teachers cannot teach tired and hungry children. Children's physical needs must be met before they can be successful at school. They should be rested and fed. I remember Joey, a twelve-year old slow learner in my classroom. Hospital records indicated that his early intellect was normal, but he had become "cognitively delayed," impacted through living in a non-stimulating, neglectful home. He was easily recognizable, as his tall, skeletal body leaned into the trash basket at regular intervals during the day. To the loudly voiced disgust of his classmates, he openly licked their discarded candy wrappers or sandwich cellophanes. He even re-chewed their disposed bubble gum. Despite school breakfast and lunch daily, he begged other children for bites of their food. Clearly, the only meals he received were those in our cafeteria. Now that his body had entered a growth spurt, he needed more food. When not foraging, often he rested his head on his desk and slept soundly. He was a hungry, neglected child, whose basic physical needs were unmet.

Without his attention on learning, I couldn't teach Joey to read or compute. More importantly, I would never be able to give him friends who respected or even liked him. Until he met his basic needs for food and sleep, he would never gain self-confidence or enjoy life. Social service workers found his single mother of eight to be barely competent, roughly slapping and shoving her own children as she fought them for food. There was no dinner, just frequent physical battles over chips and junk food. Joey, his brothers and sisters, collapsed from exhaustion late each night on soiled mattresses. Despite ongoing court threats and occasional promising moments during visits from Child Protective Services, this was Joey's home every night and weekend. His reality.

We know that children need consistency and positive parenting to trust others and to develop close relationships. Living a survival life style, children suffering daily anxiety never anticipate the reality of the next meal. Survival stress can be so severe that it's almost impossible for a child to conquer alone. Yet, help can come from unexpected places.

Smiling broadly, a wonderfully caring veterinarian explained her career choice. "I grew up in London during World War II. I was six years old and separated from my family during endless days of bombing. I was in an air raid shelter with total strangers, not knowing if my parents and brothers were alive or dead, or if I'd ever see them again. I was terrified. The only thing I had was my dog, a big shaggy old mutt. I still remember holding onto him, my face buried in his side, as bombs fell outside. I promised him that if we made it and I found my family again, I'd become a vet someday. Thank God it all worked out. I really understand how we humans love these creatures," as she stroked a small dog's head.

Her story relates the pressures outside our control that happen to the most caring and consistent families. As with world events, personal health concerns can be devastating. Many people become ill or suffer from disabling conditions. Chronic health problems of a parent or child can result in an entire family becoming depressed. Yet, parental attitudes of optimism, of well-being, are critical to give children a sense that life will be better. We can all learn from these experiences. The power of a loving, supportive family can work true miracles during the worst of times.

In my work with terminally-ill children I found that roles can reverse. Outside painful treatment times, the child may work hard to maintain a positive attitude, supporting an understandably overwhelmed parent. In a heart-wrenching scene, I observed a high school athlete consoling his parents after his cancerous left arm was amputated. Against their advice to wait a year, he insisted on completing his applications for college, commenting that he wouldn't have time for sports next year anyway. He reminded his discouraged father that no one else in their family had ever attended college, and that he had every intention of going away to school in the fall. His own strength carried them all. A few months later, I noted the return of more typical family roles as his mother scolded him for staying out with his friends past curfew the previous weekend. Their family came away strengthened by mutual, loving support during a tragic time.

Understandably, the most difficult stress in maintaining family consistency occurs when a parent suffers mental illness. From their research into resilience in families in Maui, Emmy Werner and Ruth Smith relate amazing stories of children who developed hobbies or created their own "space" in basements or attics in order to maintain a sense of psychological well-being. They looked to friends and social groups to replace the company and guidance of parents with psychiatric problems. Despite the difficulty of their home situations, many of these children were very successful, viewed as leaders by peers, and demonstrated an "up-beat" attitude that defied pessimism.

Social Stress

What wonderful lessons these children and teens teach us. But to help our children, first we must be able to identify the early stages of stress. When parents and professionals are aware that factors at home or school are upsetting children, they can lighten responsibility loads and focus on small issues before they become huge. It is easier to be proactive, preventing stress from escalating and encompassing lives,

than to be reactive when individuals are overwhelmed by circumstances. *Intervening immediately will be far more effective
than allowing anxiety and overload to encompass a child.*

My university students differ remarkably in their response
to papers, exams, and field experiences with children. Some
are considerably better at organizing their lives and workload.
They're punctual, rarely harried or complaining, and carry a
sense of competence. Yet, they find time to enjoy friends, and
many are officers in campus organizations. Above all, they're
fun to be with, popular with friends and professors. Good-
humored and optimistic, they view their future as teachers
and social service professionals with excitement and anticipa-
tion.

But not all of their lives have been easy. As they share stories of their childhoods, they tell me of serious personal conditions, such as a hearing loss or epilepsy, or of negative
responses to a divorce and remarriage. When I ask how
they've done so well academically and in maintaining a wonderful sense of optimism, almost always they speak of a person or involvement that significantly impacted their lives.

A third-grade teacher who gave the child public responsibilities so she shone among her peers. A coach who encouraged sports even when the child would never be the best on
the team. Activities such as school plays, debates, and musical performances that weren't distractions, but awakenings to
worlds of opportunity.

In contrast, other university students overreact with worry
about assignments and exams, and are frequently tense and
unsmiling, even in social situations. Victims of pervasive anxiety, they appear harried, disorganized, and unfocused. Often
on anti-depressants, they face a future of more of today's
pressures. Yet, beneath this surface, they are fine, caring
young adults who share the same goal as the rest of us: a
happy, pleasurable, and fulfilling life.

Interestingly, not all of them have experienced problems of
the severity of their less-anxious peers. From supportive
homes and loving parents, many can't point to an individual
event or series of adversities that lessened their joy in life. Yet,
their negative attitude and moodiness impact them profoundly, resulting in a pessimistic view of the future.

I believe that despite their "easier" childhood, these students are less fortunate than their peers. Often, they have experienced different types of early, less visible, stress. Rushed into daycare at an early age. Driven to earn straight A's. To excel in a sport or activity. Membership in organizations that look good on college applications, rather than the result of real interest. Often, they're afraid to risk asking or answering questions in class, not wanting to appear foolish to teachers and peers. They've missed much of the fun of childhood, always preparing for responsible adulthood. Now, as adults, they're missing the fun as well.

We must dispel the myth that stress is obvious. Adults don't readily recognize many children under extreme pressure. True, some situations are very apparent, such as a neglectful or abusive home, or the presence of chronic illness. Although hampered by lack of staff and funding, many social workers are very effective when they intervene in the most difficult situations. Despite daily news reports of families in desperate circumstances, these homes are not the norm. Most parents love their children very much.

However, without realizing it, we can create a pressured childhood. We want our children to be competitive, to be winners. Some of this is good. Without involvement in new activities and challenges, many children won't realize their potential. But when adults place more emphasis on winning than on participating, we send the wrong message.

Young children rarely understand the importance of following rules. Too young to compete aggressively, they're a joy to watch as they give a different meaning to games. They play for fun, disregard rules, and claim themselves winners, much to the upset of older children. But they love the process.

One Saturday, watching my sons play "Hide and Seek" with neighbor children on our front lawn, I was delighted by my younger son's confidence. At an assured four years, he had the game figured out. He always hid behind the car. The first few times children ran toward his spot, he dashed in the opposite direction to the oak tree, their designated "Base." His behavior was too predictable for the wiser older ones. The next time he returned to hide behind the car, they winked at each other and raced at him from all sides. Undaunted and unmoving, he placed his hand firmly on the car and shouted, "Base!!!" They halted.

"Base is the tree, Stupid! You're *It*."

"Wrong! Base is the car. I just called it."

"You can't call a new Base in the middle of the game."

"Can if I want, *Stupid!!!*"

Amidst their shouts, he walked away, head held high. Not so stupid. It was good to get out of there.

By age seven at latest, children learn that they can't create their own rules, that grown-ups decide winners and losers. And no one wants to be a loser with Dad watching. So children learn the rules, but too often, they lose the fun.

Identifying Stress in Children and Teens

Trey was a student in my tenth-grade Honors English class. The son of a prosperous attorney and a homemaker, he was an extraordinary grade-grubber. Charming when greeting teachers daily, he became furious and verbally attacking when not receiving a perfect score on an exam or paper. Trey tried to manipulate us through loud, aggressive intimidation. When he received high grades, he was our friend. A *B+* meant we had mis-graded his paper and could be bullied into correcting our obvious mistakes.

Trey's future was set. He repeated often that his father and grandfather were graduates of a well-known, Ivy-league University, one that he would attend as well. With a mocking smile, he spoke cynically of his father's brother, a nice man, but "not very bright." Despite connections, his uncle had not been accepted to the family school, attending another highly-rated, but less prestigious institute. Trey would never let his family down in the same way. In fact, his grandfather had already told him that he would pay full tuition when Trey attended their *alma mater*. Not *if*, but *when*. His parents were delighted.

Unfortunately, Trey was not a natural student, one who achieved high grades without effort. In fact, he appeared to be an over-achiever. He never seemed interested in the process of learning, at times interrupting me to ask, "Will this be on the test?" He was impatient and disdainful toward group assignments intended to be fun and exploratory. Rarely raising his hand in class, he was negative and cynical when required to respond to questions.

Trey's friends were also highly-competitive. Some involved

in sports and the arts, they focused on Academic Decathlon, where under extreme pressure, they competed against other schools in speed of recall of factual knowledge across topics. To his dismay, Trey was on the "B Team," since his rate was not as fast as his friends'. He confided in me that he chose Decathlon since it would "look good" for college.

I was surprised when Trey's mother set up a group meeting with his teachers, asking us not to tell Trey or his father about the conference. Serious, well-groomed, and articulate, her concerns became obvious as she described his increasingly difficult behaviors at home.

Trey now argued constantly with his parents over issues that had never bothered him before, such as his little sister's chatter or even the food served for dinner. His mother described an unpredictable and frightening temper, including explosive outbursts where she was afraid he would hit someone. He no longer brought friends home, saying that his parents embarrassed him. When not watching television or playing video games, Trey spent most of the time in his bedroom, locking the door to bar his family. It had become almost impossible to wake him for school in the morning, and he was progressively more resistant to going at all. A few months before, he began to experience migraine headaches. While her husband attributed these changes to a typical adolescence, his mother was very concerned. To onlookers, stress in his life should be minimal and his future exciting.

While his mother listened politely to teacher pleas to lessen Trey's pressures and allow him to enjoy the moment, his family was set in their patterns. They felt they were structuring him for a future life of prosperity and professional success. His mother emphasized how important it was for him to receive high grades, even if they were attained through his receiving extra-credit from additional assignments. She was concerned about his placement in non-Honors math classes, since they did not carry as much weight on his overall grade-point average.

Ironically, Trey's mother felt that the school was to blame for making it so difficult for him to receive *A*'s. She attributed his anger outbursts and his migraines to teachers' lack of understanding of his needs. Tragically, none of the adults in his life appreciated the achievement pressures in his home. Despite our meeting, nothing changed.

Two years later, Trey's application to the family *alma mater* was rejected. The night he received the letter, he shot himself in the head with his father's gun, suffering permanent damage to the right side of his brain. Despite months in a rehabilitation hospital, today Trey walks with a cane to balance his unstable body. His speech patterns are slurred and difficult to understand, and he has lost use of one arm. After receiving a GED, Trey began classes at a local community college. However, his stress response returned immediately, heightening his depression and encouraging another unsuccessful suicide attempt. At the advice of a psychiatrist, he dropped out of school. Jobless to date, he continues to live at home.

Early on, Trey demonstrated clinical symptoms of anxiety and depression. Parents and professionals saw them, but we did not do enough to help. Initially, Trey's problems appeared less overwhelming than those of abused or neglected children. His situation in a loving, affluent family is enviable to many we might consider "less fortunate," such as Crystal.

Living in a ghetto, her problems were more obvious. Daily exposure to life-threatening events and an alcoholic father, she certainly was at greater risk than Trey. Yet, Crystal's mother understood her needs. She was very aware of negative events and their impact on her daughter. While not passing smoothly through childhood, Crystal knew she was special, in fact cherished, by her parents. Through clearly stated life goals, they gave her direction instead of pressure. She understood their expectations. She did not have to be perfect, just to work toward healthy values and a solid future.

Trey didn't feel special. To him, adult love was conditional on demonstrating remarkable performance. He believed that a person's uniqueness comes only with extraordinary achievement. Unable to meet family expectations, he doubted his worth as a person. Overwhelmed by the possibility of public failure, he became negative and angry with the adults who controlled his world. Feeling no support and losing faith that his future would be any better, he tried to end his life.

Identifying Stress at Home

By recognizing the symptoms on the chart, we can support children's efforts to deal with stress in a healthy and con-

Symptoms of Stress in Children and Teens at Home

❏   Loses interest in previously enjoyed activities

❏   Complains of illness, does not want to go to school

❏   Expresses a negative attitude toward teachers and peers

❏   Isolates self from family

❏   Argues frequently with parents and siblings

❏   Constantly watches television or plays video games

❏   Frequently loses temper, irritable over even minor problems

❏   Insomnia

❏   Demonstrates mood swings, cries or broods easily

❏   Assumes many adult responsibilities

❏   Acts as a parent to younger children

❏   Does not bring friends home

❏   Avoids being at home, creating excuses for "hanging out" with friends

❏   Changes to a peer group with negative values

❏   Appears to be smoking, drinking, or experimenting with any type of drugs

structive manner. Years before his suicide attempt, Trey displayed a number of these behaviors. The charm he demonstrated was an attempt to woo teachers into the all-important A's that were so critical to his self-identity. While many teens have periods of moodiness, his were prolonged and marked with outbursts of anger. His negativity towards adults and ongoing avoidance of his friends were red flags that he was withdrawing into depression.

There are a few key questions to ask when determining if children are stressed. Has their attitude undergone a change? If they have become moody and argumentative with friends, parents, or teachers, something is going on. Are they irritable and complaining? While some children are more temperamental than others, an ongoing sense of unhappiness is an indicator of problems.

Physical complaints can also indicate stress and anxiety. Do children have headaches? Stomach aches? Difficulty sleeping? When these problems are chronic, parents tend to accept them as part of the child. Yet, children should be free of these symptoms. If they persist, the child needs to see the family doctor to be sure that no illness or disease is present. It's helpful to observe when the symptoms occur. In the morning, before school? When invited to friends' houses? Before exams? Emotional problems are as real as physical ones. They tell us when a child needs help.

Social patterns are very important as well. Does the child have friends? We all need people. While some children prefer a large social group, others like one or two good friends. The number is less important than the quality of the relationships. Children need to talk with others, to share joys and concerns. There is usually a reason if a child is a loner. In reports of violent outbursts, time and again, others recall that the young person seemed to prefer being alone. Yet, many children are not alone through choice, but because they feel rejected by peers and have stopped trying to make friends. Their stress may be unbearable.

Most children do have friends. Looking at children's choice of a peer group shows us how they feel about themselves. Are they healthy and positive? It's critical to so many teens to be a cheerleader or a football star, because it gives them membership in the most popular group in the school. But selection restrictions mean that most young people will be part of a different group. Academic, capable students, who may also be viewed as "geeks?" The party crowd, somewhat wild, but fun? The artsy group, daring to be emotional and creative? The dissidents, cynical and disdainful about societal values? The gang members, actively anti-social, feared and avoided by peers? Considering the image they want to portray, teens may seek membership in a particular group because of these common stereotypes.

When children choose a negative peer group, adults need to intervene immediately to avoid bad influences spreading like a virus. When children are younger, parents have more control over their friends. With other parents of similar values, they can arrange for children to play together and visit each other's homes. It's healthy for children to be with others of different economic, racial, and ethnic backgrounds, because it enriches their lives through an understanding of difference. However, parents won't want to expose their children to peers who are negative and angry. When you direct children to healthy friends early, it usually means that they'll choose friends with similar values as teens. It's wise to have children play with others of the same age. Friends more than a few years older will discuss sexual matters early and may encourage younger children to engage in activities beyond their understanding. Children develop at their own pace much more easily with friends of their age group.

Indicators of Stress at School

April 20, 1999, will never be forgotten in Littleton, Colorado. Within their own school, Columbine students Eric Harris and Dylan Klebold enacted one of the deadliest massacres in American history, killing twelve students and one teacher before committing suicide. With the sudden, tragic use of thirty home-made bombs and scores of weapons, including semi-automatics, adults had to ask, "How could this happen?" How could the signs of such deep anger and vengeance have been overlooked by so many?

Terrorized students later discussed the "Trench Coat Mafia," a small group of "losers" who finally found a place with each other. Southwest of Denver, in a middle-class suburb of 35,000, Littleton is full of health and natural beauty. Yet, this group was devoted to dark, Gothic culture and music, spending hours playing video games with menacing titles like "Doom." Often speaking German and wearing swastikas, the students staged the attack on Hitler's birthday.

A web site attributed to Eric Harris included pictures of monsters toting guns and directions for making pipe bombs. Klebold and Harris reportedly created a video of themselves murdering athletes in school hallways. Some of their friends used black lipstick and nail polish to establish group membership, along with the tell-tale trench coat, worn all day in summer and winter. Non-members indicated that the group rarely showered and were shunned in part because of body odor. Expecting teens to be different, yet needing to belong through behavior and dress, no one took particular notice of the trench coat uniform. One mother commented, "I personally thought they looked kind of goofy, but they're kids."

Followed by "copy-cat" shootings, the legacy of Columbine has horrified our nation. Since that day, countless children have been killed or wounded in elementary and secondary schools from New York to California. Many of the attackers have claimed to be profoundly influenced by Columbine. Some have been dared by friends to repeat the terror, while others are depressed loners acting out against bullies who tormented them on their campus. A tragic symptom of the times.

Why do some children fascinated by "Dungeons and Dragons" and such games understand the difference between fantasy and reality, while for others the boundaries are blurred? Why do some internalize their anger into lowered self-esteem, while others act it out against society? A huge difference appears to be the involvement of healthy adults from early in their lives. But parents can't be everywhere or recognize the significance of every symptom. When teachers and social service professionals work together with parents, they can form a team for change.

Through a negative, aggressive attitude and lack of school involvement, Dylan Klebold, Eric Harris, and subsequent attackers display symptoms of school and family stress. Their fascination with violent videos and web sites may be a cry for help, or at least a question about how far adults will let them go. They rarely communicate with their parents, or with adults in general, turning instead to equally angry peers.

Many symptoms of troubled youth can be seen in school. A bad attitude often tops the list, as children become disdainful and negative about the adult world, government, and the future. Some become apathetic about schoolwork and participating in school activities, while others "drop out" through unexcused absences. Some withdraw into themselves, while others lash out in anger.

Their arrogant and scornful attitude toward adults often masks a lack of assuredness about themselves. They appear to have little energy for productive activity at home or school, showing enthusiasm only around their friends. Unfortunately, they choose peers whose negative values match and reinforce their own behaviors.

We need to identify and work with at-risk students *before* they engage in aggressive behaviors. They usually give themselves away in several areas: comments in class, written work, and dress. When students offer negative, cynical, or threatening comments, teachers need to follow-up immediately, with a discussion with the student and other involved teachers. But the most important dialogues are between teachers and parents.

Often teaching 150 students a day, secondary school teachers may overlook a depressed or apathetic child, allowing stress and tension to build to the breaking point. Parents should contact teachers if there's a problem or major change at home, such as divorce, death of a grandparent, or illness of a family member. It's understandable that parents do not want to publicly share family problems. But educators are professionals in the best position to support children each day.

Parents of elementary students can talk directly to the teacher, enlisting the counselor if the child needs more extensive help. Instead of meeting with five or six teachers at the secondary level, it's easiest for parents of teens to call the counselor and ask that the counselor speak to teachers. Parents may want to invite individual teachers to call them if the child seems stressed or has behavioral problems.

A wonderful elementary counselor shared her "trick" for having students begin the dialogue about their personal problems. At the beginning of the school year, she went to every classroom, introduced herself to students, and described her role as *a helper.*

"I have the best job in the world," she said. "I'm a helper. You have a problem. Anything, big or little, that worries you. You come to me and I get to help you solve that problem. Then we're both happy." Her warmth and sincerity came through as she set up a "help box" in each classroom, with nearby cards requiring only the child's and teacher's names. The boxes remained there all year, with teachers checking them daily and letting the counselor know who needed an appointment. She met with the children immediately, and they shared worries ranging from dogs who died, to "bad touching" from adults. Several times, she notified authorities. But mostly, she was there to listen and give advice. With the child's permission, she called parents or spoke with teachers when adult intervention was necessary.

More secondary school counselors are using this model as they worry about violence, weapons in schools, and overheard threats. The "help boxes" are usually outside their office. Students include their names when they want to meet with the counselor, but may file an anonymous concern if safety is an issue, such as drug sales or potential school violence. Very few students complete forms as a joke. Because of ongoing concerns about safety, they respect adult efforts to help solve problems and manage crises.

Teams of teachers working together can also be very effective. One can alert others about worrisome spoken or written comments. While students' behavior is usually the same across classrooms, the structure of some settings allows adults to overhear student concerns more easily. For example, coaches and teachers in speech and drama, choir, orchestra, and art usually interact more informally, establishing environments where students express problems openly. Elementary and English teachers read students' written concerns daily, giving them a good opportunity to note problems. In schools where teachers work as a team with the same group of students across subject areas, they get to know the children well and are in an excellent situation to share concerns.

Often, solutions include involving students in extracurricular activities to broaden their friends and increase confidence, or after-school tutoring for a student falling progressively further behind. When a child has a history of problems, teachers can work quickly to select an adult in the school to monitor progress. This adult should be someone with whom the student has a good relationship and will turn to in time of stress.

Parents need to be part of selecting the best solutions. When students understand that the most important adults in their world are working together, the message alone is powerful: *We care about you enough to be there for you.*

It's time to move children from risk to a happy, positive childhood. The following chapters include ways that adults can work together to help children overcome stress. Each

Symptoms of Stress in Children and Teens at School

- ❑ Negative change in appearance
- ❑ Bad attitude toward peers and teachers
- ❑ Apathy toward schoolwork
- ❑ Lack of involvement in extracurricular activities
- ❑ Friends who are poor role models
- ❑ Aura of pessimism and negativity
- ❑ More aggressive or withdrawn than peers
- ❑ Frequent absence or tardiness
- ❑ Clothing that indicates anti-social identification
- ❑ Discussions about involvement in negative activities or groups outside of school
- ❑ Verbal or written comments indicating anger or anxiety
- ❑ Non-completion of homework
- ❑ Parents not involved with or respected by their children
- ❑ Previous school or social problems
- ❑ Lack of energy or enthusiasm toward academic and social school activities

explores a different theme to protect children from daily pressures, improving their chances of growing up happy and with strong self-esteem. I include stories of children from my own experiences as a parent, teacher, and a counselor. By exploring how some children make it despite today's pressures, we can learn how to provide emotional strength, love, and support. Adults can make a difference in children's lives.

Lessons Learned

The power of a loving, supportive family works miracles during difficult times.

Children do not have to be perfect to embrace healthy values.

Children's needs must come first.

Failure happens, but often it is the motivation for future success.

A parent's attitude toward education usually becomes the child's attitude.

Identify stressed children early, before they become overwhelmed.

Children who seem timid and shy may be afraid of something in their lives.

Children respond more to the reasons behind adult behaviors than to the behaviors themselves.

We can mold a child's temperament. The difference between an introvert and an extrovert may be how well adults accept the child's ideas.

Money has less impact when there is love and support at home.

As we handle stress, so do our children.

If your child can't sleep well at night, there's a reason.

If your child does sleep well, take some credit.

Each day, spend time together as a family.

No one gets an 'A' every time.

'Mom' and 'Dad' are the dearest words in the language.

Chapter 2

Getting in Touch with Your Children and Teens

*If a child is to keep alive his inborn sense of wonder
without any such gift from the fairies, he needs the
companionship of at least one adult who can share it,
rediscovering with him the joy, excitement
and mystery of the world we live in.*

Rachel Carson

Even in the large meeting room at the group home, mother
and child appeared isolated but proud. With silent dignity,
they sat separate from conversation. Yet the mother quietly
studied the other children at play, listening to adult admoni-
tions to share toys and hold younger hands.

She tried to ignore me as I approached them, glancing
down at the bulky child in her lap. Noisy breathing filled the
room, frighteningly loud and uneven gasps as the child's
chest heaved.

But it was not the breathing that anyone would even note.
It was the tumor. Huge, pushing beyond skin capacity, it
appeared that the left side of his face would break open with
the size and weight of it. It conquered his eye and ear, and
squashed the nose aside, forcing his mouth to hungrily suck
for air. The tumor truly was alive, angry, and mean in its
grotesque distortions.

Clearly, the mother sat away to avoid stares and questions.
The desolation of isolation. This child had no playmates. Other
toddlers fixated on his face, denying any commonality in
childhood, despite their own bald head or machine-accompa-
nied bodies. As they rocked, mother and son seemed as one,
their own universe. "And the tumor's," I thought.

It was hard for me not to stare as well. I too was physically overwhelmed, despite my weekly counseling here with families of chronically ill children. Trying anything to engage his
mother in conversation, in Spanish, I asked, "How are his
treatments going?" She wouldn't have it. She just shrugged.
"Will he be able to stay an outpatient?" The woman looked
away.

My frustration grew. I sensed that the mother wanted company, even counseling, but not all the questions about the
tumor. But how could I help if she wouldn't talk?

One more try. "Do you have other children?" Most mothers
were concerned about the impact of illness on siblings, hungry for any parenting ideas. She shook her head and rested it
on her son's curly black hair. Wrong question. I touched her
hand and left.

The next week, mother and son sat closer to the group, but
could have been galaxies away. Still holding him in the rocking chair, she avoided all eye contact. The office staff reported she asked for nothing after registering that first night a
month ago. She spoke to no one, even during meal preparation, usually a noisy, shared time at the House. Their isolation had worked. Both she and the boy had become invisible
to all but side glances or the stares of newcomers.

She rose and fixed her son's bulky body into the stroller as
she walked toward the kitchen. I followed, unsure of my
reception, but sure that she needed a friend. I decided to
ignore the obviously physical and concentrate on the real
child. It surprised me that I didn't even know his name, that
I just thought of him as the boy with the tumor.

His mother ignored me as she fried beans for dinner. Until
I knelt down next to the child and held his hand.

"Su nombre?" I asked.

"Jesús," the mother replied without looking up.

"Y de donde es?"

"De Monterrey."

"Cuantos años tiene él?"

"Tres."

All of a sudden Jesús became a real three-year old child.
Not that he touched or even looked at me. But the little boy
inside became more important than the tumor.

I playfully grabbed his toes resting in the barely-worn sandals. He startled and stared at me. I grabbed them again. He studied me intently.

His mother began to speak softly as she cooked.

"Es muy difícil para nosotros. Mi familia está en México, y no hay nadie aquí. Cuesta demasiado que mi esposo viaje. Y, en Monterrey, me ayuda mi madre."

I wasn't surprised that part of her pain had been living in a strange place without her husband's and mother's support. But I couldn't imagine how difficult it would be to make it alone in a different country with a very sick child.

"Pero la semana pasada, buenas noticias. No es el tumor maligno. Dicen los medicos que podrán elimnarlo. Necesita mas cirjujía, y meses, o años, para reconstruír la cara. Por fin, será posible que mi hijo tenga una vida normal."

Her chest heaved with relief that the tumor was benign. She was able to put aside concerns about the months, or even years, of surgeries to rebuild his face. Her son would live. Now he could have friends, and maybe someday even a family of his own.

While Jesús sat, seeming to slumber, we spoke of other things. The trip from Mexico. When she would next see her husband. No more mention of the tumor or illness.

As she spooned steaming food onto their plates, I moved to leave. I waved at the child, who only stared back. Twice more. More stares.

I started out the door but heard his mother's summons. I turned to the stroller. Jesús regarded me solemnly and waved his small hand slightly. His mother's face streamed with tears.

Children and Parents: The Strongest Bond

In my encounters with Jesús and his mother, it was too easy to focus on the obvious disfigurement and ignore the reality of the beautiful little boy inside that body. So often we put the disability before the child: *a blind baby, a dyslexic teen, an emotionally disturbed third-grader.* Understandably, Jesús and his mother wouldn't relate to me until I was able to look beyond the striking difference in his appearance. Imagine being a child whom no one wants to touch. That is, no one except your mother. As in the German proverb, "Who takes the child by the hand takes the mother by the heart," she couldn't relate to the families in the group home until they accepted her son. The tumor also distracted all of us from the powerful bond between mother and child. Her protection and nurturance not only shielded him from the stares of others, but assured him that she would always be there. Her love was unconditional, not based on the handsomeness or cute behaviors we usually seek in young children. Her lap in the rocking chair was his refuge, his place of acceptance.

Research indicates that children can overcome adversities as serious as the tumor. Their most important support is an adult, especially a parent. Strong, shared relationships depend on meeting children's physical and emotional needs, while gaining their attachment and trust in return. Children's self-esteem improves by showing them that they deserve others' attention. Our caring for children should be unconditional, not earned by grades at school or even by behaving acceptably to adults.

We are attracted to young children when they are charming and engage us through coy interactions. The five-month old in the grocery store grins with a seductive smile and we all become willing victims. It reduces normally sophisticated adults to playful babblers of baby-talk, with delighted onlookers waiting their turn! A natural phenomenon, this smile continues for months after the mother's powerfully nurturing hormones return to their normal, pre-birth level. It's Nature's way of allowing children to gain and sustain our attention so that we will continue to meet their needs.

As children become older, adults respond most strongly to those who approach us first, chatting and taking the lead in developing a relationship. It's not surprising that children who seem to most easily overcome problems tend to be extroverts. A friendly, outgoing nature attracts adults, enlists their support, and encourages them to want to help. It's more fun to work with a delightful, happy young person than with someone sullen or aggressive. Understandably, adults tend to avoid negative children because they're not very pleasant to be around. So positive children receive the most positive response. We all react most immediately to attractive, friendly, outgoing children.

Jesús was not cute or interactive. In fact, his appearance distracted all of us from even considering his personality.

Unable to talk and restricted from walking freely because of parental concerns about the stares of others, he became an Untouchable. He was dependent on adults reaching out to him.

Despite the reason, when children experience problems, their all-important relationship with parents may not develop naturally because the parent feels rejected by a baby who doesn't respond in a "normal" way. Added feelings of guilt may result in avoidance, through fewer conversations and less holding. Yet, the need for protection and support is even greater.

Adults must accept children as they are and initiate the relationship. At any age, children in need can't wait, but they don't always come to us. They expect us to be openly welcome to them. Jesús' mother knew this and accepted him totally. In turn, he gave his trust and love. Despite imposed isolation, he was able to relate to other adults if they took the initiative. He had learned that adults could be trusted, but they needed to first show they accepted him for who he was.

Many children, and especially teens, are not isolated because of physical disabilities, but as a result of their behavior. Even in the healthiest of families, children may have a low self-esteem because of personal misperceptions about themselves and their abilities. Often, they doubt their worth and feel they can't meet adult standards.

Believing that no one understands their feelings, they reject others before they can be rejected. Conversations with parents may be brief and accusatory, with outrageous demands to draw adult ire. In an effort to avoid further confrontations, adults steer clear of future conversations. Some young people withdraw, cutting off the very contacts they need to show them that they are loved for who they are.

But that's the point. Many times, we don't love children for who they are, but for who we want them to be. It's not surprising that teachers respond most favorably to those who are good-looking, smart, and well-behaved. And at home, these children also receive positive attention from their parents. But children change. Most teens are disruptive at some point in their adolescence, or even into their early twenties. Understandably, parents have a difficult time watching formerly loving children question and sometimes loudly reject family values. Yet during these questioning stages, there's one thing a child or teen should never have to question: the unconditional love and support in the family.

Mothers

Mothers are in a natural position to form a strong relationship with the child because of their extreme love and nurturance, the frequency of contact, and their ability to focus on immediate needs. Relying on mothers for their very survival, children expect their support and consistency in life. *This psychological sustenance may be the most important element of the modern day parent-child attachment.*

I love tea. I drink hot, steaming cups all day long, teaching classes, writing, during meetings with colleagues. Afternoons, students sip tea in my office, our conversations often beginning with class and ending with their personal issues around family and friends. In my clinical practice, parents share their concerns about children and teens as the tea kettle simmers.

I also collect teapots from around the world. Some come from my own travels; others are gifts from family and friends. Each pot has a story or person behind it, making it special to me, such as the one from my Aunt Kitty in Ireland. The family matriarch, and now in her eighties, several years ago she impulsively pulled out a new metal teapot from the cabinet in her farm kitchen.

"Take this one. I hear you collect them."

"Aunt Kitty, I can't. You bought it for yourself."

"I did. But one day I'll be gone. Then you'll look at it and think of me."

That shiny little teapot has a place of honor on my window sill. With the charming store sticker remaining in full view, I look up, smile, and do think of her often.

The blue enameled pot tells me my husband remembered me in China. As did my children at Christmas, with a hand-painted Japanese tea set, a woman's face delicately molded into the porcelain bottom of each cup. A tiny silver teapot dangling on a necklace reminds me of the student whose problems we worked out together those quiet afternoons. And the note cards that arrive with designs of friends sharing steaming cups carry messages like "This one had your name on it!" or "I miss you."

Tea sustains me because it reminds me of shared times with my mother. After I started school, she worked as a custodian in aircraft factories, cleaning until her raw, rough hands bled. With washing, ironing, and other chores at home, her days and evenings were very full.

But sometime each day, she would quietly ask, "Cup of tea?" During those special conversations, we sat at the kitchen table and talked. Sometimes my brother or father joined us, the first cup leading easily to the second. Other times we visited alone, discussing small things and large. School pressures, friends, gossip. Some discussions were work-directed, where she sternly quizzed me on spelling words and math facts, or listened intently as I read an essay aloud. "I don't like the way you describe that character. And you need to relax more and be less formal. I like the history part, though. Never be afraid to back up what you say."

From her I learned the Irish respect for the written word.

My grandmother's rheumatoid arthritis forced my mother to quit school early to mind her many younger brothers and sisters. But the trip from an Irish farm to a lower-middle class neighborhood in America didn't change Mom's values. Two things mattered most: her family and an education. Today, my steaming cups and my teapots bring her back, when she can no longer listen to my thoughts or critique my writing. They remind me of special times.

When parents have conversations with their children, they show them that they are important. Chatting together, listening to each other, they build a trust bond that secures children's positive feelings about themselves and adults. *Bonding with an adult is the most important factor to a child's healthy development because it both prevents and lessens stress, while helping children understand that they are not alone in solving life's problems.* But it requires time together as well as an accepting openness.

My situation was far from unique. Often, the mother-child bond is the core of future healthy relationships. Adult siblings share "Mom stories" from childhood, laughing delightedly or remembering poignantly those times unique to their upbringing. They hear themselves use phrases with their own children that they swore they would never repeat. *Clean your plate: Think of all the starving children in the world! or Close the door! Did you grow up in a barn?*

Adults remain attached to activities they enjoyed as youth, especially those that the family shared. As milk and sugar in tea, many habits or small idiosyncrasies we perform daily are not as original as others might think. They were family behaviors we experienced as children, and for better or worse, they remain with us as a tie to our past, a reminder of shared relationships. They are part of our history. When introducing them to others, particularly our own children, we modernize them to meet the needs of hurried lifestyles.

For example, with crowded family schedules, bedtime may become more important for conversation than the traditional dinner hour. Reading a book to a young child or listening to a teen's concerns about friends shows that parents care. In reaching out to children, we should look for specific times each day to share ourselves. While a busy world makes this more difficult, it also makes it more important. Often, calm and quiet moments are even more remarkable to children in contrast with the frenetic pace of their daily life.

No situation is in itself special for developing close relationships within a family. It is what we bring to that place or moment. How wonderful to hope that as adults, our children will feel a warmth about special times such as evenings, thinking back to books or bedtime conversations. There are many ways to share tea.

Even in overwhelming situations such as wartime, close mother-child attachments provide a strong buffer to lessen stress. It was heart-breaking to watch the televised tragedy of nearly a million refugees leaving and then returning to Kosovo on foot and with few possessions. Yet, they held their children tightly, as a prize, not a burden. Often with missing fathers and no knowledge if relatives lived or died, they still carried a sense of *family*, because of their mother's presence.

Fathers

But Fathers matter too. Anthropologist Margaret Mead's remark that fathers are a "biological necessity, but a social accident," clearly dismisses the really significant part men play in raising children. Indeed, fathers are not only role models, but they set definite limits on behavior and often hold higher standards for performance than mothers do.

As Robert Frost commented, "You don't have to deserve your mother's love. You have to deserve your father's. He's more particular." Mothers tend to judge children's behavior on a case-by-case basis. They try to understand why their teen over-slept for work on a Saturday morning. Wasn't he feeling well? Did he have an argument with his girlfriend the night before? Often, mothers withhold judgment and response until examining all the facts. They forgive quickly. Yet, their unconditional love and nurturing can cause them to be too understanding at times, defending the child to others when the behavior is obviously unacceptable.

On the other hand, fathers tend to be the standard-bearers. They won't accept most reasons the teen gives for missing work, instead assuming a lack of initiative that will be detrimental in life. Often, fathers set expectations for future achievement through ongoing demands. They represent adult society by not accepting excuses for poor performance. They compare the teen's actions with those expected in the workplace. While they may respond as subjectively as mothers, they do so for different reasons.

Children need both kinds of love. The mother's unconditional regard supports their esteem by showing them they are loved despite what they do. The father's sterner requirements impose societal standards so they feel a greater need to accomplish goals and gain independence.

Often fathers play more with children than mothers do. They run, chase, and encourage young bodies to climb over them. Into their teen years, youth turn more to their fathers for activities and to their mothers for consolation and nurturing.

From as young as three years, boys watch their fathers closely. Wanting to be the best "men" possible, they imitate body posture and attitudes. Often, they spend time together by doing things with their fathers, such as sports and hobbies. Action directs discussion, with comments ranging from new computer software to season touchdown passes. For males, the act of a shared conversation may be more important than the topic itself.

Young girls relate differently. They examine the relationship between their parents and note the factors Dad admires in women. They listen carefully to his words of personal approval. Does he say, "You're so pretty" or "What a soccer player"? He may show her report card to neighbors, commenting "She's really smart." In many ways, he tells her daily those features she should emulate to be a good woman. Many fathers are more protective of daughters than of sons, working harder to keep them from physical harm. Often, girls grow up with a sense of security, knowing that their fathers will not let anything happen to them.

But both for sons and daughters, fathers set levels of expectation. Through direct involvement in their children's lives, they give impressions and values that last a lifetime.

To many, Bill McCaffrey's life ended years before it was actually over. A promising young attorney newly out of military service, the world lay before him as he established his burgeoning practice. Intelligent and sensitive, he was a kind listener, surprisingly wise for his youth.

Much of that wisdom came from his father. As a young, only child, Bill was always at his father's side. Often, the two quietly conversed over issues ranging from batting averages to schoolwork. Other times, they simply shared the moment, saying nothing at all. Evenings, the tall and small figures walked hand-in-hand down busy city streets, stopping to visit with neighbors, nodding and greeting surprised strangers.

In food and conversation, Bill's capable mother nurtured both her men, remarking often at their powerful attachment.

"It's wonderful. They don't need to talk like I do. They just enjoy being together."

Years later, it was of no surprise that Bill's father was quietly there for his young attorney son when the doctor pronounced, "Muscular Dystrophy."

The disease took its physical toll quickly. Brief years passed, and with quiet emotion, Bill shut down his law practice. Confined to a wheelchair and unable to care for himself, his parents invited him to move back home. As his mother cooked and fussed, his father returned to Bill's side for evening conversations. They slipped easily into their comfortable relationship, no longer as father-son, but now as friends.

Although his muscles deteriorated, Bill's mind never lost its sharpness. He inhaled books and news reports, engaging visitors in heated discussions over literature, history, and politics. As his voice weakened, turning soft and hoarse, friends strained to learn from him. He spoke most often of the need for justice for the disadvantaged and people of color.

"Why not use my family as a model?" he asked. "My needs are tremendous, but my parents care for me. I hope I give back in turn. We can help the poor make it. We just need to change our attitude to support training and jobs. In a system of *us* and *them*, I'm afraid we may actually be the problem."

His steady stream of visitors never came out of duty or pity.

Bill was their teacher. Not only of ideas from the books he read, but through his own reflections and observations on life's lessons. He sat in his chair, deceptively removed from activity. Yet, his whispered words projected involvement, optimism, and excitement in the future. He never complained about the disease. He only praised his parents for their love and continued care.

Years passed. Bill's aging, stooped body was wheeled into a nursing home after his father died and his mother could no longer care for him. Instead of voicing anger or bitterness at his situation, Bill became the advocate for patients' rights, such as a staff member positioned by the elevator door and variety in food for individual tastes. Despite his press for services, administrators and nurses respected his role, his deep commitment to improve others' situations through enhanced safety and small pleasures.

Eyes brightly lit, his immobilized body no longer distracted visitors during intense discussions. It had become part of who he was. Long before, with his father seated next to his reclining chair, Bill had accepted the disease and himself. Others could do no less. Acknowledging his compassion, the staff asked him to write columns for the monthly nursing home newsletter, sharing his reflections with a broader audience of patients and their families. Unable even to raise his chin from his chest, he dictated his thoughts to a high school volunteer, her ear close to his slowly moving lips. His voice almost indistinguishable, she paused often to ask him to repeat a word or phrase. Never impatient, he smiled warmly at her interest.

Bill dictated the following for the Father's Day newsletter:

What's Happening

Dear Dad,

Not once did you ever tell me that you loved me. Our culture did not condone a Father verbalizing love to or for a son. Your actions, deeds and examples expressed that love more eloquently than any words.

You made no attempt to teach me anything, but I learned so much from you. You had no philosophy of life, but you lived day by day in a philosophical way.

You found good and goodness in everyone and everything. I never saw you display anger. You seemed to treat anger as a waste of time. From your view, anger was not only non-productive, but counterproductive. When the weather was hazy, hot and humid and everyone was complaining about it, you would comment, "It's hot, but there's a little breeze."

You never presented yourself in a threatening judgmental way, but as a friend who was entirely engrossed in what I had to say. As early as I can remember, I could come to you and would get your undivided attention, not because you felt that was the thing you were supposed to do, but because it was just in your nature. You taught me the value of listening. Your thinking process was always clear, precise, uncomplicated and almost childlike in nature. Your reasoning, in its simplicity, was brilliant. To paraphrase baseball parlance, you kept your eye on the ball.

I remember a particular Brooklyn Dodgers baseball game that we went to at Ebbetts Field in 1947. It was the year that the first black ballplayer, Jackie Robinson, played in the big leagues. We got there before the game and the entire Dodgers team was on the field practicing. A young boy asked of no one in particular, "Which one's Robinson?" What with twenty-five Dodger uniformed players on the field and 24 with white faces, the question appeared to cry out for the obvious answer, but as far as you were concerned, what this young kid asked was a simple baseball question and it deserved a simple baseball answer. You glanced at your score card and said simply, "He's number 42." So simple.

I was also caught up in the culture of no no's. I never once told you that I loved you. I learned very early from you that actions speak louder than words. Over the years I used your method of communication, with me sending and you receiving the message of love many times and in many ways.

When you died 9 years ago, the Pastor of the church, in preparing for his homily or eulogy, asked me if I would describe you in one sentence. My answer, "He was a very kind man."

"Honor Thy Father," the commandment goes. God! I will for the rest of my life.

Bill McCaffrey, rm. 214
Central Island Health Care

When Bill died, friends recalled that he too was an extremely kind man. He spoke of fairness and justice, never openly regretting their absence in his own battle with Muscular Dystrophy. It was only in reading this letter that others realized how closely Bill had not only modeled upon, but fully adopted, his father's behaviors. A simple reaction at a baseball game provided an example of how to ignore racial differences. Even his later advocacy for the less advantaged in the nursing home was a natural outcome of his childhood.

Bill's own lack of anger at his situation, indeed his very ability to listen to the concerns and ideas of others, were a continuance of family attitudes. Sadly, the inability of father and son to express their love for each other kept Bill from speaking the words he later wrote. How I wish his father could have heard them first-hand. No one has ever suffered later regrets from expressing love to a family member. Yet, Bill's father knew his son loved him. He listened in many ways.

When children talk to us, they entrust us with their ideas, their personal beliefs. Adults who listen undividedly and are fully attentive to what their children have to say earn a closeness that can last a lifetime. Parents also build their sons and daughters' self-esteem by indicating that what they are saying is important.

Currently, with violence erupting in our schools, we see children turning to each other for acceptance, for listening. If their friends are poor role models, they take on these negative values in order to belong, to be important to someone. When children have parents who spend time with them, engaging in conversation to clarify their newly developing values, important emotional bonding occurs. Subsequently, they tend to follow parental ideas and suggestions instead of relying totally on peers. These conversations begin when children are very young. Telling the two-year-old, "We don't hit others!" Explaining to the six-year-old why racial slurs are wrong. Sitting up late with the fifteen-year-old who is furious at being treated unfairly by peers.

Keeping Your Teen from Abusing Substances

Columbia University's National Center on Addiction and Substance Abuse has reported that teens in two-parent families who have a fair or poor relationship with their father are

68 percent more likely to use drugs than those who have good interactions with their father. Of the 2000 surveyed youth between ages twelve and seventeen, 70 percent indicated that they had very good or excellent relationships with their mother, while only 58 percent had a similar rapport with their father. Importantly, teens raised by a single mother with whom they shared a strong bond were less likely to smoke, drink, and use drugs than were children in a two-parent family where youth had a fair or poor relationship with their father.

Fifty-seven percent of teens interviewed commented that it was easier to talk to their mother about drugs, while 26 percent preferred talking to their father, and 17 percent did not know. Mothers were reported as more likely to have private conversations with their children about substances, and to influence children's important decisions three times as often as fathers.

The study also indicated that teens who never have dinner with their families have a 70 percent greater risk of substance abuse.

As with Bill McCaffrey's father never saying he loved him, there are still cultural tendencies that devalue men being involved in family life. Most fathers work hard to financially support their families, providing the food their children eat and the backyard where they play. But when parents are unable to share meals and conversations, children are the losers. Nothing a parent can do will make up for the loss of a son or daughter to drugs or alcohol. Once youth are addicted, it becomes exponentially more difficult to help them. When parents talk with their young children, they form a communication bond that continues into adolescence. When children receive good advice in early years, they return for more as teenagers. But parents have to be available to talk. Fathers as well as mothers need to be emotionally involved with children's development so that they can guide them around the allure of drugs and alcohol. Neither parent is more important. A child needs both.

Getting in Touch

In order to relate to children and help them handle modern day stress and pressures, we have to establish a dialogue. It's the inability to understand each other's feelings that under-cuts most relationships. Adults expect teens to be difficult, and often they are. Youth feel that grown-ups are unreason-able, and, at times, they may be right. We can't form a strong bond if we don't relate to each other's worlds. To relate, first we have to listen.

In cross-cultural studies, Jerome Kagen found that teenagers continuously noted that one of the best indicators of a loving parent was a listening parent. These adults under-stood that during conversations, their sons' and daughters' comments were more important than their own. Teens try out new concepts by discussing them. They hear the sound of their own evolving ideas, quickly consider their reasonable-ness, and look to listeners to agree or disagree.

Yet, every parent and teacher knows that disagreeing with a child, and especially a teen, can be perilous to our health! Initially, youth may seem doggedly stuck in an idea, sure that they're right, and angry that others don't see it their way. A few days later, adults may hear an entirely different, even opposing, viewpoint. A questioning, "But you said..." results in "I did not!" Usually this dramatic turnaround happens after the teen rejects first impressions or talks to friends who dis-agree. Since teens believe the way they see things at the moment is the way things have always been, they may not even fully remember the strength of their original belief.

Responding with a pseudo-sophistication about the world, teens may become self-righteous and angry when adults dis-agree with them. They feel very knowledgeable because they have "seen it" on television or videos. They have "heard it" from friends or in explicit song lyrics. Often, teens don't real-ize that parents experienced similar feelings during life situa-tions, providing them a perspective. When parents try to explain issues involving sex, alcohol, or drugs, bored teens may become impatient, rolling their eyes and looking superi-or as they make adults feel foolish.

To the detriment of family relationships, some adults dis-miss teen fashion and language as fads. From the teen's per-spective, parents and professionals may appear unsophisti-cated because they don't wear stylish clothing or use the cor-rect "in" term of the moment. Since these trappings are all-important to youths' acceptance by peers, teens view adults as naive and inexperienced in understanding what matters in today's world.

Why should they listen to an adult who claims never to have used drugs? This parent can't possibly know what it's like to live in a world where there are drugs available, not just from street corners, but from friends' lockers. Adult opinion seems farcical anyway, coming from one who wears worn shoes and old sweaters. Today's teens are excited by the young and new. Anything "old" is questionable because it is not current, not in harmony with the times.

Teaching Children to Use Better Judgment

In addition to dismissing parents and professionals as out-of-touch with their fast-moving reality, modern-day children may confuse opinion with fact. They believe that if they feel something strongly, it must be true. In an open, non-traditional society, this is easy to understand, since adults consider young people's ideas from an early age. We ask their opinions about food and clothes, preference in friends, and choice of family activities. We encourage them to speak openly and we value their ideas. It's ironic that as we build their esteem, we may be leading them to believe that their way is the only way. At home and in classrooms, many children become annoyed if their viewpoint is not accepted on face value. They confuse feelings with logic, often giving emotional responses to matters of fact.

When making critical decisions, these quick responses to life situations result in poor judgment. Children who feel that their parents aren't "with it" dismiss adults and don't consult them about important issues. They feel they know the best way to behave because they and their peers agree. Hormones become stronger in adolescence, encouraging unchecked, heightened emotional responses, and our own children do things we would never expect.

Teaching Children to Control their Impulses

In a study commissioned by the Metropolitan Educational Research Consortium in Richmond, Virginia, researchers interviewed 62 resilient, academically successful children about the reasons behind their excellent school performance. Despite their being at-risk due to problems in their homes, these students indicated that they had been able to develop strong internal controls over their behavior. The younger ones attributed their success to the guidance of teachers and counselors. The older ones pointed to one or more adults who had helped them manage and take responsibility for their actions. Interviewers identified impulse control as the critical overall factor in students' abilities to handle upset and crisis.

Usually, parents are in the best position to teach these skills, helping children learn from an early age that their feelings and urges can mislead them dramatically. Young children tend to chat away at times, with busy adults not listening closely to their words. Yet, we should never ignore what children say. They are sharing with us their developing values and their understanding of the way the world works. When a child talks about wanting to hurt another, the parent can respond, "We don't ever hurt other people. It's wrong. What happened? Let's talk about why you're so angry and what you can do." Through these conversations, adults help children understand the importance of self-control when dealing with adversity.

Everyone loves a story, especially about real people showing bravery or responding to unlikely situations. But stories can also underscore how we should behave and ways to curb our urges. The reason adults retell the worn story of George Washington and the cherry tree is that it portrays the value of honesty despite the threat of punishment, a real concern in children's lives. We relate it when we catch children lying, guiding them around an impulse to escape by using the easy way around problems.

Children may supply facts when they lack understanding of phenomena around them. Four-year-old Mark excitedly shares, "That train went ten million miles an hour!" His parents can have him tell this to other adults, who will laugh at his cute exaggeration, based on lack of understanding of numbers. Or they can say, "You're right, it's really fast. A train can't go ten million miles an hour, but I bet this one's going about eighty miles an hour." At this age, the difference in speed won't mean anything to him, but he'll learn the lesson that his first impressions are not always correct. Later, pleased with his new factual knowledge, he will greet grandparents with "I saw a really fast train. It went eighty miles an hour!"

Knowledge flourishes from a deep basis of exploring possibilities and solving problems. Without realizing it, teachers reinforce that factual information isn't important when they encourage "inventive spelling," dismissing correctness for the creative act of writing, or permit the use of calculators in elementary grades so students can move on to new ideas quickly. Some secondary schools allow students to write term papers from brief Internet searches, not requiring them to examine the knowledge base or reputation of the author. "Yahoo" or "Lycos" becomes the source. Throughout schooling, adults must expect children to support beliefs by examining all sides of an issue and the quality of the information behind each viewpoint. Then young people can make better judgments about their lives.

We have to respect children's feelings as their own, as personal and indisputable. Yet, we must teach them that in science, math, history, literature, and the arts, great thoughts have existed for centuries and we are all smarter for using these ideas to develop our own thoughts. We wouldn't want the surgeon to remove our gall bladder based on her intuition about where it might be in our body. In bad weather, we wouldn't want our pilot to land where he felt a runway should be. Children need to know that the best-received opinions and the most successful actions are based on facts, not on emotions or intuition.

Then, moving to the personal, we can underscore factual reasons behind values, relating issues to their own lives through logic and discussion, asking them to reflect on tremendously important issues. Why don't we hurt others? What are the physical and personal outcomes of drug use? How will my future be impacted by pregnancy?

Combatting the teen sense that adults are old and out-of-touch, many schools have successfully brought in speakers whose lives have been altered by poor judgment, based on emotions of the moment. When Magic Johnson announced that he was HIV-positive, teenage boys took note because they look up to him. When the public scrutinizes young movie stars for eating disorders, girls talk about it. Yet, it's sad when children and teens relate more to a famous stranger with whom they've never had a conversation, than to their own parents, who want to communicate and understand their experiences.

Quantity vs. Quality Time

Today's hurried world provides fewer opportunities to be the type of parent most adults want. We speak of *quality time* instead of *quantity time*, acknowledging that work and other demands have won the battle of the clock. I believe that we need to re-examine our priorities, that we need to improve both the quality and the quantity of our time with children. We have to be there more often and we have to be more involved in their daily lives.

The problem with "quality time" is that it evolves around parents' schedules, rather than when children want us to be there to talk or listen. Teens like to talk at night, but adults need sleep for work the next day, making it difficult to stay up until midnight. Children might be worried about a test or a potential confrontation at school that day, but parents have to rush them through breakfast and off to the bus stop. No time to talk. So we don't learn what's going on in the teen's life, and the younger child develops a stomach ache.

While adults have to work and are involved in a busy life and schedule, we really do have more opportunity daily to improve the quality of even brief times spent with families. It saddens me to visit a household where children aren't talking to brothers and sisters or their parents, instead sitting totally focused on a television program. Parents may be fixing dinner or doing laundry, feeling that their children are safely occupied.

Instead of occupying children's time, it's better to fill it with enriching conversations and activities. When parents are driving teens with headphones to an activity, they're losing valuable sharing time while the young person may be listening to lyrics with angry messages. How sad to replace conversations with wrath. Teens will pick up on the messages they hear. Words from a parent are better than words from a song.

Child Privacy vs. Child Secrecy

There are many ways to enjoy our families. From carpools to visiting while doing chores, parents can talk to their children and teens, staying in touch with their worlds. However, when young people isolate themselves in their rooms with a telephone, television, VCR, and stereo, they can experience many harmful influences of which parents are unaware.

Children have more rights than ever in today's society. Used in a healthy manner with parental guidance, they can grow up to savor their independence and become stronger adults. But frequent exposure to permissive violence and sex teaches them a different message. When they know they're viewing or listening to messages their parents wouldn't normally allow, many young people become secretive and stay in their rooms or at friends' houses, becoming "hooked" on the sensational.

Some after-school talk shows promote the outrageous in order to entertain viewers. Children are mesmerized as adults scream at each other, describing horrible personal situations. Children learn what they see and hear. Several years ago, a group of teens was arrested for cruelties they committed as part of a young satanic cult in their community. Their primary defense was that they had heard specific acts of mutilation discussed on television by members of an adult satanic cult. One boy testified that he felt that his desire to perform torturous acts on animals and people was supported since adults had corroborated it on a popular talk show by describing their own similar behaviors.

Cities such as Atlanta have started "Teen Talk Radio" to combat the trend toward isolation and to provide positive media input. Each day, teenagers anonymously call in their concerns and problems, discussing them with other youth, parents, and authorities such as the police. As one young man commented, "It's good to know you're not alone." Without a preachy tone or a goal other than offering support, such efforts have met with immediate success among young people who want help in dealing with daily problems. Interestingly, the majority of callers convey concerns about school success, problems with peers, and personal safety. They report less frequent fears about drugs or violence as a daily part of their lives.

It's normal for teenagers to spend more time with friends than with adults. They tell parents not to invade their privacy by looking in their rooms or inquiring about their social life. While most parents avoid searching rooms unless they suspect drug or weapons use, they should keep interactions open through daily conversations with teens about their activities. If drugs or weapons are found, or if their children are "hanging out" with others who use them, adults must not accept *any* excuse for this behavior. Your child's denial of involvement is not enough. The proof is in their behaviors and their friends.

When these situations occur, counseling can be very beneficial. Youth who normally refuse to meet with a psychologist or religious counselor often agree if the entire family goes. At the same time, parents should tighten rules, personally remove all weapons or substances from the house, and regulate the teen's activities and friends. Meeting with the school counselor and working with teachers to redirect the teen into extracurricular activities will help school become an important stabilizing factor.

It is easier to *prevent* isolation from the family into secret activities than to deal with it once it occurs. The suggestions on both charts describe healthy family patterns that will encourage openness among all family members. When these patterns are set in younger children, the teenage years usually are much easier. If your child has already become secretive and withdrawn, it is important to set firm curfews, know where the child is at all times, and get to know friends' parents. Looking for a hobby or interest to share and making time to talk daily will also encourage a stronger bond with adults. While young people may be quiet or seem disinterested at first, they warm quickly when the parent shows genuine interest in their lives without being dogmatic or pushy.

Taking Charge at Home

As part of establishing healthy home patterns early, parents need to carefully structure the family's daily routine for children and teens. As noted in these charts, children benefit from a specified time and location for homework each evening, away from interruptions such as television and telephone. An organized week begins on Sunday night, when children and parents arrange notebooks and discuss upcoming schoolwork and activities. Together they can set a schedule for when chores such as laundry and cleaning should be done.

A daily routine is critical to establishing a comfort level within hurried schedules. Children should rise with their own alarm or radio, not with parents' continual prodding. Breakfast is critical. If the family had dinner at 6 P.M. the night before and the child skips breakfast, it will be eighteen hours before the next meal at noon! While we adults can grab a snack between meals, children can't do this at school. It's hard to concentrate on learning long division when your stomach's growling. Hungry children are distracted, lowering their academic performance. Claims that they would rather sleep in than eat breakfast usually signify that children need an earlier bedtime. Both their rest and morning meal are important to their health and school success.

Often, parents report that children will not get up on their own in the morning, or that they refuse to turn off the television during homework. In these situations, parents need to regain control of the family. Adults can award or withhold privileges based on how independently children wake up and get dressed each morning. We can also turn off the television and restrict hours of phone calls, signaling that homework is important.

Seated next to each other on a flight from Washington, a Congressman and I talked about childhood and the art of raising healthy children. He noted that he, his brothers, and sisters were all happy adults, doing well personally with their families. Noting that some were in blue-collar and others in white-collar jobs, he said that it wasn't their occupational level that gave them satisfaction, but a sense of being in control of their lives.

Laughing, he described an incident from his childhood, where his family finally bought a color television.

"I know it makes me sound ancient, but we were country folks, didn't have a lot of money or things, so this was really a big deal.

"Well, all five of us kids wouldn't leave it. We didn't want to go outside much anymore, and we even argued with my mother about having dinner at the table. We fought with Mom about watching it during homework. She'd turn it off and we'd turn it back on. We figured we'd wear her down eventually."

Shaking his head, he continued.

"Dad came home one night and found Mom crying in the kitchen. She said that the television had taken over, that she couldn't stand all the arguing, and that the kids refused to listen to her any more.

"He came into the living room, where we were all glued to the set. Without saying a word, he unplugged it and carried it outside. We all ran after him screaming, including my mother.

"To our amazement, he carried it up the hill that marked the end of our property. And he threw it off the hilltop! He just threw it away, and we heard it smash into a thousand pieces.

"Then he looked at Mom, who still had her mouth open, and he said 'There, I think that should solve the problem.' He turned and walked back to the house.

"We cried, we yelled, and as I recall, we didn't speak to him for weeks. He didn't even react. He just ignored us and went about his business. We didn't get another TV for years, and we all followed the family rules that time.

"Today, it's become a family joke, and we still tease Dad. But he made his point. He wasn't going to let anything take away our focus on the important things in life. And he taught us that children can't be allowed to take over the family. Adults have to keep control and set guidelines."

As he told me that story, I imagined scores of parents on hilltops, tossing over televisions and video game equipment. We may not have enough hills to meet the desire! One of the most common complaints I hear from parents is that videos and the Internet have taken over their children's lives. The Congressman's father yielded to his own impulses to make a point. Yet, there has to be a calmer, less-destructive way to handle this sense of technology overwhelming the family. Without throwing things over a hilltop, adults can turn controls off. It's not always popular to be a parent.

The true voice of American wisdom, Ann Landers, commented, "Television has proved that people will look at anything rather than each other." Even within families, adults have to show children how to talk to each other by providing opportunities for shared conversations. Interactions are much poorer when family members are looking at a television instead of each other when they are speaking. These body messages indicate that the televised message is more important than the thoughts of spouses, brothers and sisters.

When we model and enforce behaviors from the time children are young, they integrate these behaviors into their own habits. Later, as teens, when they test rules such as turning off the television during dinner, we can remind them that "In this house..." we behave a certain way.

Getting in Touch with Children

❏ Carpooling: Listen to children's conversations with each other. Informally ask about school and activities.

❏ Bedtime: Assemble clothes for the next day. Read stories together or just talk. Avoid being critical of the child's behavior that day. Hugs and "I love you" are always in order!

❏ Television and Video Games: Watch and discuss TV with children. Monitor their shows and compare content with family values. Avoid allowing children to watch too much TV or to spend hours at video games. Decide in advance which shows and games are allowed, limiting the number each day, after homework is completed. TV or video games in a child's room discourages focus on homework and family. TV should be turned off during reading and conversations.

❏ Homework: Schedule homework at the same time, early each evening. The child should complete all reading assignments before attempting written work. Parents should not complete the child's homework, but review its correctness. Quiz before tests, explaining unclear concepts. Have the child arrange papers and books to take to school the next day.

❏ Chores: Household chores are more fun when done together during scheduled times, daily and weekly. Informally ask questions about school and activities. If children are non-communicative, chat about light, social topics. Compliment them on how well they are working ("I like the way you're setting the table" or "Thanks for the good clean-up after dinner tonight").

❏ Dinner: Have children suggest and help cook meals they enjoy. Let the child prepare part of the meal, asking your advice and taking pride in the results. Turn off the TV during preparation and dinner, allowing for better conversations. After the meal, clean up together. Prepare next day's lunches.

Getting in Touch with Children (cont.)

❏ Mornings: Because everyone is rushed, mornings are rarely a good time for close conversations. When parents get up early, mornings are calmer. Children should not turn the TV on before school, as it distracts them from getting ready. Reminders about carpools and after-school plans prepare the child for upcoming activities that day. Informally sharing newspaper items (i.e., significant world and domestic events) makes children less self-involved and more competent as world citizens. At school, they gain respect by discussing this knowledge.

❏ Sunday evenings: Informally discuss field-trips, exams, and after-school activities, preparing for the upcoming school week. Together, organize notebooks, file papers, collect supplies. The child will feel more secure with things in order and will learn important planning and organizational skills.

❏ Every day: Schedule an undemanding family time (at least 15 to 30 minutes) to spend with each child individually. Turn off the TV and ignore the telephone. Let children know that they have your undivided attention. Save this time for informal conversations and activities you both enjoy (i.e., games, crafts). Parents should not allow other children to interrupt, explaining that they will have their individual time as well.

❏ Weekends: This is a good time to complete chores together and schedule family activities that everyone enjoys (i.e., movies, bike rides). If children are involved in sports or performances, it is important for parents to attend. Part of Saturday and Sunday should be for quiet relaxation, both for parents and children.

Getting in Touch with Teens

❑   Late at Night: Unfortunately, teens are natural night animals, and prefer discussions late in the day. Often on the phone with friends earlier in the evening, they are more open to share personal thoughts with adults.

❑   Carpooling Younger Teens: Parents' last chance before teens are driving, this is a good opportunity to ask questions about their social concerns, encouraging open conversations.

❑   Weekly: Flexibly schedule time each week for a shared family activity (i.e., a movie, dinner out together). Together, parents and teens can select what they would enjoy. It's important that family-time not conflict with friends' activities.

❑   Television: Watch TV shows with teens, openly comparing family values to those observed. Ask teens their ideas about what they are watching. Watch an in-depth news report every day, one including a range of stories about people from around the world and their experiences (i.e., from war to sports). Discussing TV opens conversation about ethics and acceptable social behaviors.

❑   Hobbies and Activities: Together, continue a hobby or activity enjoyed from childhood to a more sophisticated level. Have teens teach you games they enjoy. Watch sports and arts performances, videos, and movies.

❑   Shopping: Notorious shoppers, teens will discuss styles and fads as you accompany them in buying clothes and personal items. Frequent trips for small purchases are better than one long shopping trip where everyone becomes tired. Shopping provides a good opportunity to discuss budget, savings, and credit card use. Teens often model on parents' spending habits.

Getting in Touch with Teens (cont.)

❑ Weekends: Parents should be at home when teens have friends over. Chat informally as you supervise them. Check to assure parental supervision when teens are at a friend's home. Stay up to be sure your teen meets curfew. Many times he or she will want to talk when coming home from a party or activity. Schedule weekend times for shared family activities the teen enjoys.

❑ Computers and Internet: Learn how to use new software together. Share Internet searches, looking up information for school, travel, and of general interest. Don't encourage your teen to engage in solitary activities such as playing video games alone or engaging in chat rooms. Making the Internet a joint activity will allow you to supervise information.

❑ Meals: Talk about your own day, welcoming teens to share comments about school and activities. If they are non-communicative, discuss social and world issues. Ask their opinion. Do not use mealtime to criticize their behavior or schoolwork. Mealtime should be based around mutual schedules. If teens routinely miss dinner, it is best to reschedule the meal. Snacks provide a good opportunity to visit informally. Food and the kitchen are wonderfully conducive to conversation.

❑ Chores: Do chores together during a set time. Plan and carry out large, joint projects such as re-painting their room. Show teens how to fix things by working together around the house. Ask their opinion about even small re-decorating projects. Compliment their involvement and performance. A major part of the teen's allowance should include completion of weekly errands. But it's more fun when parents and teens do them together.

Supervision

The suggestions in the charts include interactive ways to share time both during scheduled activities and relaxation. Yet, in all these situations, parents are actually supervising behaviors. Supervision comes in many forms as adults and children interact. When carpooling, if children voice angry or prejudicial statements, parents can redirect them immediately. If teens like to shop too much, managing money poorly, parents can help them set up a budget as well as determining their need for a job. When children spend hours playing video games, adults should set rules for the amount of time allowed daily or weekly.

Quality time occurs when parents are there for children, guiding them through life's logistics and experiences. As with Jesús and his mother, some of the most important times are when the child understands that the parent will be there for support despite what happens. Or, as with Bill McCaffrey and his father, quality times can be spent together without speaking at all. Sometimes parents' presence is more important that anything spoken. Other times, what they say guides children in gaining their own resilience. When adults accept responsibility for supervising their children, they set standards for compassionate and ethical behavior.

Yet, we can certainly share fun at the same time. Parents and children of all ages enjoy activities together, ranging from crafts and sports to hikes and games. Teens are most willing to continue family times if they've enjoyed certain activities from childhood. Working on bicycle repairs is a natural compatibility for working on cars together later. Joint cooking and baking activities, building models, and shared computer software gain excitement as the young adult reaches new levels of sophistication and enters into friendly competition with parents.

These times are excellent opportunities for conversations about personal matters or about the activity itself. Parents should never place pressure for heavy conversations during shared times, or their children will refuse any future involvement. If the child has a learning disability or a behavioral disorder, it's natural for adults to focus much of their time discussing the problem. Yet, the child must come first. It's more fun for everyone if the problem is not always discussed, allowing a normal relationship to develop.

I met with a father who was concerned because his son, Keith, now away at college, never wanted to talk to him on the phone. The boy called his mother at her office, and at the end of their lengthy conversations, offered a lame "Tell Dad *Hi!*" When the father phoned, after a few brief comments, his son always needed to go somewhere.

During Keith's semester break, his father finally confronted him about the avoidance. The boy's response was very honest.

"You only care about my learning problems. That's all we ever talked about at home when I was growing up. Now, you still ask me if I'm organizing my time and studying enough for tests. I hate talking to you.

"Mom wants to know how I like the campus and what activities I'm involved in. She treats me like a real person, not a dummy."

The father was shocked. Trying to prepare his son for independence, he emphasized problems instead of successes. While these conversations were necessary, they became the primary focus of their relationship.

Father and son struck a deal. Keith agreed to receive tutoring and academic support through campus services. During phone conversations, he would bring up schoolwork when he wanted his parents' opinions. At the end of the semester, if his grades were low, the family would sit down and discuss alternatives, adults together solving a problem.

His father felt immediate relief at turning a nagging issue over to Keith and the university.

"I still bite my tongue when we're on the phone. I want to throw in a quick question about how classes are going or if he's having problems researching his papers. But I'm getting better. The first time he called home and asked to speak to me, I felt very emotional. I don't want to mess that up. I'm just sorry we didn't do more things together outside of schoolwork when he was growing up. But we're enjoying each other a lot more these days. He's really a good kid and I've decided to get to know him better."

The Best Parents

Staying in touch with children is the most important way to help them through troubled times. As the saying goes, we were given "two eyes and two ears, but only one mouth," encouraging us to observe and listen before reacting. Yet, responses should clearly indicate that we are there to help young people gain and keep control of their lives through making positive choices.

By exercising good judgment, adults provide a model. By teaching children to question impulses, we teach them to take charge. From a young age, we can show them how to handle problems, even crises, through reasoning and understanding consequences.

The best parents are there for children, both in the quantity and the quality of time together. They establish healthy relationships by showing children they want to be with them, to enjoy life together, and to solve inevitable problems. What parents do now can truly last a lifetime.

Lessons Learned

Spending time with your children shows you love them.

Children do not have to be perfect to embrace healthy values.

The most resilient children have a strong, supportive adult in their lives.

Anytime a teen wants to talk, listen.

We must love children unconditionally, not because of behavior or grades at school.

Children need both quality and quantity of time.

Television will never take the place of a caring parent.

Mothers and fathers show their love differently, but children require both kinds of love.

Never ignore what a child says.

Correct children when they are wrong.

Never let children take control of the household.

Being a good parent may mean saying "No" more often than "Yes."

Each day, schedule a specific time to spend with children.

Listening and talking are the best ways to stay in touch.

Anger and hormones cause teens to do things their parents would never expect.

Children should never go to school tired or hungry.

Good parents are good supervisors.

Sharing hobbies and interests is fun for parents and children alike.

Children need guidance and understanding, along with a firm set of rules.

Chapter 3

Grandparents, Stepparents, Sisters and Brothers Together

From what we get, we can make a living.
What we give, however, makes a life.

Arthur Asche

It was four o'clock in the morning when they finally heard the key scratch repeatedly in search of the lock. Andrea stumbled in, swaying drunkenly toward the sofa, front door left open behind her. Judy and Doug groaned as they pulled themselves out of bed, anticipating another scene. But tonight would go beyond their worst nightmare.

"Where's the baby?" Judy looked quickly around her daughter's passed-out body.

No response.

This time her high-pitched voice gave way to months of anxiety. "Andrea, damn it! Where's Katie?"

The prone body lay silent. His usual gentleness dissolved, Doug pulled his daughter quickly upright, holding her shoulders forcibly and speaking loudly.

"Where's Katie, Andrea? We need to know now!"

Judy raced to look outside into empty darkness, the rough wind and pounding rain tightening her chest with worry. A four month-old infant didn't stand a chance out there.

"Tired. Lem'me sleep," Andrea responded grouchily. Shaking her groggy head, she tried to lay back down.

"Where's the baby?"

Slurred, "The baby? Dunno. Lost. Lem'me alone."

"You lost your baby, Andrea? Like sunglasses or a camera?

She's your baby. You don't lose her!" Judy's increasingly shrill voice filled the room.

"Probably cocaine again, along with the booze." Anxiety lined Doug's face as Andrea sank with dead weight into the cushions. "This time she's gone too far. Let's get on the phone."

Despite the hour, Doug and Judy called all of Andrea's friends' houses. From groggy and annoyed parents, they learned that several of the sixteen year-olds weren't home yet. No one knew their whereabouts, although they tried to be helpful once they awoke to Katie's danger.

Police report filed, they pressed coffee on Andrea, unable to hold back their contempt. Sick and miserable, she could not remember the later places she went that night. Nor the last time she had seen her baby.

"Everybody was holding her like a doll. I don't know who had her when we left. Look, I'm sure she'll show up. What about me right now? Why is it always *Katie* around here? I need some food. Mom, get me something. I feel like hell. Then I'm going to bed."

The last straw broke. Judy and Doug's heads jolted up, as their eyes met purposefully.

Doug's response was quiet but determined. "No, Andrea. Get your own food. But let's find your daughter first. Your mother and I've been talking. Since you quit school, you'll have to get a job if you want to live here anymore."

"Dad, hello in there! I have a baby. I can't work."

"You have no baby. You lost her, remember. You're not up for Mother of the Year, Andrea. From now on, we'll help you raise her, but only if drugs and drink are out. No discussion."

In high emotion, Andrea threw accusations at her parents, while they watched the clock worriedly, waiting for news about Katie.

At 9:03 the phone rang, but it was not the police.

A woman's subdued voice. "Is this Andrea's house?"

Judy held her breath. "Yes. Do you have news about the baby?"

Relief. "Actually, I have the baby. The kids raced through here last night when I was in bed. When they left at about two, I heard her crying on the sofa. No bottle or diapers, of course. I took her to the all-night pharmacy and fixed her up.

She's fed and sleeping now, but I didn't know whose she was. My son just got home and told me." A long hesitation. "I'm surprised Andrea didn't come back for her."

"I'm not. My husband and I will come get her ...."

That terrible night changed their lives forever. Desperate for her adolescent freedom, Andrea agreed to Doug and Judy's terms and found a job as a waitress. Doug went with her to AA and drug counseling, as much to assure her attendance as to give her support. As grandparents, they began the long road so many experience today, that of raising their children's children. Continuing the power struggle, Andrea refused their pleas to adopt Katie. She knew they would always be there as long as she kept the baby.

But when Sam was born two years later, Doug and Judy had to acknowledge their limitations. With no father or financial support present, they insisted she take responsibility and begin caring for the children. Their hearts broke as Katie said good-bye to her "Mi-Maw" and "Poppy," moving with Andrea and infant Sam to their new apartment.

In their engaging innocence, Katie and Sam have been the easy ones. It's the adult Andrea who continues to move from one crisis to another. In and out of substance abuse programs. Terrible judgment in friends. Heavy credit card debt. Job loss after loud confrontations with employers.

The past three years have seen even more problems than Andrea's troubled youth. Male and female friends flow in and out of her tiny apartment, some living there for days, others for months. Doug and Judy's occasional visits end in arguments over the children. Katie's Kindergarten teacher describes bullying behavior, where Katie swears at and hits other children. The sweet little girl Judy and Doug remember is now angry and aggressive, with a temper that flares without obvious provocation.

Sam's body engine is in constant high gear. He snatches food, refusing to sit at the table. His impulsive hitting and shouting indicate emotional problems that Andrea refuses to acknowledge. Already he's been forced to leave two daycare centers after biting other children.

Yet, Katie and Sam's powerful bond with each other is obvious to all. He's her shadow, racing behind, his legs a blur. When his mother or one of her friends yells at him, Katie's

"C'mon, Sam" and her yank on his arm direct him to their cluttered toy space. Hands cupped, she whispers in his ear and he laughs delightedly. Together, they glare suspiciously at others from their private, inseparable world.

They also gang up on Andrea, first ignoring her commands, then screaming and demanding if she persists. When she loses her own explosive temper, they run screeching out the door, pleading with her not to hit them. Katie places her body in front of Sam, threatening to call "Poppy" if Andrea slaps them.

Doug and Judy are at a loss at how to intervene in Katie and Sam's lives. Ready to give up on Andrea, they realize that she holds the key that lets them see their grandchildren. They also know that the children's behaviors will accelerate if they don't receive help now.

What can they do to lessen the power struggle with Andrea and help Katie and Sam grow into resilient, happy children?

Grandparents Raising Grandchildren

In situations as extreme as this, grandparents may be tempted to "throw in the towel" and believe there's nothing they can do. Yet, some of the healthiest children I know have been raised by grandparents who guided them away from drugs and poverty. Not always by choice and often stepping in to avoid catastrophe, their parents' parents raise them to overcome adversity and live healthy lives despite a difficult childhood.

So many times the toughest of youth have told me that if they did drugs or engaged in crime, their grandmother would kill them. Not the law, but their grandmother, from teens whose side of the street we'd avoid at any cost! And when a grandfather is present, he provides that wonderful caring relationship that teaches a boy how to be a man, or encourages a girl to be a special young woman. Frequently, grandparents have questions about their role, whether in chaotic families such as Andrea's, or in happy, adjusted homes, where they simply want to be part of their grandchildren's lives.

Grandparents can have a special impact. In the most difficult of times, they save young lives through caring and redirection. In the best of circumstances, they share an unconditional love that shows grandchildren their worth, that they deserve being loved. In her wonderful autobiography, *Blackberry Winter*, anthropologist Margaret Mead notes that children who have been raised near their grandparents carry a broader, multi-generational perspective. Having been directed by wisdom and experience instead of immediate needs, they understand and deal with life more appropriately.

When crises occur, the courts often award custody of children to grandparents and other close relatives, recognizing the importance of kinship ties. Or, in less extreme situations, adults experiencing difficulty raising their own children turn to family members, especially grandparents, for help and support. While this is natural, it can create financial and personal burdens. There's a lack of information about how relatives can raise healthy children, especially when the biological parents are problemed.

Keys to ongoing success for grandparents are based on perseverance and a positive attitude. Judy, Doug, and other caretakers have to initiate and be consistent in their contact with their grandchildren, providing a sense of security. They must follow through with promises and planned activities. They have to rid children's lives of unpredictability. In unscheduled homes, disorganization prevails. Children are unsure of when they'll have their next meal or if adults will be able to handle even the most basic logistics of daily life.

In considering how children develop *Emotional Intelligence*, Dan Goleman describes the Stanford University *marshmallow tests* that explored which children might be more socially and personally competent later in life. While the experimenter "ran an errand" for fifteen or twenty minutes, a group of four-year-olds were given the following choice: They could have one marshmallow immediately to eat while he was gone. Or, if they waited until his return, they could have two. This daunting choice for any four-year-old was designed to measure impulse control and the ability to delay gratification. Some grabbed the single marshmallow immediately, while others covered their eyes or engaged in spontaneous activities to distract themselves so they could wait longer and receive the greater reward.

When researchers tested the same children upon graduation from high school, they found significant emotional and social differences. Those who had resisted impulses at age four still demonstrated more self-control. They were better able to handle stress and pressure. They had well-defined, long-term lifetime goals, indicating they were still able to delay gratification. As adolescents, the one-third of the children who had snatched the marshmallow tended to have fewer positive social interactions with peers, lower self-esteem, and were more easily irritated and overly responsive to stress. They still were impulsive, tending to provoke fights and arguments stemming from envy and mistrust of others. Their academic records and SAT scores were far poorer than their less-impulsive peers. They demonstrated less ability to focus on immediate tasks or to set goals for the future.

It's clear how Andrea's son, Sam, would have performed on the marshmallow test. But his situation raises an interesting question. Would he have immediately snatched the single marshmallow because he was impulsive, or because he was unsure when he would eat his next meal? Indeed, researcher Abraham Tannenbaum found that children in poverty or from unpredictable homes more often give into immediate gratification because they don't believe adult promises, even for food. They develop realistic survival strategies, such as grabbing what's available.

When teaching children with serious emotional problems, I watched their anxiety increase dramatically on Fridays and before vacations. Despite claims that they couldn't wait for time off from school, they became more agitated as the afternoon progressed. Mondays required the full morning to calm them down to our tight classroom routine. While some of their homes were troubled, they were not all abusive or neglectful. My students' insecurity was in response to the more basic issue of predictability: Who would be living at their house that weekend? When would they eat? Who would watch them? Would they get to see friends? Go to the mall? Most often, their family life was unscheduled and disorderly. These children were all grabbing the marshmallow before it went away.

The following chart includes suggestions that grandparents can follow to enjoy time with their grandchildren. When the parent's situation is difficult, these should help establish consistency and structure in children's lives. If Doug and Judy help Andrea schedule meals, reasonable bedtimes, and household logistics, such as laundry and shopping for food, Sam and Katie can expect that their needs will be met. With help, when Andrea better organizes her day, the new household structure will lessen the children's stress level and help stop anger outbursts.

"But Andrea won't listen to us!" is Doug and Judy's likely response. They're entering the caretaker role with a major drawback. Their relationship with Andrea is already confrontational, and she's using her children as part of a power struggle to control her parents. Sensing this at age five, Katie is already threatening her mother about calling her grandfather.

Clearly, Judy and Doug are justified in their upset with Andrea. From abusing drugs and losing track of her daughter to her ongoing record of bad judgment, Andrea is every parent's nightmare. But Sam and Katie aren't. While their current behavior is disruptive, it doesn't have to remain that way if adults intervene by offering love and structure.

The only way the grandparents will play this significant role is if Andrea lets them. Therefore, instead of angering her through their criticism, they'll have to develop a supportive, more positive attitude. If they pick up Sam and Katie from daycare, baby-sit some weekends, and watch them when she's busy, Andrea will see the benefits of the relationship and become more cooperative than combative. While Judy and Doug will want to schedule specific weekly times to spend with Katie and Sam, they may need to be available to take them when Andrea becomes stressed or when no other adults are available to supervise them. This protects the safety and security of the children, preventing neglect and abuse.

When parents seem negative or disinterested, grandparents and extended family members may have to work to keep their attitude positive. Even when they feel discouraged about things outside their control, they must never be critical to the children about the parent. Anything that grandparents say goes right back home.

Grandparents welcome grandchildren by creating personal space in their home, by listening and responding to their ideas. It's important to remember to *have fun* with children. When life is difficult, laughter adds a wonderful dimension. Everyone enjoys playful interactions. Libraries and zoos are

Guidelines for Grandparents

- ❏ Nurture children of all ages.

- ❏ Never be critical to children about their parents.

- ❏ Keep interactions positive with the children's parents, even when you disagree with their lifestyle.

- ❏ Do not "team up" with the child against his parents.

- ❏ If the parent is having drug, alcohol, or psychiatric problems, help arrange for counseling.

- ❏ Have children stay with you if their parents' behaviors are out-of-control.

- ❏ Volunteer to take the children when parents are stressed or children are unsupervised.

- ❏ With parental approval, help create personal space for reading and hobbies in the child's home.

- ❏ Don't wait for the child to come to you. Initiate the contact.

- ❏ Be present in children's lives. Check in frequently by phone as well as personally.

- ❏ Don't shower children with gifts, but with time.

- ❏ Create warm, welcoming personal space for the child in your home.

- ❏ Engage in caring conversations with children, listening and responding thoughtfully to their comments.

- ❏ Monitor children's television shows, movies, and music. Limit their time with these distractions, encouraging conversations instead.

- ❏ Be firm in your discipline. Never allow a child or teen to be rude to you. Require them to follow household rules.

- ❏ If children or teens become impatient with you, tease them out of it.

- ❏ Let children know that they should talk to you about their problems and that you will always be willing to listen and help.

Guidelines for Grandparents (cont.)

- ❏ Take children to the library and for inexpensive treats (i.e., ice cream).

- ❏ Do not loan children money. Instead, share your time and care unconditionally.

- ❏ Constantly let children know that drugs and alcohol are bad and that they will disappoint and anger you if they use them.

- ❏ Contact the school counselor immediately if the child experiences behavior or attitude problems.

- ❏ Attend teacher conferences. Help the parent follow through on teacher suggestions.

- ❏ Enroll children in after-school activities.

- ❏ Attend school events for teens as well as for younger children.

- ❏ As often as you can, hug grandchildren of all ages.

---

good places to share, as they broaden the child's interests and language by exposure to new ideas and experiences. But talking and listening are the most important.

Children always seek limits. As with any caregiver, Judy and Doug need to establish acceptable behaviors. Grandparents can explain their rules, respond with rewards when children obey and refuse to give privileges when they don't listen. It's important to avoid spanking children so they don't model aggressive behavior. Instead, Katie and Sam can earn activities, such as a story, depending on how well they follow the rules. When grandparents take on parenting responsibilities, it's necessary to put aside the stereotype of being pushovers. Their stricter role may be critical for enforcing socially acceptable behaviors.

Children listen more closely to discussions than lectures. However, the firmest conversations should be about drugs, alcohol, and gangs. Today, *all* children are at risk through exposure to substances and negative peer influences. The true "zero tolerance" policy has to come from every significant adult in their lives.

Unsurprisingly, stressed and angry children act out in school. Yet, grandparents may feel it's not their place to talk to teachers. It is always best if the parent attends school conferences and brainstorms how to improve the child's behavior. However, if the parent is reluctant to go or wants their input, grandparents should go along for support. They can encourage ongoing close contact with teachers, since parents need to understand how restructuring their home will positively impact children.

When Grandparents Live Out-of-Town

Living in a different town or city make being a grandparent easier and more difficult at the same time. It's easier without the day-to-day stresses of being called on to watch the children when you have other things to do. With less daily involvement, grandparents avoid problems such as being caught in the middle of disagreements over how to raise the children. They can send presents, make phone calls, and plan fun visits. When grandparents leave, the children are sorry to see them go and good memories remain to fill the void until the next visit.

But it's difficult to love those grandchildren and not get to be with them more often. Videos and telephones can't replace first steps. Grandparents want to see them hit a home run or dressed for the prom. But they live miles away and hear second-hand reports days later. When there are problems, such as divorce or a child doing poorly in school, grandparents want to be there to help. Visits may tend to be rushed and emotional. They envy those grandparents who have a crib in the extra bedroom or take their children "trick-or-treating" on Halloween. While Doug and Judy could escape Andrea's problems by living out-of-town, they would worry constantly about the children. Despite everything, they prefer living close by.

Yet, there are ways to be a wonderful grandparent without living down the street. This requires planning, visits, and ongoing contact despite the miles. The ability to get on well with adult children is critical in any grandparenting situation. While seeing them less often, visits usually are intense because everyone is staying in the same home. Another good and bad situation: Grandparents are able to catch up more easily on children's lives by experiencing their activities, but if the visit is too long or if they become critical, irritations emerge quickly.

As finances allow, it's best to plan more frequent, short visits. Weekends are enjoyable and usually filled with activities without work pressures, allowing everyone to relax and talk.

It's less expensive and not as demanding on children for visits to be at their house. Yet, grandparents can prepare meals more easily and treat their adult children to some time off when visits are in their own home. Few families enjoy a one-sided arrangement, where grandparents or children are expected to visit the other all the time.

Friends of mine have worked out an arrangement everyone enjoys. With grandchildren four hours away, they alternate visits between homes one weekend each month. The grandchildren have a special area for toys and sleeping at their grandparents'. Their own parents enjoy a weekend away and free babysitting while they go out to dinner or sleep late. When grandparents visit the children's home, they help out with household projects for the family and get to spend quality time with their grandchildren, naturally more relaxed and on-schedule in their daily environment. As the children gradually become involved in weekend activities, adults will change the schedule to be flexible.

That's the key to grandparenting, no matter where anyone lives: flexibility. Visits go more smoothly when grandparents are careful to be positive and to avoid criticism. "Rolling with the punches," it's important to fit into the grandchildren's family without making personal demands. Neither should grandparents constantly have to make personal sacrifices to be available at their children's schedule. As adults, we bring the most to relationships when our own needs are satisfied. Cancelling weekend plans to baby-sit last minute can cause resentment. Being a grandparent adds a facet to our lives, but it should not be the only thing we do. The best grandparents are happy and fulfilled with a busy life and many calls on their time. They bring a perspective to their family because they're involved. Open conversations with adult children and the ability to say "No, sorry we can't," puts their needs in perspective.

When with grandchildren, it's far better to listen and nurture without much comment. They and adult children want

Guidelines for Out-of-Town Grandparents

❑ Call grandchildren. Don't wait for them to call you.

❑ Call routinely, but especially on days important to you and children (first day of school, important game).

❑ Call when children are ill or you are worried about them. Avoid constant calls, even during difficult times, or you will intimate that they can't take care of themselves.

❑ Plan visits flexibly, based on the best schedule for both families. Frequent, shorter visits are better.

❑ When you visit, don't spoil children by allowing rude or unacceptable behaviors. Talk to them directly, explaining the behaviors you expect.

❑ Do not complain about grandchildren's behavior to their parents.

❑ Never undermine what parents say, even when you disagree. Discuss your concerns later when they involve health or potentially damaging effects on the child. Don't worry about small issues that have little impact.

❑ Wait to be asked for advice.

❑ If their parents are experiencing ongoing problems, advise counseling.

❑ Explain to your children that you'd like to be an active part of grandchildren's lives and discuss the best ways for you to be involved, despite distances.

❑ Send presents for special occasions, such as birthdays. Occasionally send a note or small, "fun" present to children, showing you're thinking of them. Send parents treats too. Everyone enjoys a surprise.

❑ Ask parents to recommend best presents/sizes.

❑ Include books and educational gifts.

❑ Give more love than money to adult children and grandchildren.

❑ Avoid loaning adult children and grandchildren money. It builds resentment if they don't repay you.

love and support. Typically, they don't want advice or opinions. Yet, it's never appropriate to allow grandchildren to misbehave. It's always helpful when grandparents and their adult children discuss in advance what role they should play in discipline. Usually, parents will decide to be in charge when they are with the child, but will give this role to babysitting grandparents. By telling the child the behaviors parents expect, adults avoid children pitting grown-ups against each other.

Grandparents can ask, "What is he allowed or not allowed to eat for lunch? If she acts up a bit, how would you like me to handle it? How much TV do you let them watch?" When the parents direct the discipline, they support other adults implementing it and tend not to listen to child complaints. The child benefits from a consistency of behaviors that all adults expect.

Yet, everyone loves to be spoiled a bit, and nature gives grandparents this delightful role. But it's important to never leave out-of-control children behind after a visit, having suspended all family rules. Parents complain that it can take weeks after a grandparent's visit to "straighten children out" again, getting them back into a steady bedtime or following rules.

When feeding my beautiful three-month-old granddaughter, we developed a game that made her laugh delightedly. When her initial hunger was past, I popped the bottle in and out of her mouth teasingly. After a few attempts, she responded by pushing the nipple out of her mouth with her tongue, waiting expectedly for me to put it back in. We played this game for days. She loved the attention and I loved her giggles.

I went back home, and her father had a different response during 4 A.M. feedings. Waking him from a sound sleep, she would fill her immediate hunger and then start pushing the bottle nipple out with her tongue. She waited for him to respond. To no one's surprise, the hour and an impending workday made him a less enthusiastic player. She always cried and stayed awake when he put her back in her crib. Understandably, for the next few weeks, I lost my favored grandmother status in their house!

Out-of-town grandparents enjoy sending small gifts, thoughtful remembrances for the children. Yet, these presents can also be a source of resentment if grandchildren don't say "Thank you," or if they don't seem to enjoy them. Again, consulting with their parents is the key. What can children use? What would they like? This way, children are excited and adults are working together. When finances are stretched for grandparents, they should send small fun presents and notes. If their adult children are having money problems, clothes for grandchildren are usually a favorite.

If children don't acknowledge the present, the grandparent can call and ask directly if they liked it. Most children will respond immediately and gratefully that they did. Gifts must be given freely, not to receive thank-you notes. It's important not to complain to their parents about this social lapse or presents will begin to have a negative tone in their family, the opposite of what you intended.

Brothers and Sisters

Within the family, children bond to each other as well as to adults. In addition to caring grandparents, brothers and sisters can thrive because of their strong ties to each other. While siblings are naturally competitive and teach each other many difficult lessons, they also share a daily life that no one else understands as well. Usually, their relationships are intense and highly emotionally charged, both positively and negatively. No one knows your abilities and your flaws like your brother or sister. Sharing good and bad experiences, you watch each other struggle through childhood, forming the foundation for who you will be as adults.

I grew up in a working class family that loved to read. We frequented the library at least weekly, searching for "finds" we hadn't already discovered. Bookstores were simply too expensive, outside our reach. When I was twelve, for Christmas my brother gave me the first books I ever owned. A complete set of Shakespeare, in wonderful hard-covered, individual blue volumes. Not only did I have my own book, I had my own library. To my mother's upset, I spent Christmas day removed from family, skimming volumes in my room and preparing for some serious reading.

Kevin also left me a surprise Easter basket and a towering chocolate rabbit the year my parents decided we were too old for this family tradition. When he learned to drive, he invited me bowling and to movies frequently, even when his friends were along. We played non-competitive tennis on Sunday afternoons.

Yet, despite these special times, he and I teased each other constantly, at times hurting each other's feelings badly. We taunted back and forth, cruelly and without provocation.One particularly difficult weekend of furious name-calling and arguments, I was terribly discouraged and went out for a walk in the packed snow. Suddenly, a group of older boys appeared from around the corner. Spotting me, they laughed gleefully and began pounding me forcefully with painful balls of snow and ice. For protection, I fell to the ground behind a hill of plowed snow, screaming for my brother.

He dashed outside in shirtsleeves. Immediately appraising the situation, he quickly formed large iceballs and began pelting my three attackers mercilessly with his practiced first-baseman's arm.

"She's *my sister*. Leave her alone!"

It only took a few minutes. Swearing at us, the leader called the others after him and they raced off down the street.

His arm around my shoulder, my brother walked me back inside the house.

Maybe that's what it's all about. Despite bouts of helpfulness and meanness, when you're in a family, you belong to each other. You can pick a fight with a sibling, but no one else can. When others try, you become protector to the death.

Research on homeless children shows us that they lack just about everything necessary to grow up successfully. Living daily with dysfunctional adults, often in and out of shelters with exposure to poor role models and serious illnesses, stability and consistency are missing during their developmental years.

Yet, they do have each other. Ties between homeless brothers and sisters tend to be even stronger than in stable homes. Tragically, these troubled children cruelly beat and abuse each other as they adopt the language of the streets. Yet, more often, in the absence of reliable parents, the older one raises the younger, who remains fiercely loyal. Indeed, their brother is their protector in an overwhelmingly frightening environment.

In Andrea's chaotic family, Katie and Sam's strong bond may be similar. Based on instability in the home, she protects him from threatening adults, including their mother. In turn, he provides her company and worships her competence and acceptance. The esteem of both children benefits from the relationship. Yet, their interaction isn't normal. Based on survival, it lacks the natural give-and-take of dealing with life's situations under parental supervision. They depend on each other for more than either child can give. Adults need to intervene to guide brothers and sisters into healthy relationships.

Raising Brothers and Sisters to be Friends

Parents might think about the type of relationships they would like their children to have as adults. Friends or competitors? Confidantes or adversaries? Involved in or removed from each other's lives? For example, most parents want their children to remain friends throughout life. They'd like them to enjoy each other's accomplishments at any age, sharing opinions, and helping make difficult decisions. Keeping in mind these goals, they can set early patterns to steer their children in that direction.

Parents who require cooperation also teach compassion. But few children ever share easily or naturally. As Dr. Benjamin Spock noted," There are only two things a child will share willingly—communicable diseases and his mother's age!" Entering preschool, first-born or only children find for the first time that others want the most exciting toy just as much as they do. When siblings are around, children learn the lesson much earlier. Yet, sharing doesn't mean using and losing a brother's favorite CD or taking a sister's clothes without permission. I know adults whose relationship is still cool because the younger "borrowed" the elder's clothes during adolescence, often ruining or not returning them. It's important to teach children the differences between sharing and taking.

The chart includes suggestions for how adults can help their children develop a good relationship. It's clear that brothers and sisters will always disagree over some things. In fact, early competition can teach them how to "hold their own" later in life. Yet, physical fighting or cruel comments are not behaviors we want to see in adults. Therefore, we can't permit them in children.

It's very important to all hold children equally accountable to family rules. Siblings of children with disabilities require counseling far more often than those without a disabled brother or sister, primarily because they resent the special time and treatment spent with the "less able" family member. A disability can't be an excuse for rudeness or bad manners. When adults with disabilities lose their job, typically it's because of problems with working with others, not because of their ability to perform the work. It's critical for parents to require all their children to follow family rules, preparing them for adult social and professional interactions.

Similarly, one child can't receive the majority of parental attention. When students have learning problems, they may dominate parents' time each evening over homework. To the neglect of their other children, parents tutor, threaten from frustration, and eventually dictate correct answers. Night after night. The children who are "better students" don't receive this attention because they seem more capable. Yet, they strongly resent their sibling's pull on parental time.

Rather than spending their evenings doing work with a child, it's better for parents to meet with teachers and hire a tutor. Parents can check the child's completed homework along with his brothers' and sisters'. When parents say, "But she won't (can't) do if I don't stand over her," it usually means the child is powerfully manipulating the family. While all adults like to be needed, spending too much time with one child reinforces demanding behaviors for a lifetime, creating expectations for similar involvement in adulthood. Since children often gauge parental love by the amount of time spent with them, focusing on one family member creates sibling rivalry, with the sense of "They always loved you more."

Children with behavior problems may get attention by causing such powerful disturbances that all family members react. They monopolize mealtimes through incessant talk or refusal to eat. They argue and complain, and are irritable or unpleasant to be around. They're are hard-to-please since their goal is attention, which they receive as others try to satisfy them. When the house seems calm, they burst into their brother's room and write on his favorite football poster. Or go through his bureau. Even punishment gives them the attention they crave.Instead of trying to please or punish children, it's better to have firm rules and consequences. Usually, the most effective response is sending them to their room when

Ways to Help Brothers and Sisters Help Each Other

- ❑ Never allow children to fight physically.

- ❑ Monitor what children say to each other. Don't allow cruel comments or teasing.

- ❑ Avoid having older brothers and sisters be fully responsible for younger ones. Encourage them to have their own activities and interests.

- ❑ Yet, establish a sense of caring helpfulness of one child for another.

- ❑ From an early age, encourage sharing. Yet teach each child not to take another's personal items (i.e., clothing, toys) without permission.

- ❑ Do not type-cast children into roles (i.e., "smart one," "pretty one"). This encourages competition and discourages children from attempting to try areas where they may be less competent.

- ❑ Expect all children to follow family rules. Don't be less strict with a child who is disabled or experiencing problems.

- ❑ Yet, allow children to be different, pursuing their own areas of interest in school and extra-curricular activities.

- ❑ Do not criticize one child to another.

- ❑ Divide your time equally among your children. Do not ignore other children to focus on a child with special problems.

- ❑ Include all children in conversations. One child shouldn't dominate or be ignored.

- ❑ Never allow one child's misbehavior to disrupt the family continually.

- ❑ Meal times are for sharing. Don't allow children to argue or complain, turning the meal into a negative experience.

- ❑ Encourage brothers and sisters to play together from an early age. Yet, schedule times when each plays with friends outside the family.

Ways to Help Brothers and Sisters
Help Each Other (cont.)

❑ If an older sibling is having a negative impact on younger brothers and sisters (i.e., drugs, gangs), keep them apart. Instead, enroll both in school and community activities where they are surrounded with positive peers and adult role models.

❑ If a younger sibling engages in negative behaviors, enlist the assistance of older brothers and sisters to talk with the child and to model appropriate, alternative behaviors.

❑ Never trust a teenager with full supervision of younger brothers and sisters.

❑ Do not allow teens to take younger siblings to their parties or to "hang out" with their friends.

❑ Don't have older siblings constantly baby-sit younger ones.

❑ Create individual space for each child's privacy.

they annoy the family. One warning, including a statement of what the child should be doing, and then immediate placement in the room.

"Chris, you don't talk to your sister that way. You need to speak to her nicely and without teasing. Go to your room now."

No excuses or discussion. No more chances. For younger children, ten to twenty minutes is usually effective. For teens, an hour. When children are removed from the ability to gain attention through negative behaviors, they usually change their actions. But parents must respond immediately, consistently, and not be talked out of the time-out. Otherwise, an individual child takes control of the family, building resentment among brothers and sisters.

If older siblings join gangs, abuse substances, or have a bad attitude, parents need to limit their interactions with younger brothers and sisters. They should not be allowed to supervise younger children or take them to parties or "hang-out" places with their friends. In the presence of older children or teens, the younger will usually engage in the same negative behaviors through fear of appearing foolish. This begins their own path into trouble.

Even when teens are involved in healthy activities, parents might consider the appropriateness of their taking younger brothers and sisters along. Watching your older sister play soccer is fun. Hanging out with her and her friends as they meet boys at a party puts you at risk. The older sister doesn't want to be the perpetual "baby-sitter," and after a while will ignore her sibling in social situations. Both appreciate the parents' sense that children need to have their own group of friends so they can develop social skills outside the family.

Stepparents

Awaiting an international flight, a fifteen-year-old girl sat next to me, her short orange and purple spiked hair pointing into the air. Rings protruding uncomfortably from her nose and tongue, she sported two bands of snake tattoos around her upper arm. Her body was forced into skin-tight black spandex. Purple lipstick accentuated the frown that said, "Leave me alone."

"Where are you off to?" I asked, pushed by irresistible curiosity.

"Wha-at?" she snapped, with a quizzical, clearly annoyed look.

I repeated the question, with an added comment about how much fun it was to people-watch in a crowded airport.

"Right. To Rome, with my father and his new wife." A sarcastic tone with an added roll of her eyes showed how she felt about them both.

"For how long?"

"As long as they can stand me. I live in Atlanta with my Mom. A few times a year, Dad takes me along on one of these bonding trips. He calls it *quality time*. I call it *guilt*."

Surprisingly, she continued.

"I hate my new stepmom. She thinks I'm weird. She makes fun of my clothes and hair. Thinks everyone should dress like her. At least sometimes my Mom listens. But Dad found a bimbo who's smarter than the rest of us."

"What'll you do to get along with them on this trip?"

With pride. "Absolutely nothing! I can be very offensive if they push me. He even sent me home once."

"I'll bet you can really give them a turn or two!"

Startled, she hesitated for a moment and then burst out laughing.

"Yeah! Wait until she sees my new tattoo," pressing her forefinger on the evil face of the rattler poised to strike hatefully from her arm.

We laughed together and chatted about the different types of clothes passengers wore, identifying their native country. She was kinder now, very open about wanting to travel more, to broaden her experiences. I found her to be intelligent and delightful.

As her long-faced father quietly sat down during the conversation, he looked back and forth between us in surprise.

"Made a friend, Cara?" he asked her. No response as her expression went dead.

Looking at me, he continued. "I wish you could go along on the trip. My wife joins us tomorrow and it'll get pretty bad in a hurry. Cara will do something outrageous to offend her and my wife will be furious with her the whole trip. They can't even be in the same room together. They've never talked for more than two minutes before shouting at each other." A sad, slow head shake from an obviously caring, frustrated father.

To my surprise, Cara winked at me from under thick black eyeliner, obviously enjoying their game.

Taking her Dad's arm as they walked toward the plane, she kissed him quickly on the cheek. Hugging her tightly, he kept his arm protectively around her shoulder as they boarded.

Like Cara, many children show their angry and confused thoughts through aggressive, antisocial behaviors. Open belligerence toward her stepmother was her way of demonstrating upset with a variety of situations, such as infrequent visits with her father and a sense that no one paid her much attention. Cara was emotionally needy. Through appearance and behavior she took the lead in rejecting adults before they could reject her.

She wore a tough attitude along with unattractive clothes and tattoos that keep adults away. If they weren't going to listen to her, she had nothing to say. She manipulated their attention through behavior that became increasingly outrageous, until they reacted loudly and in anger. Cara engaged in a power struggle with the world. Unfortunately, as she won each battle for negative attention, she further lost the war for a happy childhood.

She projected a sense that she knew everything, but really didn't believe it herself. She spoke of places she wanted to go and was quizzical, rather than condemning, of people who dressed and spoke differently. I felt that she really was gaining a lot of knowledge from these "bonding" trips, and her father knew it. But he was at a loss for how to change her antisocial behavior.

Yet, appearances couldn't hide the affection Cara and her Dad felt for each other. Her kiss didn't surprise him. She enjoyed his hug and his protective arm. Cara needs more of her father, not less. Time together for her to talk, for him to go beyond her appearance and listen to her words. If he reflects non-judgmentally on what she says, she will open up to him, trusting him further. If Cara's opinions were heard and discussed, over time she might become more flexible and responsive to other adults.

But first her father needs to ask himself why he lives in a different city. Is work so important? Can't he live closer to be with Cara more often? Certainly, he can call her frequently, just to talk. Finances permitting, he might plan some weekends just for them. They need more time together to establish a healthier relationship for a lifetime.

Guidelines for Raising Stepchildren

Cara's reaction to her stepmother mirrored Mark Twain's comment, "Few things are harder to put up with than a good example." She baits her stepmother into being openly critical so she can return in kind. Likely, her real feelings include jealousy over her father. But the issue has progressed into a power struggle over respect. Both she and her stepmother are losing.

The chart includes a series of suggestions to ease the natural divisiveness after a parent remarries. It's critical for everyone to understand that *there is no such thing as an instant family*. Biological parents and their children have a lifetime bond and a history together. Stepparents, along with stepbrothers and stepsisters, form a new family and must prove themselves to others who may not want them in the picture at all.

Remarriage destroys the dream that your parents will get back together. New family members compete with you for your mother or father's already limited time. It can take years for bonds to develop. Children, and especially teens, rarely initiate this process, because too often they want the new parent to go away. *Unsurprisingly, conflicts over children are a major cause of second divorces.*

As with any type of parenting, it's necessary to put personal resentment aside and place needs of the marriage and child first. Likely, Cara and her stepmother are worried about the same issue: Attention. Both may be threatened about sharing and possibly losing her father's affection. When he takes Cara's side in an argument, the stepmother bristles. Cara's pushing toward constantly more outrageous behavior may be a test of how much support, or love, her father will give her before he sides with his new wife.

Stepparents are often as resentful as are their stepchildren. Why should they spend money to support a child who ignores, or even worse, confronts, them? Why does the biological parent seem blind to obvious misbehavior? How can the ex-spouse say such mean things, inciting the child against the stepparent? While their opinions may be justified, constantly expressing them to their spouse or stepchild only deepens the crevice within the new family. As author William James commented, "The art of being wise is knowing what to overlook."

Stepchildren need limits, but these are best explained and enforced by the biological parent. Before misbehaviors occur, spouses can create household rules for all children, with positive and negative consequences applied immediately. These rules might be shared with the ex-spouse, encouraging all adults to work together and provide consistency in discipline. It was fun to hear a flustered teenager tell his mother, "Now you've got me going to bed early at Dad's house too. I thought you two were supposed to be divorced!" How wonderful to dispel another stereotype.

Children are creatures of practicality. Their attitude is "Don't tell me about this wonderful new closeness we'll have. Is my room as big as her kid's room? Who gets to choose TV shows? When can my friends come over?" Informally asking stepchildren's opinions and listening to their ideas is critical, especially when establishing new family logistics. Stepparents can win a good deal of respect by showing children that their needs will be met.

Guidelines for Stepparents

❑   Never discuss the child's natural parents critically.

❑   Establish a plan with your spouse about who will enforce discipline. Often, children listen more to the biological parent.

❑   In order to establish consistency between homes, have your spouse discuss household rules and expectations with the former spouse,

❑   Say less instead of more.

❑   If your stepchild tries to "bait you" into an argument, change the topic or walk away.

❑   With your spouse, create household rules for all children. Reinforce them immediately and consistently, with positive and negative consequences.

❑   As a couple, supervise teens closely. Know their friends' parents. Enforce curfews.

❑   Do not attempt to buy children's regard through expensive presents.

❑   Never use children to send messages to former spouses.

❑   If you are the non-custodial parent, live close by the child in order to develop a more natural relationship.

❑   Attend school functions and extracurricular activities

❑   Remember that your spouse loves the child. Do not complain and put him/her in the middle. The biological parent will usually defend the child's behavior.

❑   Develop an activity or hobby to share with your stepchild, encouraging the development of a joint interest.

❑   Even when the child is being difficult, be non-judgmental and non-critical in your attitude.

❑   Look for things to praise, not criticize.

❑   Refer to blended family members as "our children."

Guidelines for Stepparents (cont.)

❏ Children watch for signs of favoritism. Treat your own children and stepchildren equally.

❏ Never complain to your own children about the stepchildren, or you will initiate feelings of resentment.

❏ Spend individual time with each stepchild, listening and talking.

❏ Offer to help the stepchild when other adults don't have time (i.e., driving, shopping, completing a school project).

Elsa Schiaparelli's comment, "A good cook is like a sorceress who dispenses happiness," is particularly apt in stepfamilies. Food is a wonderful way to win over stepchildren and change the sorceress image. Discovering their favorites, preparing a special dessert, and stocking the house with their cereal and soda shows you care about them. Resisting the temptation to complain about children's terrible diets, stepparents can ask for help grilling hamburgers or ordering a pizza with the right toppings. Food is a critical aspect of life for children. They have strong preferences. Including their favorites in a meal encourages them to eat a bit of salad or try a few vegetables. It's better to turn another area of potential confrontation into a pleasure the family can enjoy together.

Stepchildren are very concerned about fairness issues, especially when new siblings are in the picture. Avoiding a natural tendency to favor their own, successful stepparents work at sharing time and enforcing the rules equally for everyone. Even when stepchildren don't live in the house all the time, they expect to be treated with the same importance as any other family member. This is their second home. It's important for stepparents to avoid complaining about them to their own children or their spouse, dividing the family further. Saying less is always better.

The hardest part is reacting appropriately to the child whose actions are pointedly rude and unacceptable. It's time for Cara's stepmother to stop being pulled into an escalation of negative behaviors. The game needs to end. As startled as she may be, it's important not to respond to the snake tattoo trick Cara has already devised to set her off. Better to smile and shake her head, or to laugh and ignore the attempt to bait her. "That's really something!" would take the wind from Cara's sail. As W.A. Nance commented, "Never answer an angry word with an angry word. It's the second one that makes the quarrel."

Through insult or confrontation, when Cara pushes her too far, the stepmother should look at her directly and say, "That really hurts my feelings. Let's get beyond this." If Cara responds with more insult, the stepmother should turn and walk away. *It's hard to continue an argument with someone who won't argue.* The next time she and Cara are together, she should ignore the previous conflict and talk about topics of interest to the both of them. "Did you notice that...?" It will be impossible for Cara to continue to play the game alone.

Relationships

In the best of worlds, there's an expanded family or neighbor- hood that supports children and their parents, a type of safe- ty net for people when they fall. But we can't rely solely on others, especially when their own busy lives distract them with daily demands. We have to turn within the family. When children are at risk, grandparents, stepparents, brothers and sisters take on new responsibilities. Together they can guide children around land mines, such as drugs and gangs, to a happier adulthood. Nurturing and listening remain critical, but consistency and discipline are just as important.

If children's parents are unresponsive or troubled, the risk grows. Yet, most parents love their children and want the best for them, including protection from their own pitfalls. By developing a non-judgmental attitude, other family members show them they want to help, not criticize. Early struggles can become the stories of later years, as children realize how for- tunate they are to have surrogate parents in their lives. More can be better, especially when adults are all working together to raise the children.

Lessons Learned

Compliment children each time you see them.

Shared activities between neighbors create friendships.

It is good to be loved by your parents, but it is even better to be loved by more people.

Always emphasize the "grand" in "grandparents."

Independent children become independent adults.

Children thrive when we meet their needs consistently.

Help is easier to accept when the helper has a positive attitude.

Children need rules to live by.

No one understands our history better than our brothers or sisters.

Brothers and sisters should be friends for life. We set the patterns early.

All children in the family deserve equal time and love.

Disabled children are enabled when we hold them accountable for family rules.

Compliment children for behaving well and they'll strive to please you.

Stepparents and stepchildren all need hugs.

When children are in earshot, say positive things or nothing at all about former spouses.

Introduce change slowly into children's lives.

Families take time to develop, but they're worth it.

Chapter 4

Building Self-Esteem: Everyone a Winner

He turns not back who is bound to a star.

Leonardo Da Vinci

I loved Angie. I thought of her as I supervised my own children's homework, during family dinners, and soccer practices. Yet, limited by my teacher role, I had no power over her daily life outside our classroom. Her foster parents were good people, but the placement was temporary. Could anyone undo those four years?

She came to me in a body cast. Back broken, ribs fractured, heart emptied. A fragile thirty-six pounds of wasted child. Cigarette burns on her bony arms and shoulders had not yet begun to fade. What could have happened in her life to engender such misery?

But her quietness disturbed me most. Angie simply refused to speak. She looked around intently, staring at times. Yet, she had no affect. Wounded beyond emotion, she never smiled, showed upset, or said a word.

Because she couldn't walk, I carried her on my hip. She never held onto me, not even putting her arms around my neck when I lowered her gently to the floor. She sat and watched the other children play. No eye contact, no desire to be part of their adventure. A coma of rejection.

Angie's history read coldly from a clipboard. The middle daughter of a severely depressed mother and a schizophrenic father, her early developmental milestones were normal. At five months, she suffered mild brain damage from what appeared to be Shaken Baby Syndrome. Nothing proven, she was released to her father. Several more hospital visits for broken limbs and a severe concussion. Meanwhile, her six-year old sister was diagnosed with Childhood Schizophrenia and the two-year old with mental retardation from environmental factors.

Then the big one. A neighbor called police, reporting domestic violence. They found Angie in her shared bed, unable to move. One sister hiding in a corner and another screaming uncontrollably, the parents were arrested. Her mother was carried to the ambulance in a fetal position while her father swore at his "attackers."

Not your typical American family, I hoped as I read the incidence report and awaited her first-day arrival. I regretted my callousness when I encountered her huge, unfocused brown eyes.

"C'mon, Sweetheart," as I lifted her slight body. "No one here will hurt you." It was months before she believed me.

Angie and her sisters were in different foster homes now. Her mother in a psychiatric hospital and her father out on bond, Child Protective Services enrolled her in our special speech and language program. But you can't teach language to someone who won't speak. Her heart needed to heal first.

So I carried her. And I talked. In my life, I have never chatted so aimlessly, discussing the color of chalk or Manny's new haircut. I conducted full discussions, graduate seminars, on sunshine, Maurice Sendak pictures, sandwiches versus tacos.

I whispered secrets to her. "Watch, here comes the Principal and I think she has a new dress," or "Sonia will be so disappointed if she can't blow out all those birthday candles." Silence resounded.

Despite daily attempts, my children never learned to pronounce *Waldron* easily. Lisping starlings, heads and voices raised to singularly capture my attention, they chirped, *Miss-Wa*. My name had never sounded so charming. With Angie on my hip or balanced against a huge patchwork pillow, in unison we bestowed names on objects, pictures, letters. Seven loud voices, one profound silence.

I greeted Angie every morning at the van. As assistants chased other toddlers to breakfast, I carried her through the line discussing options.

"Chorizo con huevo tacos are great today! Look, Mrs. Herrera made her empanadas—to die for, Angie. Fresh naranjas—orange juice for us!"

Nada. She startled me daily with her non-communicative resolve. Starving, yet she never even pointed at a sugared buñuelo. Later, I wondered how she endured those moments until she finally stuffed her mouth full, gobbling food so hungrily she choked.

While others clambered into my lap during lessons, Angie sat by apathetically. No jealousy. No involvement. No speech.

"Marcus, I see two blue objects in our circle. Show us."

"Rachel, como se llama *hombre* en inglés?"

"Jaime. This is a hard one. I'm thinking of three soft things we ate for breakfast. What are they?"

So it went. Her unfocused eyes spoke of buried concerns. Was her lack of speech from fear? Suffering? Or did she have nothing left to say?

A few months later, when her cast was removed and she tread painfully across the floor, her diminished body moved slowly and silently. Somehow I had equated mobility with recovery. A mistake. Now I missed the closeness of her on my right hip, pats on her stiff back, our one-sided chats. I felt as if I had lost her.

Until that Thursday morning. My son sick at home, I rushed in late to school. Arranging files for our weekly staffing, I forgot to meet the children's van. An assistant by her side as Angie walked slowly to my room, I was hidden by the cabinet and never saw them enter.

The most beautiful voice I have ever heard strained hoarsely.

"Miss-Wa! Miss-Wa!"

I peered to the side where she finally saw me. Her tiny body wobbled as she ran unsteadily to my open arms. The assistant and I wept openly as Angie hugged my neck, inhaling deep sobs. It was weeks before she left my hip again.

I want to end her story here, to write that she recovered and I or someone else adopted and cherished her. I don't know her full story. I can only tell you what happened next.

It was during a morning lesson celebrating animals that she first pronounced a few treasured gems of unintelligible syllables. My heart stopped as she joined the gleeful group pairing animal names and pictures. Lost in the activity, she carefully expelled sounds following deep breaths. She retired into solitude as the lesson ended.

Days later, clearly touched by joyous music, her face broke its usual stoic composure. I watched Angie mouthe lyrics she would not speak. Her favorite was the "Candy Man":

The Candy Man can,
'Cause he mixes it with love,
And makes the world go 'round.

Newly freed from the cast, her body swayed and an intuitive smile appeared. Brief liberation from pain. As weeks continued, she sang openly, even loudly at times, amidst adult glances and grins at each other. She also began to study videos intently, especially ones with animals. She wept as if her heart would break during "Bambi." It took hours to console her as I comported her once again upon my right hip.

Her only tantrum occurred when Marcus wanted his show-and-tell spaniel back. Having held the warm brown body on her lap for just minutes, Angie screamed and almost pulled Sandy apart before she relinquished him. She didn't need Freud. She needed a puppy.

I have never fully appreciated rodents. Where I come from, we set traps for them. But I've learned that the power of a hamster can be profound. When put in charge of Herbert, Angie took on characteristics of both Mother Theresa and Hitler. Speaking more articulately daily, she hugged and petted him constantly, as she chastened him to "Sit still" and "Stay here." When forced to share him with others, she shouted loudly, "Don't hold him so hard!" or "He doesn't like that. Stop it!" A few months earlier, she wasn't speaking. Now she was shouting. Non-traditional language therapy.

When Herbert and Harriet mated and our "Heavenly Hamsters" resulted, she was almost overcome. Responsibility geometrically increased, she required "Happy Helpers" to care for the babies. She was a natural, but relentless, supervisor.

"He doesn't want to be held now. Careful! Watch out for the other baby!"

With surprisingly few complaints, my young students assumed Angie was in charge of animals and began asking her permission to hold or pet them.

"For a minute." "She's tired now." "His Momma says 'No!'"

They never questioned her knowledge of hamster gender,

suggesting names like 'Louie' and 'Krissy' for her approval. They accepted her as the interpreter of hamster hunger and communication patterns. She was a comfortable expert, and they trusted her with their charges. She never let them down.

Her new role on her shoulders, now she walked without pain and with purpose into our building each morning, checking that all was well in the cage before she went for breakfast. There she sat with the other children, even joining in conversation. More and more, Rachel and Janie rushed to chairs next to hers. Their three young heads bobbed in a close circle as they shared girlhood secrets.

The court date approached. We completed the paperwork about progress Angie had shown and our recommendations for continued treatment. We were filled with trepidation.

For good reason. The judge gave Angie and her two sisters back to her parents, who had recently had a baby boy. The conditions were that they would move into a two-bedroom apartment and try to attend family counseling. Since they did not have a car, we knew that the counseling clause would be voided immediately. Actually, it was after two visits.

Mistrustful of our center and its close relationship to Child Protective Services, within days Angie's father broke my heart. He withdrew her from the program. Terribly sad that morning, I witnessed one of the most poignant scenes of my career.

Angie stood between us as I tried to coax her father into allowing her to remain. His anger mounting, he became adamant about signing the withdrawal papers. Angie did not seem to understand what was happening, but she did know that she wasn't getting the attention she wanted.

"Miss-Wa! Miss-Wa!" She pulled on my skirt.

"Just a minute, Angie. I'm talking to your Dad."

"Miss-Wa!!!" she yelled more loudly than I could imagine. I ignored her.

Her right hand next pulling strongly on her father's pants pocket, she shouted, "Dad!!!"

"Be quiet!!!"

Amazingly, she punched him in the lower left leg! She began kicking his ankle with vehemence, grunting loudly with frustration and exertion.

Swiftly, he reached down with one muscled arm, grabbed Angie around her torso, and raised her several feet into the air. Face close to hers, he stared menacingly. Then he moved his arm away and dropped her down to the floor with a resounding Thump!

By now, the security guard, two assistants, and numerous children looked on in horror.

Observing the scene and feeling no guilt whatsoever, I played my final card.

"Angie, Herbert, Harriet, and their babies need you here to care for them. Janie and Rachel really like to play with you. Your Dad doesn't want you to come to our program anymore, but I do. Please tell us you'll stay."

She turned her slight body and silently looked up at her father.

Visibly, he worked at regaining self-control. Leaning down to her, he softened his voice as he looked directly into her eyes.

Unsteadily, "Angie, no more hitting, 'cause it makes me really mad. OK?"

Silently, she stared back at him.

"C'mon with me. This is a lousy program anyway. At home you can watch the kids while Mama sleeps. Everyone says you're a good babysitter. Your sisters miss you and you haven't even seen your baby brother yet."

His words were almost whispered. "We're your family and sometimes we're crazy. But we need you. It's time to come home to us now."

She studied his face intently. Then she raised her head upward to me, her huge brown eyes bright with tears. Slowly and wordlessly, she turned to her father and nodded. Sliding her tiny fingers into his massive hand, Angie turned and silently led him out of the building. She never looked back.

The Body, the Mind, and the Child

Since my experience with Angie, I have strongly questioned a system that knowledgeably allows children to live in dangerous homes. By observing her during our months together, I learned so much about the harmony of physical and mental health. After her father's abuse, Angie gave up on the adult world. She stopped talking because she felt nothing she could say would change her situation. She had no reason to trust anyone. Her emotions too were almost dead.

Medical care fixed her body, but it couldn't heal her broken spirit. She needed to feel both loved and respected. Angie gradually bonded to adults at the Center because we gave her unconditional caring and the gentle touching she needed so badly. But these new relationships could never compete with the ties that held Angie to family. Although damaging and punitive, they were already strong and would last a lifetime. As I watched her take her father's hand and leave us, I thought, *Sometimes children bond to the wrong people.*

Language is based on the need, and the desire, to communicate. Unaware of re-entering the world of language, Angie sang with us before she spoke to us. Rekindled by feelings of safety, acceptance, and well-being, she gradually melded into the group of children. Children naturally want to be with others and share in daily social activities. When young people cut themselves off, there's always a reason. Developing their talents can restore their emotional security by giving them a sense of control over their environment. When others turn them into leaders, their abilities are reinforced and they stand taller. Angie received respect from peers because she earned it. But it was the adults in her environment who created situations where she could shine.

While unable to replace her family's strong pull, our program supported her emotionally as she developed a sense of personal competence and self-worth. Her body and her mind both mended as she received respect from peers, evolving into her first friendships. Angie's ability to supervise her sisters and mother, along with a natural affinity for animals, gave her confidence in handling responsibility. Likely, she realized that both her family and the pets were even more vulnerable, more helpless, than she. They all needed her strength. Her father understood this when he pleaded with her to return with him and take charge. Her physical and emotional well-being jointly restored, she felt confident in her ability to move back home.

Emotional Intelligence

Despite her language shut-down, Angie had strongly-developed feelings of empathy and compassion. Indeed, it may have been her sensitivity to others that both caused her to withdraw in shock when abused and then to reach out to pets, and eventually, her family. Logically, she should have chosen to stay at our Center, where she was safe and respected. Emotionally, she chose to go where she felt most needed.

Clearly, Angie didn't have a healthy way to express her feelings. At first, she bottled up fear and anger, cutting off all interactions to avoid further pain. Once her faith in adults was restored, she didn't know how to ask for their attention. When she yelled and pulled at me and then punched and kicked her father, she understood we would react negatively. She was even willing to provoke his usual violent response just to have him notice her.

Emotions are often ambiguous and hard to define. But adults help children respond appropriately by guiding them in sorting out their feelings. In his *Emotional Intelligence (E.Q.)* theory, Dan Goleman emphasizes the importance of each of us getting to know who we are as people, what makes us happy and sad, and how our behavior impacts ourselves and others. He argues that while educators and parents tend to consider children's *I.Q.* as the most important indicator of future success, instead it may be their *E.Q.* that makes others want to be their friends or eventually work with them on professional teams. He feels that intelligence may not be as important as self-understanding and the ability to get along with others. Understandably, we all prefer being with self-confident, friendly people.

After 20 years of studying children who overcame the most difficult of situations, Werner and Smith concluded that recognizing and handling emotions, empathizing with others' feelings, and forming caring relationships are critically important for happiness as adults. Many children such as Angie, whose parents are mentally ill, have been surprisingly invulnerable to the psychological problems present in their homes. The most competent of these children distance themselves from their parents' behaviors and reach out to other adults who are healthier role models. But they need to have at least a basic sense of self-assuredness in order to take that first step. They have to feel that grown-ups will respond.

In any family, it's important for children to recognize, and not confuse, their own feelings and behavior. Angry or depressed girls may tend toward eating disorders as they mix up hunger with emotions. Some children lash out at others when their own low self-esteem is the real issue. I've worked with families where young people are labeled as having *Attention Deficit Disorder* or *Hyperactivity* when the actual problem is stress or anxiety from an overly pressured family lifestyle.

Emotional Intelligence includes understanding that it's all right to be sad when a friend moves or a pet dies. It's normal to be scared when your parents fight or your boyfriend says he's breaking up with you. And that you can become angry and say things you don't really mean to someone you love. But in order for children to acknowledge their real feelings, adults have to accept them too.

Helping Children Understand their Real Feelings

Four-year-old Bryan was a difficult child to raise: bright, busy, and temperamental. In our afternoon sessions, his mother was primarily concerned about his temper. Angry when he didn't get his way at home, Bryan repeatedly shouted, "I hate you!" and ran to his room. He wasn't penitent after these anger outbursts, calling Kathy "mean" for hours as he sulked. Yet, she was a wonderful mother, spending her days providing all kinds of stimulation, and was devastated that her son felt that way. How could he hate her when she loved him so much? She knew she shouldn't give into his demands, but she was worried about the long-term impact of his negative feelings.

Sixteen-year-old Glen's parents had a similar concern. When they told him he needed a job to pay for his car insurance, he was furious. None of his friends worked and he wanted to spend after-school and weekend hours with them. Feeling unfairly treated, Glen informed his parents that if they forced him to work, their relationship "would never be the same again." Having said this, he ignored them and refused any further conversations. Since they were less affluent than many of the families at Glen's school, the parents were afraid they were embarrassing him. Were his anger and reaction justified? Should they insist on his working and risk losing him?

In order to avoid becoming victims of emotional blackmail, Bryan's and Glen's parents needed to acknowledge the real feelings at play. Both boys recognized the strength of their parents' love and used it to get their own way. They manipulated their demands around threatening to withdraw their own affection. Instead of focusing on the impact of giving in to their children, adults understandably worried about long-term outcomes if Bryan and Glen did indeed "hate" them or develop a negative relationship.

George Bernard Shaw once commented, "There are two tragedies in life. One is not to get your heart's desire. The other is to get it." Most children, and especially teens, are very immediate. They concentrate on getting what they want at the moment and can make the family's life miserable until parents give in to their demands. Young children in the grocery store are a good example. They see a candy bar or a sugared cereal and insist they must have it. When parents refuse, often the children throw temper tantrums or cry loudly, assuring everyone around them that they're being mistreated and will never be happy again. The wise parent knows that once outside the store, with the treat out of sight, the child usually settles down quickly.

Teens who call home at midnight for an extended curfew and are turned down may be furious at the moment, complaining to parents and friends about unfair treatment. Yet, despite temporary anger, they know the parents care about their safety and well-being. Indeed, while never admitting it, they may feel relieved from being pressured by peers into uncomfortable, or even dangerous, situations. One mother told me that she and her fifteen year-old daughter established a code. If the teen called with a request to go to someone's house or for a later curfew, on the phone the mother asked, "Do you really want to go?" If the daughter's friends were nearby, she simply responded, "Yes" or "No." Upon a negative response, the mother told her to come home, allowing the teen to complain about her overly-strict family as she left the group. A great idea!

In Bryan and Glen's families, adults and children need to recognize the actual emotions at work. When four-year-old Bryan didn't get his way and told his mother that he hated her, she needed to respond to his feelings and actions, not his threat. She was most successful when she told him firmly, "You may not (eat the candy, watch late television) because (it's time for dinner, you need to go to bed now). You're really angry since you're not getting your way. I won't give in. Stop shouting and settle down." If he continued, she sent him to his room. Removing her own fear of long-term negativity enabled Kathy to respond to the actual behavior. Each time, she briefly explained the reason why she was not giving him what he wanted and told him that his outbursts wouldn't be successful. With only one warning to stop misbehaving, she reacted quickly and showed she meant business by sending him to his room. She also taught him to recognize his feelings as disappointment and anger, not hatred. Consistently following through every time he had a temper tantrum, Kathy stopped the behavior after several months. As she found, it can require considerable time and a good deal of consistency by parents to change behaviors that have worked previously for the child.

The same type of recognition of real feelings is effective with teenagers. Glen's parents felt apologetic for not making as much money as his friends' parents. They were afraid that requiring him to get a job would single him out as poorer, eliminating friendships. Yet, in our sessions, his father spoke with pride about having helped support his own family as an adolescent and then paying his way through college. "Times have changed," he noted, shaking his head. "Kids today don't work." The parents relaxed as we discussed how Glen's self-esteem could benefit from a job, making him more independent and less reliant on appearances to impress others. They expressed their concerns at their son's values and noted that they didn't like many of his friends because of their attitude of entitlement. There were a number of unacknowledged emotions in the family, ones that were masked by Glen's loud anger and their own guilt.

The parents handled the situation by requiring a very annoyed Glen to sit with them as they elaborated their real feelings. Importantly, they did not apologize for their income or their belief in the value of work. They told him they recognized he was angry with their insisting he do something that would make him appear different from his friends. But they felt that holding a job was an important responsibility as he became a man. They advised him to look for work in an area he enjoyed, taking into consideration the one or two times a week that were most important for him to be free to go out with his friends. They added that while he needed to save three-quarters of his salary for car insurance and college, he could use the remaining quarter for personal spending, subsequently increasing his weekly allowance. Glen's parents acknowledged his anger and need to be with friends, along with a teen's natural desire for additional cash to spend. They also discussed their own values about work.

Glen remained angry and continued to withdraw affection toward his parents for about a month. When they ignored his overt behavior and repeated their feelings, he gradually came around. After a year of working in a movie theater, now he gives passes to his friends and proudly drives a pick-up truck. His parents are delighted that he has expanded his group to include several new friends from work. Glen is more responsible now and his esteem seems much higher. Ironically, as he threatened, his relationship with his family has never been the same again. It's been much better!

Raising Children and Teens to Care about Others

Glen and Bryan needed to become comfortable with who they are, how they feel, and appropriate ways to meet their needs. Parents helped them do this by acting as mirrors reflecting on their children's behaviors. Ironically, adults attempting to show young people how important they are in the family can inadvertently make children feel *too important*, encouraging self-centeredness. A strong self-concept does not come from always being the brightest, the richest, or most talented. In fact, children who feel that they are the center of the universe may fail to develop the empathy and compassion that is so critical to healthy moral and ethical development. Very often, spoiled children become spoiled adults, never going beyond their own basic desires to appreciate the needs of others. To the contrary, compassionate children often become caring adults, because they have integrated a sense of treating others as they would like to be treated in the same situation.

Jana is an amazing woman to be with, but only if you're not in a hurry. She stops to visit with the homeless, knowing many by name. With a boisterous, "Hi there!" and a broad, clearly genuine smile, she greets the shyest of children. At the elementary school library she directs, colleagues remark on the personal and professional care she brings to the office.

"How's the baby feeling?"

"Do you want some help unloading those books?"

"I love your idea!"

Always supportive of others, she still saves time for personal work-outs at the gym and visits to the church. But interactions with adults and children clearly sustain her.

Unless you noted her occasional absences from work, you wouldn't know about the terrible history of Jana's health's problems. First breast cancer and then severe flare-ups of rheumatoid arthritis. Her illness has been no secret. She talks about it when people ask. But she's usually so involved with her nieces, nephews, and ailing neighbors that the topic rarely comes up.

Jana's selflessness pre-empts bitterness. Friends waited for her depression and withdrawal after she recently began to rely on a cane, the stiffness in her knees and hips bringing unspoken pain to her eyes. Instead, she became busier, sensing that her physical activity may eventually become more limited.

"Of course, I feel angry at times," she reflects. "I want to shout and scream at how unfair all this is. Then I think of everything my mother overcame, and I know I need to keep my focus. It's people who matter, not these terrible setbacks. I have wonderful friends and family. Others are alone and have worse problems. I have to keep my attitude going."

To know Jana is to know her mother. In the hospital after delivering her third child, Mary was shocked to see her husband collapse, orderlies rushing him to the emergency room. A construction worker, he had been carrying double shifts in bitter January weather to pay medical expenses. Infected by a terrible virus and refusing to rest, he had run high fevers for days. With his wife looking on in horror, he never regained full consciousness and died when the baby was two days old.

Left with three children under five years and no insurance, Mary's life seemed hopeless. Friends and volunteers from her church brought food and clothing. A proud woman, she was appalled when they also brought forms to apply for public assistance.

"Welfare! I can't do that. It's too embarrassing. People will laugh at us!"

But they didn't. Instead, they drove her to job training and baby-sat the children. Later, they loaned her clothes, gave her advice, and took her for interviews. Before the second anniversary of her husband's death, she received her final welfare check and became a telephone operator, a job lasting more than thirty years.

"Mom never forgot how everyone helped her," Jana reminisces with a smile. "Even when she worked full-time, we stayed in our tiny apartment and barely had enough for school clothes. But she'd invite people who were practically strangers in for dinner. Our home was packed constantly with neighbors' children, 'to give their parents some time off.' And when we were older, she started the church's program to serve dinner to the homeless. She didn't use babysitters, but took us with her. She made us talk to everyone with the same respect, from the Center's director to the man with tremors from drink. Mom never remarried, but maybe she didn't have time. She was so busy giving back that she never seemed to worry about herself or her own needs."

Jana continues that legacy. Raised fatherless, never having children of her own, and now fighting a debilitating disease, she follows in her mother's footsteps. She learned compassion and empathy as a child. Now, in her own dark moments, they sustain her.

But Jana didn't become kind just by watching her mother. She was included as a worker, given jobs to do for others, and expected to show equal respect for everyone. She learned how to be compassionate. It's a misconception to believe that some people are born more resilient, patient, or nurturing. When they see their parents and teachers care about others, they value kindness.

Developing Empathy and Compassion in Children and Teens

The chart includes a number of techniques parents can use to develop empathy and compassion in children and teens, but parental attitude determines their success. Young people are amazing in their ability to perceive sincerity. They love pets because an animal's regard is both uncomplicated and unconditional. They quickly spot a "phony" adult or child, seeing through pretense at warmth and friendliness. Observing their parents' real motives through close daily contact, they sense genuineness. So if the parent responds as Jana's did, reaching out to support others, the child appreciates the naturalness and repeats the behavior.

Developing Empathy and Compassion

- ❑ Immediately point out when children have hurt another's feelings and discuss how they can make amends and/or avoid these behaviors in the future.

- ❑ Emphasize that people are more important than material things.

- ❑ Discuss how it would feel to be denied access to something you really want because of race, religion, gender, or beliefs.

- ❑ When children hurt another verbally or physically, discuss how the injured child feels.

- ❑ Own pets and teach children how to hold them, talk to them, and treat them gently. Never allow a child to mistreat an animal.

- ❑ Ask children *why* another person may be angry or upset.

- ❑ Discuss specific ways to treat grandparents and the elderly with care and respect.

- ❑ Read/share books with children, discussing how characters in the story felt.

- ❑ Stop children when they engage in gossip or malicious talk about others.

- ❑ Do not gossip yourself.

- ❑ Help young people develop ways to include normally excluded children in social situations (i.e., the disabled).

- ❑ Require kindness in talking to others, both family and non-family members.

- ❑ Teach children to remember others' birthdays and special occasions.

- ❑ Engage in volunteer work and take children along, giving them a job to do.

- ❑ Children should be involved in at least one service activity (i.e., Scouts).

- ❑ Take children to museums and movies that demonstrate the outcomes of prejudice and fanaticism (i.e., Holocaust Museum).

- ❑ Never allow children to "talk down" to people in service occupations or with lower incomes.

There are different ways to experience empathy and compassion: through actual feelings, conversations with others about the person, and direct action. When we feel someone's grief or happiness, their emotions become our own. By its very nature, this true empathy overpowers jealousy, competition, and negative responses. We simply are sad or glad for others because we can put ourselves in their place. Or we talk about people in their absence, sharing positive things and remarking on strength and character, while avoiding gossip. This is hard to do, because we all thrive on a bit of gossip about others, especially with the added treat of personally passing on the information. Lastly, we can directly reach out to help people in need. Some extend their hands to individuals, as Jana did with friends and strangers. Others become part of efforts to reach groups through joining associations and sponsoring charitable functions, as her mother did with the homeless.

People who engage in one of these types of compassion usually are involved in all three. Mary repaid kindness through bringing others into her home. She spoke well of people, even those "down on their luck" and defenseless, insisting that her children treat everyone with equal respect. And she reached out organizationally, starting a community program for the less fortunate.

We can use these stages in teaching children compassion:

1. First, we can help them empathize with others they know personally.

2. Then, we can model and include children in activities where they lend a hand to the less fortunate.

3. Finally, we can make them part of a broader outreach to groups in the community.

The order is important. If children don't understand the loneliness of many elderly, then singing holiday songs in a nursing home is a meaningless chore. Children will tolerate the visit as part of "community service" requirements for an organization, receiving credit for their efforts. But if they picture their grandmother in the home, they'll feel more of an attachment and a commitment to the activity.

Adults can teach a sense of empathy through discussion. If children hurt others, it's important to talk about how the person feels. This includes gossip, a special problem with teens, where a reputation can be ruined or young people excluded permanently and unfairly.

Unless they're taught not to engage in gossip or malicious conversations about others, children and teens may never learn compassion.

Robin was a beautiful high school senior who cried with hopelessness in my office. Despite obvious looks and intelligence, she said that her high school years had been "pitiful." She had no close girlfriends and the boys who asked her out were "losers" who only wanted sex.

"How did this happen?"

With a sigh, "My Sophomore year. She said it was me breaking them up, but it wasn't. She made it up. It was a lie."

"Tell me the story."

"Kyle was my neighbor forever. We were best friends as little kids when I was a tomboy. Then he played Freshman football and I was on the Dance Team. So our group was the jocks. About seven or eight of us hung out together. He dated Belinda. She was a year ahead of us and really popular, already Assistant Captain of the Dance Team. I didn't care who Kyle dated, since I was going with Jeremy." She shook her head while I waited.

Continuing, "I never wanted to date Kyle. He was my friend. Jeremy and I broke up that summer, but Kyle and Belinda stayed together. Once he told me that I was lucky to be free again, because Belinda was too serious and he wanted to go out with somebody else. I could tell it was Joanna, because he always talked about her.

"Well, school started and it was same old thing. Most of the girls on the Dance Team had lunch period at noon, so we ate together everyday. Kyle and a few of his friends ate later, after Football P.E.

"A friend told me one morning that Kyle told Belinda he wanted to go out with somebody else. Then she went crazy. She's really beautiful and always gets everything she wants." Robin's voice dripped with sarcasm. " You know, I think she was embarrassed that a little Sophomore dared to break up with her." A deep sigh and she started to cry again.

I waited, but it was pretty clear how this story ended.

"So stupid me wanders into the cafeteria that day with the usual disgusting meatloaf on my tray. I was a few minutes late because I came from a math test. Everyone was already at the table, talking big-time to Belinda, who's crying her eyes out. They stared at me and got real quiet, looking back at Belinda. As I put my tray down, she nodded and they all stood up on cue and walked away. They left me alone at the table and went and sat down somewhere else!

"I couldn't figure what was going on, so I can't believe I did this. I followed them! I actually went to the new table and tried to sit down.

"Then Belinda looked at me and screamed, "You stinking whore! You stole my boyfriend. It's not enough you've been sleeping around with everybody else, you wanted him too. Well the both of you deserve each other. You'll probably give him your Herpes too!" And then they got up again and walked to the back of the cafeteria, leaving me standing at the table with my mouth open. I looked like a real idiot to about 1000 students sitting there watching me. And they heard what she said."

"Are you sure?"

"Oh, yes! Some kid I didn't even know, shouted right then, 'Herpes! She's sleeping around giving everybody Herpes!' For weeks, strangers called me 'Miss Herpes' across the hallway. In class, a few wise-ass boys told teachers they didn't want to sit next to me, but couldn't say why."

"What did you do?"

"I went to my friends and they said they knew it was a lie. But Belinda was Miss Hot Stuff and nobody would go against her. I think that if they'd told her not to say it that day in the cafeteria or if they'd sided with me, she would've shut up. But even Carrie, my best friend, stayed away for weeks. Later Carrie said that it was because she was so embarrassed at leaving the table with the others. But if she'd stood by me, at least some people would have known Belinda was full of it.

"When Kyle heard, he was really upset. He called Belinda and chewed her out, but she said it was true. When he told the guys it was a lie, they just laughed. They believed it. Pretty soon Kyle started going with Joanna, and between that and football, I almost never see him any more.

"I stopped going to lunch and went to the library the rest of the year. Even now, I rarely eat in the cafeteria. There's nobody I want to sit with."

"Did you tell any teachers?"

"Yeah, Miss Patterson. She sponsors Dance Team. She said everybody knew I was a nice person and nobody would believe I was sleeping around or anything. She was supposed to talk

to Belinda, but I don't think she ever did. I finished the season that year, but didn't try out my Junior year. Belinda was
going to be Captain and I couldn't take it."

"Your parents?"

"Mom was furious. When it happened, she called the
school. The counselor told her these things usually pass and
to let it be. Then Mom called Belinda's mother, who was really rude on the phone. She told my Mom that if Belinda said it,
it was true. That I'd obviously been sleeping around and she
should keep an eye on me! Mom was almost sick over it, so I
told her to let it be.

"That was almost two years ago. I see Carrie sometimes,
but we've never been close again, and I don't have any real
friends. I do a few things with kids in my classes, but I still
feel they're looking at me wondering. The real problem now is
that Belinda's in her first year at Tech and that's where I really want to go next year. But I'm afraid that if I do, it could start
all over again."

I was amazed at the depth of Robin's concern, since Tech
has over 40,000 students. "She can't talk to that many people. What do you think is the real issue for you right now?"

"I can't deal with it anymore. I feel like she's ruined my life."

Robin eventually decided not to go to Tech, but to a small
college where she could make close friends more easily and
experience some of the times she missed in high school. She's
a cheerleader there and joined a sorority. She's told me that
she loves the fresh start, but takes her social life less seriously now. Understandably, she's wary about trusting people.
She came to know the world's cruelty at an early age.

The gossip about Robin seemed unstoppable. Once the
words were spoken, she couldn't un-break that egg. Because
of others' wary respect for status and power, Belinda was
allowed to ruin Robin's adolescence. When adults said that no
one would believe the gossip, they misjudged its impact. In
situations like this, Belinda's mother could have played the
greatest role. By setting higher standards early, her daughter
might never have considered ruining someone else's reputation because of her momentary feelings of rejection. The
mother's harsh response to the accusation Belinda had lied
demonstrated that she wasn't a compassionate person herself, that her daughter's image was all that mattered.

Once the situation occurred, Belinda's mother should have reacted sternly, considering with her daughter all options to right this wrong. Apologize to Robin, one-on-one? Have Belinda tell their friends that she had spoken in anger, not truth? Invite Robin back into the group, treating her kindly in the future? Certainly, Belinda would do none of these on her own to avoid admitting publicly that she lied. But with a parent's insistence and possibilities of negative consequences at home, likely she would have followed through. Allowing Belinda to get away with these behaviors gave her a sense of power she would use again. Most importantly, she's been allowed to go through life thus far in a self-centered way because of looks and intelligence. She hasn't had to develop a sense of kindness or responsibility for others.

Robin's mother could also have influenced her daughter's behavior more positively by encouraging her to consider all of her options and then shape her own direction at school instead of feeling powerless. Robin could decide to become more assertive in her response to Belinda, remaining on the Dance Team. She might choose to try other activities until she found her niche. Since she enjoys physical activity, she could sign up for a sport. And by joining school and community groups that support needy children and adults, Robin would be better able to put her own problems in perspective, help others in more serious situations, and meet compassionate young people who would disregard the Belindas of the world.

Wearing Someone Else's Shoes

Empathy and compassion need to be supported by experience. Years ago, I had mixed feelings about the United States presence in the Vietnam War. I understood the poignancy and sacrifice for the first time only when I visited the Vietnam Memorial, in Washington D.C. I wept openly as I watched family members trace a loved one's name as a treasure. A woman in her '60s placed a rose in front of the row with her dead husband's name. She wore no wedding ring these days. How great her loss must have been. Arms around each other's shoulders in support, a family of five stared quietly at a soldier's name. Finally, they dropped their eyes, hugged each other, and sobbed.

On another front, we all learned in our schoolbooks how

the United States bombing of Hiroshima forced the Japanese to surrender in World War II. Yet, as my sons and I stood at the site in the Peace Memorial Park, the attack took on new meaning. More than 200,000 people died, many of them children. Victims who survived the immediate bombing later suffered the terrible aftermath of radioactivity, with hair loss, bleeding gums, and a decrease in white blood cells, ending their lives with leukemia or other forms of cancer.

The statistics had no real meaning until that day, when I looked up at the *Statue of the A-Bomb Children.* A young girl stood poised with her arms outstretched. Rising above her was a crane, the bird symbolizing longevity and happiness in Japan. The statue represents the true story of a young girl who suffered the effects of radiation after the bombing. As an almost-destroyed nation followed her poignant health decline daily, she vowed to create 1,000 cranes in origami, the Japanese art of paper folding. She believed that reaching this number would acknowledge her devotion to peace and see her well again. She never reached her goal, folding just 964 before she died.

But her story continues to be an inspiration to the Japanese. Our visit was during the annual commemoration of the bombing. Thousands of colorful streamers of paper cranes surrounded the statue, creations of schoolchildren from across the country. Ironically, one Japanese child walked around the memorial wearing a Chicago Bulls tee shirt, and another, a New York Yankees baseball cap. Yet, despite the Americanization of a former enemy, even the children's moods were somber as they looked up at the girl reaching toward the crane.

Most experiences such this trip happen once-in-a-lifetime, because of prohibitive distance and cost. But there are many local places in our cities that allow children to experience the pain and promise of humanity. From museums to videos, children need to relive history and the impact of critical decisions on real people.

A high school teacher couldn't afford to take her students to Washington, D.C., for the incredible display of quilts honoring AIDS victims. Instead, she showed her students close-up pictures of pieces commemorating the specialness of the many who died. "The kids needed to see that these were real people, with families and friends who loved them. It made students realize how this disease could happen to them too. Several cried as they read the messages on the quilts." At first she felt that their tears meant that she shouldn't have shown the pictures. Then she realized that a strong emotional response was necessary to gain understanding of another's plight.

Sometimes we avoid these activities because we don't want to depress young people. In doing so, we deprive them of experiences that can develop their empathy for others' situations. Part of creating strength in children is having them understand that others need their help. Visits to shelters for abused children or the homeless, or even videos about their situations, expand the world of youth beyond their own daily activities. They begin to care about others, focusing less on their own needs.

Community Business with a Social Conscience

But it's the job of all of us to care about each other. Individuals can only do so much. Through a shared commitment, business needs to support individual efforts to reach out. Any time I feel discouraged about modern-day commercialism's impact on children, the best pick-me-up is a visit with Jack and Laura Richmond. Our conversations fill me with the Richmond's wonderful combination of generosity, corporate savy, and common sense. Jack and Laura own Pizza Huts on the north side of San Antonio. When a competitor across the street from one of their busiest locations shut down years ago, I commented to Jack that he once again had overcome the competition.

"Actually, I'm sorry they closed," he reflected quietly. "Competition is good for us. It makes us perform at our best."

As business people and community citizens, Jack and Laura always do. For years, they have supported countless programs for at-risk children and teens, focusing on preventing drug abuse and school dropouts while providing safe havens for families that have nowhere to go. They emphasize success through improving young people's self-esteem and assumption of responsible behaviors.

The Pizza Hut "Book-It" program is immensely popular. Children who go beyond school expectations, such as reading 100 extra pages a month, receive a coupon for a pizza. When they pick up their prize, they receive a medallion and personal congratulations from employees. This program extends for five months a year. Last year, in San Antonio alone, 100,000 children participated.

This program is important because of what it tells children. While many school libraries are stocked with books, too often students take them for granted, reading only as much as required by parents and teachers. In "Book It," they have to go beyond expectations and meet a more demanding reading requirement. As Jack says, "The critical issue behind all of our sponsorship is an attitude that people want to help themselves." They create this desire in children, with the goal of it lasting a lifetime.

Similarly, at their own children's former high school, the Richmonds underwrite "Lee Legacy," targeting approximately 50 high-risk freshmen each year. Designed to reduce the drop-out rate, identified students receive counseling and extra attention from teachers. Expectations are clear: good attendance, improved grades in classes, and reductions in tardiness. Every six weeks, achieving students are rewarded with $20, two movie tickets, and a pizza. Ongoing teacher praise and recognition play an important part in program success.

Results have been excellent. The majority of students adopt these initial behaviors and expectations as they continue through high school, even with the discontinuance of external rewards after their first year. They get the message that responsible behaviors bring rewards. Importantly, they take charge of their own success through making positive choices.

Nothing builds self-esteem more than a sense of personal accomplishment. Reading extra pages and improving grades at school make children and teens feel better about themselves. They earn the respect of others when their achievements are recognized publicly. This success can be addictive. Moving from monetary or tangible rewards to an internal sense of self-congratulations encourages young people to set even greater future goals.

Jack and Laura don't just write blank checks. They help sustain "people who can make an impact and programs that work." Each of the agencies they support has an already-established track record of success. The Richmonds point out that Pizza Hut is not in the business of starting programs, that there are many wonderful ones that already work and need ongoing support. Their motivation originates through others, the teachers and volunteers who work daily with families in adversity.

Having watched teachers provide goals and direction to endless overwhelmed young people, the Richmonds continuously support schools. Through Pizza Hut, they also sponsor Scouts. Since 1977, each ticket to the annual Scout Country Fair has a coupon attached for $2 off the price of a pizza. Because tickets only cost $2, purchasers can go "for free." As a result, attendance has tripled at this important event where Scouts have the opportunity to publicly share their projects and accomplishments.

For years, Pizza Hut helped fund "Midnight Basketball," a community favorite. Youth between the ages of seventeen and twenty-four played late-night basketball at city gyms several nights a week, keeping them off the streets and out of gang activity. Coaches volunteered their time, with only the officials being paid. Again, participants had to "earn" their right on the court. For every night they played, they came an hour early for classes in fundamental areas such as hygiene and completing a job application. Approximately 350 young people were involved in this program.

But the Richmonds moved to higher impact support through the "Pizza Hut-Spurs Drug-Free Youth Basketball League." Created in 1991 by Frank Martin, President of Kids Sports Network, and Gregg Popovich, Coach and General Manager of the San Antonio Spurs, 1,100 youth participated the first year. With enormous popularity, the League currently enrolls 16,000 children ages 7–16, at 75 locations throughout South Texas. An expansion grant from the Robert Wood Johnson Foundation supported creation of Drug-Free Leagues by the Portland Trailblazers, the Golden State Warriors, the Indiana Pacers, and the Denver Nuggets. An estimated 10,000 additional children now participate in Portland, Oakland, Indianapolis, and Denver.

Supported by numerous agencies such as the YMCA, Department of Parks and Recreation, Boys and Girls Clubs, the Police Athletic League, and the Salvation Army, the purpose of the League is to transmit an anti-drug, alcohol, and tobacco message to children.Team coaches and administrators attend training on working with youth in a sports environment and on best ways to discuss substance issues. Most teams have a practice and a game each week, with a pre-game dialogue about the consequences of drugs, alcohol, and tobacco use. To lead these discussions, volunteer coaches receive a fieldbook containing lesson plans. Along with their young basketball players, they also recite a pledge to be drug, alcohol, and tobacco free. Spurs' coaches and players conduct clinics for participants and visit game sites during the season. In addition to numerous other awards, in 1992 President Bush presented the prestigious Point of Light to this innovative program modeling children's sports with a social theme, through the cooperation of community volunteers, service agencies, and business.

Parents have been very supportive of the Drug-Free League because it provides information on substances from additional adults their children respect. Young people feel special to be included as team members, enhancing their esteem and sense of self-worth. But their commitment to a healthy lifestyle underscores their right to participate.

Jack speaks for the many League volunteers and parents when he verbalizes concerns about the personal and societal costs of addiction: "The curse of our society is drugs. It ruins families and grows like a cancer. There is no person on drugs who doesn't want to be out of it."

In additional efforts to encourage a shared social commitment by business and the community, the Richmonds have helped sponsor the work of a number of religious organizations, agencies, and volunteer groups. Through grants matching public support, Urban Ministries is able to sustain programs for latchkey children, St. Vincent de Paul continues its outreach to economically poor families, and Christian Alliance Ministries assists families and individuals with nowhere else to go.

The philosophy is that children need support to overcome adversity, but that neither business nor agencies should be singularly responsible. Businesses match the monies pledged by the public. Volunteers and agencies provide the workforce to implement programs. Children participate actively and take responsibility for decision-making in their own lives. Motivation for a program comes from need, with support at all levels. Once recipients show positive results, business, community agencies, and the public can share their success. But children are the real winners.

The Richmonds are quick to point out that Pizza Hut is only one of the many businesses across America that has "a social, a community, conscience." Their philosophy is that support starts, but doesn't end, with management, that businesses have a critical role in encouraging all employees to give of their time, becoming role models as they serve the community and their own families simultaneously. Maybe that's what it's all about: Businesses as extended family members who motivate and encourage all of us to be role models for the young.

Children with Natural Talent

Whether through school performance, extracurriculars like the Drug-Free Basketball League, or by just observing children informally, it's important to see where they shine. Nothing improves self-esteem so much as doing something well and having others recognize accomplishments. But there are many additional advantages to children immersing themselves in meaningful activities. In their research on resilient children, Werner and Smith repeatedly found that engagement in a natural talent, hobby, or skill not only distracted children from their problems, but also gave them an emotional outlet to express themselves. This was certainly true with Gabe.

They noticed it first when Gabe was too young to remember. His mother sang to him, and his young body moved in delight. Arms flailing, legs kicking, a full joyousness in response. The music continued to move his spirit. To adult amusement, he danced freely and tinkered with toy xylophones and bongos. For him it was not diversion, but life.

As other children jumped across the dance floor to Hank Williams, Gabe's feet moved intricately. He swayed smoothly to a waltz. He hummed Mozart without knowing why. Rachmaninoff was inside him before he learned to read. He always slept better when a tape lulled his senses.

And then life was out of his control. He had loved living in the country with birds and dogs as his friends. But when he was three and his parents separated, they moved into town. Gabe didn't tell anyone that the music stopped for a time, that all the tapes in the world did nothing to touch him. But one day at preschool, the teacher played some haunting music that gripped his mood. He reported to his mother that the composer was someone named "Beth Hoven."

"Can you believe he was *death*?" he asked.

Now his music was somber, but it filled his emptiness. And as times became busy with lessons and play, he put aside his sadness for another day. When Sesame Street prompted lyrically, "What's the Name of that Song?," he hummed for hours. When his older brother had trouble spelling weekly words, they practiced with horrible operatic voices and doubled over with laughter. Albeit off-key at times, his voice had returned.

All the naturalness was spoiled by a call from the preschool. "Gabe has real musical abilities." Piano lessons. The teacher was friendly but conventional. She wrote (he later said "rote") the music books, emphasized scales and children's songs. He brought her his own composition, notes and all. She said, "That's nice." He hated the recitals in a shopping mall. He sat with others, all waiting to make public mistakes. His heart was in *Cats* and *Phantom of the Opera*, while he played nursery rhymes.

Only his cockatiel made piano sufferable now. Mornings as Gabe practiced before school, Charlie sat on his shoulder in rapt attention. When he paused to turn the page, the bird sharply pecked on his ear. Gabe later claimed that this was where he first learned to swear freely. But even Charlie couldn't save him from the routine piano boredom. Another teacher, more scales. His feet began to tap to the rhythm of the football field. His mother made him a middle school deal. He could give up piano and play football if he joined the school choir.

Seemed easy, until his jock friends caught wind of his other after-school activity. He struck a different deal with his teacher. He would not perform in concerts, but he would compete in the solo voice competition. "You don't even have to stand in front of anyone and sing," she promised. "In the studio, you'll just make a tape for the judges." Despite ongoing complaints, his voice filled the house for weeks, dissolving school crises, weariness, and solitude. He won first place. It didn't matter. Just the songs in his head and heart.

When his brother left for college, Charlie and he filled the hours shrieking to raucous rock music. With the house strangely silent one night, Gabe's mother opened his room door quietly. He was motionless in bed, with the bird standing guard on the headboard. She screamed as Charlie flew at her in attack, closely missing her eye. The protective bird understood first that Gabe was very ill.

He wanted only darkness and quiet as the meningitis ravaged his body—but Charlie began to sing. Relentlessly, he chirped and screeched. Unallowed to sleep, Gabe woke often to this piercing voice. Finally, when he swore at the bird, they knew he was safe.

High school years passed on in a blink. Beer, car wrecks, and broken bones from the field. Yet, he sang joyously in *Oklahoma* and *Showboat.* Combinations of innocence and testosterone. Gabe tried his voice in debate and drama. But it wasn't the same. Only the songs.

When the girl broke his heart, he went back to the piano. Wiser now, he sang his own songs. *The Piano Man* and *Memories* slowly spread their ointment. Sitting on the lonely bench, Gabe could not yet imagine the Army uniform or nights at karaoke bars and Oktoberfests. Nor could he see the strangers turn to him in smiling wonder as his voice soared.

Multiple Intelligences

Had Gabe depended on life's daily experiences to heal his wounds incidentally, likely he would have remained depressed and angry about his parents' divorce. Even the piano teacher tried to restrain him with her inflexible, rote teaching, fitting him into her own structure without molding lessons to meet his needs. When children have natural abilities and loves, they have to develop them in personally meaningful ways. Forcing talent into a set curriculum can destroy joyfulness and even the child's desire to pursue innate abilities.

We help children such as Gabe reach their potential by encouraging their natural skills, or even just their interest in pursuing a hobby or fun activity. Not only do they have a diversion from the negative experiences in their lives, they also have the opportunity to do something well. Their self-esteem grows through feelings of personal accomplishment and recognition by others. Talents have to be encouraged by adults who can create situations for children to pursue natural aptitudes. Gabe was pulled to music. But if he hadn't been in an encouraging environment, he might never have sung or played the piano.

In studies of adults who reached world-acclaimed status as mathematicians, artists, and athletes, Benjamin Bloom found that their parents sought tutors and specialized training, often at tremendous expense to the family. His interviews revealed stories of parents who bought a piano instead of a badly needed car, of mothers who drove their children for hours each day to the best private instructor. Yet, he also tells of the artist who set up creative art space for her daughter and displayed her young artwork everywhere around the house. When asked about how the child was doing in math at school, the parent was puzzled: "Fine, I'm sure." Yet, she wasn't *really* sure. Because of her own interests, the mother encouraged and nurtured skills that were most important to her personally. In order to discover talents, we have to go beyond our own experiences and look at children as individuals. Sometimes their strengths are very different from ours.

In an athletic household, a teen may be more interested in drama or debate. In a family of scientists, a child might prefer writing poetry. Even with parents who are teachers, a young person may not be involved in academics, instead shining socially. If we expose children to our interests without discovering theirs, they can become apathetic and uninvolved or jealous of siblings who perform better at the preferred family activity.

With our modern day interest in psychological labeling, adults may consider children "passive-aggressive" or engaged in a power struggle over activities, when in actuality they simply have different preferences from parents. Young people are not being non-compliant or showing behavioral problems when they want to do something else. The key is to be sure that the interest is healthy and involves peers with strong moral and ethical values. Whenever possible, the parent might try the child's activity, learning something new and having fun at the same time. Children so enjoy being the teacher. I love to see a parent roller-blading or flying a kite with sons and daughters. It's never too late to enjoy the pleasures of childhood.

It's also fun to look at children objectively, observe their preferences, and discover their strengths. Once we do this and encourage them to participate in new activities, we'll see them develop pride in accomplishment and a willingness to risk new things. A child who has played a good soccer game may be more positive about math the following week in school. Anticipating a family fishing trip excites a child for days. Interviewing peers for the school newspaper requires a take-charge attitude from the "reporter," who may usually be shy. When involved in successful experiences, children develop a positive attitude that can spill over into unrelated areas.

We can find children's strengths by considering the ways their mind approaches new ideas. Some learn best by listening or observing. Others need to touch and do. Some are logical in solving problems, while others are more immediate and intuitive. In his theory of *Multiple Intelligences*, Howard Gardner goes beyond the usual reliance on academic success, vocabulary, and memory as key indicators of intelligence. Instead, he discusses a breadth of different types of intelligence. People with *Linguistic Intelligence* are sensitive to the structure and meaning of language, writing and speaking well. These children usually read at an early age and express themselves with ease, often startling adults with the wisdom, humor, and sophistication of their remarks. *Logical-Mathematical Intelligence* exists in children who more easily understand relationships among both ideas and numbers, handling long chains of reasoning with ease. Computers, science, and math usually come more easily. I remember a middle school student who immediately solved a computer problem stumping a group of adults. While he had never worked on that type of machine before, he was undaunted, commenting, "It's only a computer." He left minutes later, with the embarrassed adults wanting to strangle him!

Most people appreciate one or more types of music, but fewer respond by creating as well as listening. In our story, similar to composers and performers, Gabe had *Musical Intelligence*, an ability to perceive and create rhythm, pitch, and tone. *Spatial Intelligence* is common among artists, photographers, engineers, and architects, those who understand the visual-spatial world and can go beyond their immediate perceptions to create new ways of seeing things. Young children build unlikely Lego structures, while older ones draw or design unusual combinations of objects, clothing, or machines. Their pictures show marked sensitivity to light and movement. Athletes, dancers, and sculptors have *Bodily-Kinesthetic Intelligence*, controlling movements with grace and natural direction, often while manipulating objects. While we think most easily of the football player catching the pass or the ballet dancer in a pirouette, surgeons and sculptors alike possess these skills.

Similar to the theory of Emotional Intelligence, Howard Gardner views relating well to our own needs and those of others as ingrained skills supporting self-esteem. *Interpersonal Intelligence* is the ability to understand how others feel and respond appropriately. Children strong in this area are social, popular, and often selected as leaders. Appreciating the needs of others, they are compassionate and "street smart" at the same time. Children with *Intrapersonal Intelligence* are comfortable with their own feelings and emotions, understanding their personal strengths and foibles. From a young age, they are independent, comfortable being alone, and march to their own drummer. They have a strong confidence in their abilities.

Those who are sensitive to Nature and enjoy informally studying the sciences demonstrate *Naturalist Intelligence.* By observing the natural world, from insects to rocks to clouds, these children demonstrate the survival traits of hunters, explorers, and farmers. Inborn scientists, as adults they may choose professions that develop modern-day consumable items, from clothing to medicine or cosmetics. At times these applications can exploit their tendency to freely examine the natural. Their heart is in the out-of-doors and exploration of living things.

Howard Gardner is currently considering additional types of intelligence, underscoring the extensive possibilities for children and adults to demonstrate special abilities. The chart lists each of the intelligences thus far, with a series of behaviors that demonstrate each area. You might take a moment to consider which of these types best suits your child. Likely, he or she has some strengths in each of these areas. We all need some of each intelligence to experience life fully. While one of us is pulled to music and another to math, each of our lives would be lacking if we couldn't enjoy a concert or manage a bank account. Gardner feels that we favor or are naturally better at some ways of thinking. On the chart, the strongest areas are the ones where your child has the greatest number of characteristics.

These behaviors are interesting to observe across all ages. As I watch Doug move and tap on the desk during class, I try not to take it personally. He's our star football player and uses his kinesthetic intelligence best on the field. Sitting in that chair is hard for him. Ruby wins awards for teaching children with emotional problems. She quietly exudes competence and gives them the sense she will let nothing bad happen to them. My older son first beat me at chess when he was four, sitting on two phone books to reach the table. Both of us relaxed and chatting, I jolted when his "En garde" call cost me my Queen and he seriously explained his reasoning to achieve checkmate. Not yet appreciating his logical intelligence, my immediate response was annoyance, turning quickly to laughter.

Being aware of areas where children excel helps us encourage activities where they can be successful, improving their self-esteem. But labeling can also limit a child's activities. Gifted children especially tend to have many wonderful skills across all areas. To categorize them is to discourage their marvelous breadth of interests. Their greatest problem should be selecting a future profession because they are interested in so many areas. Calling one child "the athlete" and another "the reader" infers that they are boxed into that description. Conversely, it's as important for children with strong social abilities to complete their homework as for those with the best academic skills.

But it's just as important to note those areas where children need support. Marie may refuse to participate in the arts, saying "I can't draw." Yet, with recent technology, it's hard to take a bad picture. She may surprise herself with at least passable photography, especially when her efforts are complimented. Joe may view himself as non-athletic because of his long, thin build. What a wonderful surprise to find out that he's not a bad swimmer. Or Ellie says she's "a loner," which really means she's shy. Encouraged to have friends over and show off her new puppy, she's never seemed happier. Reviewing the charts can indicate not only where children are strong, but also where they need support and parental encouragement. Children blossom when adults guide activities around natural interests and encourage attempts in areas of difficulty.

Everyone a Winner

Self-esteem is a misnomer. We get it from others' regard, not just from ourselves. It starts at home with positive parenting

Discovering Multiple Intelligences in Your Child or Teen

Directions: Review the behaviors listed beneath each type of intelligence, noting the ones that describe your child most often.

<u>Linguistic Intelligence:</u>

has a good vocabulary

writes ideas in an engaging way
likes to talk
enjoys telling stories and jokes
reads well
enjoys listening to others' ideas and stories
has a good memory
sounds more mature than his or her age

<u>Spatial Intelligence:</u>

has good drawing skills
builds or diagrams sophisticated structures
prefers pictures to reading
easily completes puzzles and mazes
has a good sense of direction
reads maps and diagrams easily
is mechanical, good at fixing things
focuses on understanding how things work

<u>Bodily-Kinesthetic Intelligence:</u>

has good fine motor skills
touches objects as if to understand them better
excels in at least one sport
gestures frequently when speaking
is a good dancer
body is in frequent movement, even when seated
would rather show than explain
enjoys working with hands

Discovering Multiple Intelligences
in Your Child or Teen (cont.)

Logical-Mathematical Intelligence:

   enjoys strategy and board games
   solves math problems more easily than peers
   associates and categorizes ideas
   handles abstract concepts from a young age
   draws mature conclusions
   thinks in an orderly, organized manner
   enjoys computers beyond games
   uses advanced applications on the computer

Musical Intelligence:

   sings well, naturally on-key
   enjoys hearing music, may stop other activities
   has good body rhythm
   drawn to play musical instruments
   hums or sings to self
   remembers words and melodies of songs
   bothered by off-key sounds
   "tuned in" to environmental noises

Interpersonal Intelligence:

   frequently socializes with others
   enjoys school activities and extracurriculars
   makes friends easily
   gets on well with adults as well as peers
   is popular and a natural leader
   shows empathy and compassion for others
   helps peers with problems
   competitive, but not overly-zealous

Discovering Multiple Intelligences
in Your Child or Teen (cont.)

Intrapersonal Intelligence:

is comfortable being alone
accepts self as special and unique
displays strong self-confidence
pursues personal interests and hobbies
is aware of and expresses feelings
understands own strengths and weaknesses
makes independent decisions
works toward personal goals in life

Naturalist Intelligence:

prefers the out-of-doors
shows a sense of pleasure in animals
likes camping and hiking
asks questions about natural phemenoma
enjoys hands-on science at school
sees cause-effect patterns in scientific behavior
studies plants and their uses
expresses a sense of wonder

and stretches through our lives with each new accomplishment. Through recognition from others, we begin to appreciate ourselves. People who are the most assured usually have fulfilled lives, actively embracing new challenges. Risks are easier if you feel failure won't diminish you.

Feeling good about ourselves usually means feeling good about others. Empathy and compassion are teachable, especially in childhood. Adults can model positives such as speaking kindly and considering feelings, redirecting children from the self-centeredness to which they may be pulled naturally. A childhood of helping others can create a lifetime pattern.

But these are busy times where parents can't do it all. Children need to be involved in activities and hobbies where they can shine. With the breadth of wonderful offerings of academics, sports and arts, there truly is something for every interest. These involvements not only keep children out of trouble, but also immerse them in skills and talents that can last a lifetime. After school, no young person should go home to an empty house and television or video games. There's too much out there: games to play, practices for performances, social activities with friends. Involvement and pride are what it's all about.

Lessons Learned

Safety, acceptance, and well-being help children blossom.

Physical and mental health cannot be separated.

Expose children to strong role models. Otherwise they may bond to the wrong people.

Businesses, agencies, and parents can become the village for the child.

Self-esteem thrives when we understand who we are as people, what makes us happy and sad, and how our behavior impacts others.

Children who feel they are the center of the universe often don't develop empathy and compassion for others.

"School smarts" are not as important as the ability to get along with people.

Often, children who talk down to others try to build their own esteem by making someone else look foolish.

While gossip is temporary for the sharer, it can be permanent for the subject.

Give children experiences that allow them to share others' pleasure and pain.

Every child needs an activity or hobby: It's hard to focus on life's negatives when you're having fun.

All children have strengths waiting to be discovered.

No one benefits from a label.

Forcing talent into a set mold can destroy its joyfulness.

Children's and parents' interests can be very different. It's fun to learn something new.

When proud of their accomplishments, children are more willing to try new things.

If we feel good about ourselves as children, we'll feel good about ourselves as adults.

Chapter 5

Raising Responsible Children and Teens

Make yourself necessary to somebody.

Ralph Waldo Emerson

She glanced around her own classroom surreptitiously. Within easy view, Annie sat quietly, though looking up frequently from her math. Inviting distraction, her birdlike body seemed ready for flight in any direction. Janet Macaulay moved toward her, placing a gentle hand on the child's fragile shoulder.

"Glad to see you here working on those fractions today. Looks good so far, Annie."

As she spoke, Janet looked directly under the desk and at the open backpack. Nothing visible. But that didn't mean the new Dr. Seuss books weren't there. Or Michael's missing multi-color sports car.

"You've been out a lot lately. What's going on?"

"Nothin'. Jus' sick."

"Anything bad? We didn't get a note from your Mom."

"No. Jus' sick. She been busy."

Annie returned studiously to her computations, body language indicating they had suddenly become incredibly important. The conversation was over.

Janet shook her head as she walked to another desk. Instinctively, the other fourth-graders ignored Annie. Yet, she had never been a behavior problem. She was absent often, sometimes for three or four days. No phone at home. No notes from parents. Social Services had gone to the apartment a few times, but no one was ever there. Or, at least, no one opened the door.

From the beginning of the year, Janet was concerned about Annie's appearance. Disheveled, often dirty, she had a few wrinkled clothes that she wore without washing, stains and all. Annie's tiny body resembled eight, not her eleven, years. Always a kind child, quietly she helped a few slower students, from checking difficult classwork to reminding them to button their jackets against the cold.

Despite absences, Annie was not that far behind in her own work. While she used street vocabulary and occasional sexual terms beyond her years, she loved to read. For completing onerous tasks such as writing and math, Janet discovered that Annie's most favored reward was lying on the beanbag with a colorful book. She revelled in brilliant pictures, laughing aloud at Curious George. But Seuss was her favorite. She recited *Green Eggs and Ham* by heart and sometimes whispered lines as she practiced spelling or math facts. Amazing contrasts as her small body quivered in amusement inside her dirty dress. She didn't seem to need anything else.

And then things disappeared. A knit cap. Magic markers. Colored rods for math. Favored scratch 'n sniff stickers. And books. So many books were missing.

Quickly, the aura changed in the room. At first, pairs of students had whispered about *The Thief*. Then wide-scale disgruntlement set in, a semi-paranoia about perceived possibilities.

"*The Thief* took my pencil."

Located inside the desk minutes later, "*The Thief* put it back."

"*The Thief* could take the gerbil, Miss. Spot would be real scared."

"Do you think *He's* here in the morning waiting for us?"

"Has *He* ever hurt anybody?"

Reluctant to assign blame, Janet watched the children carefully. It was obvious that no malintended thief slipped into the room at midnight, stealing Legos from the game table, exiting quickly into darkness while leaving everything else intact.

No clues until Monday, when Michael whispered angrily, "It's Annie, Miss! She didn't want to give back my sportscar Friday. Later it was gone from my desk."

"Did you see her take it?"

"No. But she's sneaky." It was obvious from intense onlooker eyes that Janet was not the first Michael had told. Annie wrote her spelling words studiously.

As the children walked to lunch, she kept Annie in the room. "Did you take Michael's car, Annie?"

"Bastard's a liar."

"Don't swear. Did you take the car?"

"NO! And if that stinkin' S-O-B says it one more time, I'm gonna sue his ass!!!"

The vision of a suited-up attorney standing behind Annie in her dirty blue dress and smudged arms almost made Janet laugh aloud.

"Well, right now, fair or otherwise, you've been accused. The best way to prove you didn't do it is to help him get it back and to be sure you're not around anything else that disappears." Janet wasn't prepared for the old, cold eyes or the strange response.

"There's a lot you people don't know. About this or anything." Fiercely, she ran out of the room.

Shuddering uncomfortably, the teacher went through Annie's desk quickly. Nothing. She decided the law probably didn't allow her to search the backpack. But curiosity prevailed as an eye seemed to peer from inside the half-zippered pouch.

"Oh, Lord."

It was Lucky. Spots everywhere, they adored him. The class Dalmatian looked out-of-place inside the tattered school bag. Certainly, Lucky was more than a stuffed animal, even more than a mascot. Janet bought him for the room after the class earned the "101 Dalmatians" video through a week's good behavior. Still excited by the movie, at first they fought over holding him.

When Shana found out she didn't have to move, and when nobody in their class caught chicken pox, Lucky earned his name. If good things happened, it was because of him. When Bob broke his arm and later, Katie's cat died, the class decided that they could have Lucky on their desk. So other bad things wouldn't happen.

Great! We learned superstitions this year, Janet had reflected uneasily.

Then Crystal's precarious health worsened. Absences for dialysis became more frequent. Worries about finding a new kidney. Holding the stuffed dog above the small desk, Janet remembered with a start that it was Annie who suggested Crystal be allowed to keep Lucky with her whenever she was at school.

In her interesting combination of wisdom and street talk, she said, "Ain't nobody needs more luck." Since then, Crystal and the Dalmatian became inseparable, the child even rubbing him absent-mindedly as she did her schoolwork.

So why would Annie steal the dog now, knowing that Crystal would be inconsolable when she returned from this round of treatments?

Happily, the class hadn't noticed his absence from his home on the shelf where he awaited Crystal these days. Returning from lunch, Annie didn't blink when the teacher pointedly referred to Lucky. Studying the non-reaction, Janet sadly remembered Michael's words. "She's sneaky."

Her after-school conversation with Annie encountered only disbelief and denial. "Wasn't in my bag. Why'd you go in my bag anyway? You do that to everybody when they're not around?"

She's good, thought Janet. *She's got me feeling like the thief.*

Since that episode, no Annie for three days. Then she reappeared this morning, looking like a beggar woman. Strangely old, edgy, and stooped. Janet decided to let the situation sit for awhile. Hopefully, it was over.

Math completed, she told the group about her parent conferences this term. "I'm sending home the schedule for your parents to come to the school. But if they're working or can't come during their time, have them call me or write down a better time." *I'll bet Annie runs home with the schedule.* She immediately regretted her sarcasm, since no one had ever seen the mother at the school.

As Annie left that day, she stopped at Janet's desk. "Teacher, you ever go to somebody's house?"

Jolted, Janet responded, "Sure."

"Come Saturday morning then."

"Don't you want to check with your Mom first?"

"She'll be home. Come on..."

Saturday dawned chilly and overcast. *I bet no one's even around when I get there*, Janet worried. But her mood softened as she surveyed the filthy complex. Trash and broken bottles bespoke an active Friday night, as Janet walked around a young man, his head resting in sleep on a plastic bag in the alley. *What a place for children to grow up...*

Annie opened the shabby door, holding a baby on her bony hip. Television blaring, more young eyes quickly appeared at the door.

"This your teacher, Annie?"

"Janie, stop pushing so I can see!"

"Then move, stupid!"

Janet could see a ragged boy of about seven angrily shove a younger girl. Dancing with excitement, the small child observed Janet through huge brown eyes, her near-naked body shivering.

"Can I come in, Annie? Your sister looks cold."

"She's always cold. Needs some clothes." Annie turned and they moved into the tiny living room.

Loud television predominated, with a filthy sofa opposite, no carpet on the dirty tile floor, scattered toys, and empty bags from chips and pretzels. Children's magic-marker drawings brought surprising shocks of vivid color to low areas on otherwise neglected, smudged walls. Roses in a basement of rats.

Two more children scurried over, one attaching herself immediately to Janet's leg, while the other stood back and looked mistrustfully.

"Is your mother home?"

"Right behind you!" Annie laughed.

Janet startled to see a huge woman seated on a chair in the tiny kitchen.

"Momma. Get over here and meet my teacher."

Surprised by Annie's bossy tone, Janet watched the woman rise slowly and move awkwardly toward them. She had a friendly smile, but vacant eyes.

"Miss Macaulay, somethin' you need to know. My momma likes everybody but she don' say much..."

Attention abruptly turned to Annie's hip. The small body she held exuded pain suddenly, coughing violently. As his hacking chest expanded with interspersed wheezing, he pitched his curly head back and forth gasping for air.

The mother moaned. Yet she made no attempt to take the baby, who by now almost threw himself out of Annie's grasp.

"Make him stop it!" she shouted at Annie from her huge frame, tears coursing down her face.

Janet quickly grabbed the baby, whose rasping breaths were now the only sound in the room. She walked about the tiny quarters, rubbing his back, talking to him softly.

"Where's his medicine, Annie?"

Her head hung. "Don' have none."

"How long has he been coughing like this?"

"Awhile. A long time."

Thumb in mouth, the two-year old climbed into Annie's lap, her slightly older sister watching from a distance. Janie and Sam resumed argument over the television channel. Annie's mother went back to her chair in the kitchen, saying nothing.

Janet's glance began to take in familiar objects. Next to crumpled stickers, assorted Dr. Seuss books on the floor. Annie appeared disinterested as Janet walked over to pick up some familiar math manipulatives, noting a box half-full of magic markers on the sofa.

The wheezing baby needily close to her body, Janet felt especially moved by the children's pictures hung jauntily on the bare wall.

"Who did these?"

"Janie and Chrissy. I teach them numbers too. Chrissy's real quiet, but she's smart. And it keeps Janie out of trouble with Sam."

"Do you read to them?"

"Yeah. The girls like it, even little Boo here." She tickled the toddler curled in her lap. "I wish Sam could read better 'cause he could help. But he don't go to school much. We take turns. But since the baby's been sick, I'm afraid to leave Sam here. I think he's sorta' slow anyhow, like Mama." She nodded across the room at her mother, now relaxed back into watching television.

How old was this person in a skinny child's body?

The tiny chest on Janet's shoulder heaved mightily as a new coughing round began.

"Teacher, the baby's really sick. My brother Tommy, he died awhile ago after coughing a lot too. And he was big, even older than Sam. I'm scared the baby's gonna die too."

Looking back, Janet would remember this day as a blur. A home call to a Child Protective Services friend brought two adults to interview the mother and stay with the younger children. While shadowing Janet's every step, Annie refused to relinquish the baby until the emergency room nurse promised she could stay with him. Quickly diagnosed with pneumonia, he was admitted to the children's hospital. The nurse's eyes questioned Janet's when Annie claimed she was old enough to sleep in his room. The teacher nodded. Clearly it was both or none. With a shrug of resignation and a quick word, Janet decided it might just as well be all three of them.

On Monday, her classmates each wrote Annie a letter wishing for the baby's recovery. (Janet made Michael change his "Dear Thief" opening.) Newly back from her dialysis, Crystal insisted Janet take the Dalmatian to Annie. Again, Lucky worked his magic.

Ensuing weeks saw each of the younger children, even little "Boo" and the baby, enrolled in neighborhood daycare. Annie and Sam re-entered school. A temporary court order kept the children together with their mother during a trial period when a social worker visited the home to teach shopping, cleaning, and cooking. The Court hired a neighbor to take the children to daycare every morning. A final decision was pending.

Annie had other changes awaiting her at school. On her first day back, she seemed nonchalant as she noted the returned Seuss books and Michael's car. But her usually nonplussed countenance started when Janet led the class to the school's newly initiated Care Room. A huge closet, its floor to ceiling overflowed with an amazing array of jackets, dresses, shoes, and pants of every size and color. Bookshelves spilled over with a cornucopia of books, colored paper, markers, and toys.

Astonished gasps. Annie and her classmates hungrily gaped at a Thanksgiving feast.

"Can we have these, Teacher?" Michael asked, eying a Red Sox cap greedily. His face fell when she shook her head.

"No, you can't have them. But you can earn them."

"Oohhh." Delight turned to caution.

"The Care Room is full of donations from parents and friends of the school. The clothes are barely worn and the materials brand new. But people worked hard to bring this to you. You have to work hard to earn these things.

"You'll see that everything here has a number of points attached. Let me know in advance what you're working for, and you have one week to earn those points. If you do, it's yours. If not, the article goes back for someone else to earn.

"How do we get the points?"

"Through work and behavior that you and I set together."

She noted the direction of Stacey's stare.

"If math is hard for you, but you crack down and answer questions without skipping any, you can earn this great sticker book."

A glance at Chris.

"If you have trouble finishing your homework every night, but you do it anyway, you'll get this Yankees shirt."

A look at no one.

"If you don't steal anything, but earn it instead, you can take home this whole collection of Dr. Seuss. It's your choice."

Humbled, the class walked back to the room quietly contemplating options. As more seconds passed, their hearts bursting, they shouted, "Miss, I want the bear...the Legos...the pink shirt." Annie said nothing.

At the end of the day, Janet Macaulay watched Annie linger as others departed. "Did you decide what you want to earn?" she asked quietly.

"Miss, you done a lot for me, but I gotta ask one more favor," her eyes peering hopefully from beneath weary eyelids.

"Yes, Annie."

"If I promise I won't never steal again, will you hold those Seuss books for me 'til later on? Right now, I got a sister who needs some clothes."

Responsible Children and Teens

Annie was the most responsible of children. In fact, she was too responsible, realizing that her family's very survival rested on her shoulders. She parented all of her sisters and brothers along with her own needy mother. Knowingly, and beyond her years, she made life and death decisions. Already having lost one brother, she learned to call out for help to save another. Annie never would have invited the teacher to her home if the baby weren't so sick, but she understood that he too could die. Acknowledging her mother's limitations, she turned to a competent adult outside the family.

Because she felt she had no other choice, Annie naturally adopted all of the roles of a caring parent. She became a physical caretaker, even putting her sister's need for clothes over her own desire for books. She also was an intuitive teacher, formally instructing the younger children and hanging their colorful work about the dirty apartment, illustrating pride in the midst of squalor. Sensing Sam's "slowness," she wouldn't leave him to care for the sick baby and she served as a peacekeeper so he didn't hurt Janie. Her own life was such a far cry from the colorful Dr. Seuss books she coveted. The playfulness of the rhymes must have helped give her a perspective, or at least an alternative, to her otherwise bleak and worry-filled life.

Yet, Annie naturally carried her helpfulness into the classroom. She sized up Crystal's need for Lucky, the mascot. She supported "slower" children academically and personally. Viewed as kind by adult onlookers, her behaviors may have been more a result of integration of responsibility for the needy. She displayed the helpfulness that researchers Werner and Smith found in the most resilient children they studied. Initially helping others more by necessity than choice, these young people adopted reaching-out behaviors as they developed stronger identity and self-esteem. Taking control of otherwise chaotic lives, they found that peers and adults alike respected them when they demonstrated competence and caring.

As Abraham Lincoln noted, "To ease another's heartache is to forget one's own." There was no time for Annie to be self-absorbed in her worries, concerned about the new or clean clothes she didn't own, the books she couldn't have. She had to take care of her family, even if it meant compromising a moral code for their survival. Likely, she gave very little thought to the social reactions of being labeled a thief. Her family was her priority. Without compunction or emotion, she took whatever she felt they needed. It was so telling about Annie that books and school materials were among the cherished stolen items. She enjoyed school and wanted to share her pleasure, even taking time to encourage her quiet, but noticeably smart, sister Chrissy.

Without adult intervention, the Annies of our world may grow up amoral and outside the law because social conventions don't give them what they need. As adults they continue to feel family loyalty strongly, but may lie and steal or worse because they see no alternatives. It is critical for involved parents and teachers to understand the demands of a child's home and to create a balance of responsibility and childhood.

In reading Annie's story, parents might feel, "My children would never be able to do all the things she did. They're too into themselves." But adults might be surprised at what their children could and would do if the need arose. During a consultation about their teenage son, Stan and Dana shared some concerns about his apparent helplessness. They complained in disbelief, caring parents who were willing to sacrifice anything for their family, but were baffled by Luke's indifference.

"He can't get up in the morning. He'd never even find his shoes or get to school on time if we didn't lean on him. He has no sense of responsibility for himself or anyone. We worry a lot that he'll never be able to make it in the real world. We're not even sure he cares for us or his sisters. He treats us like annoyances instead of real people. He just tells us to just leave him alone."

Indeed, in our first two sessions, Luke appeared apathetic and unmotivated. His parents were bullies, trying to force him into the professional world. He wasn't sure what he wanted. Teachers only cared about math or science. Was any of that really important? He found the adult world purposeless, but had no replacement. So he vegetated after school and on weekends.

Just weeks later, life imitated fiction as I read Luke's name on the front page of the newspaper. Luke the Hero. Leaving the shower on a school morning, he heard his mother's screams from the garage. She had opened the door to pick up the morning paper and returned to find a strange man with a knife waiting for her. Her husband and younger children gone, she was captive to a rape, burglary, or both.

At his mother's shrieks, Luke ran to the garage and found the intruder attacking her. Luke tackled him, suffered a terrible knife wound, yet still managed to knock the attacker to the ground with fierce blows to the head. Grabbing the knife, he screamed for his petrified mother to call the police. Finally jolted into motion, Dana made the call while an injured Luke pinned down the intruder.

Hospitalized for a few days, Luke later returned home to an appreciative family. I was delighted by Dana's phone call.

"Luke was like a crazy man. He held the attacker down until the police came and kept screaming *No one hurts my mother.*" With a surprised laugh, she added, "I guess we won't need any more sessions. I think he'll make it OK on his own."

I thought so too.

Meaningful Responsibility

Like Annie, Luke showed survival responsibility by immediately responding to a terrible, threatening situation. Neither he nor Annie should ever have been in the circumstances where life placed them, but they took charge as well as any adult. Luke showed his true colors to his family. Viewed as lethargic and helpless, he actually cared enough to put his own life at stake.

He hadn't felt daily school or home activities meaningful enough to give him a purpose. So he stayed disconnected, finding little worthwhile. How sad that with opportunities for involvement surrounding him, Luke spent each day watching television and playing video games.

From Annie's and Luke's stories, we see that children can be responsible if they are in demanding situations. Yet, duty and childhood shouldn't require extenuating or survival circumstances to see what children really can do. No child is born more or less capable of accepting responsibility. But many children are required to do less and continue to take life's easy road unless adults intervene. With an understandable attitude of "Why should I work if I don't have to?" they continue through a childhood of entitlement while adults scurry to make them comfortable and happy. Often, adults complain, "We give and the kids take." We can stem that tide in our own homes.

Avoiding the Parent Abuse Syndrome

But adults can't do everything. Indeed, sometimes we do too much. It's a common conversation that begins with "Kids today...," and usually finishes with an adult disappointment in children's behavior or lack of caring. In response to constant letters of parental complaint, columnist Abigal Van Buren wrote, "If you want your children to keep their feet on the ground, put some responsibility on their shoulders." Psychologist B.F. Skinner agreed, underscoring the importance of work in providing a sense of self-esteem and comfort in our own competence as human beings.

It's not just the child who doesn't make up her bed or the one who ignores his laundry for weeks. It's also the toddler in the grocery store who hits his mother when she won't buy him candy. Or the ten-year-old who tosses her backpack at her mother and says, "Here, you carry this." Or the teen who speaks more nicely to his girlfriend than his parents.

There are many types of responsibility, ranging from daily chores to social interactions. Children or teens who don't respect parental requests to complete chores or homework rarely respect adults outside the home. Too often a sweetened tone of voice toward a parent precedes a request for something expensive or an additional privilege. Laughing with siblings and peers about how to get around Mom or Dad, many young people learn to work the system at home as their primary training ground.

Indeed, while no child should ever experience the tragedy of neglect or abuse, there appear to be many more abused parents than children today, their personal needs for respect and attention neglected. The syndrome begins by not requiring small children to be accountable for their behaviors, allowing them to interrupt adult visits and phone calls as they place their own needs first. Children are naturally egocentric. But unchecked and undirected, "Me First" children become self-centered teens and selfish adults. It may seem many years and behaviors between the three-year-old who ignores the parent's requests to go to bed and the fifteen-year-old who breaks curfew. But as veteran parents note, those years pass very quickly. Young patterns become teen patterns in a blink.

Hurried lives help create the Parent Abuse Syndrome. It's faster for adults to do chores. No one wants to waste time arguing about meal preparation or taking out the trash. Children too are hurried by daily practices and busy schedules. Adults want them to relax and have some unscheduled time, so they're reluctant to interrupt a favorite television show to ask them to pick up toys or their clothes. When parents work and try to run a household, there isn't enough time to get everything done. In the scheme of things, it doesn't seem that important if chores wait or the parent quietly completes them. And when a child ignores requests, argues, or does a poor job, parents may give up.

Guilt is another reason behind letting children "off the hook." Since most parents work, the stay-at-home Mom is often a person of the past. She did the laundry, cleaned the house, and had dinner ready. She took pride in *being there* for her family. But even parents who choose to stay at home today know that life isn't that simple. They spend mornings organizing the household, afternoons driving children to activities, and evenings supervising homework. Working or not outside the home, there's little time to do everything. Even women with full-time jobs may spend hours each day doing housework. In addition to driving and supervising children, they accept responsibility for running the household. It doesn't seem to matter if women work outside the home or not— so many still try to do everything.

While fathers are doing increasingly more housework each year, some spend less than an hour daily in direct interactions with their children. And the majority of this time goes to telling them to brush their teeth and finish their homework. Because most men don't have the mother's history of believing housework to be their job, in many homes they delegate chores to children more easily than women do. If they've worked all day, they feel less guilt in asking a teen to do dishes or a toddler to pick up toys. But it's not easy on Dads either. As a father told me, "It would be fun to just sit and have a conversation with my daughter, to find out how school went and what's going on in her life. But she's usually at extracurriculars until seven, getting a hamburger with friends afterwards. Our evenings are spent with reminders to concentrate on her homework while she's mad because I won't let her use the phone or watch TV. I'm the bad guy when I'm just trying to be a good parent."

Requiring Helpfulness

To avoid the Parent Abuse Syndrome, we have to create children who are responsible for caring behaviors. Many parents and caregivers read books such as this about how to do the best job in raising children and teens. Understanding that in these demanding times the most important skills in life may not be intuitive, but learned, they accept the responsibility and work hard for the family they love. But while many of us study how to be good parents, young people don't study how to be good children, grandchildren, or students who cooperate with teachers.

Understandably, we expect children to learn these things by modeling on adult behaviors. Yet, they may not see many responsible situations on television, where acts of violence are routine, or even on "sit-coms," where actors receive laughs for being dishonest and "beating the system." In our secondary schools, with classes as large as forty, teachers don't have the opportunity to reach everyone, so students often model on peers' behaviors.

To avoid the Parent Abuse Syndrome and to teach responsibility, the best time to start requiring helpfulness is when children are very young. But it's never too late. For example, we may expect our own parents to be generous to our children without ever teaching young people ways to be a responsive grandchild. When Amy's grandfather calls, she should be required to speak to him even if she says she's "busy." Once into the call, she's usually engaged enough that the conversation becomes fun and a reminder of his love and concern. If the grandparent is ill or lonely, parents should help her initiate the call, explaining how much it will cheer him up. Weinreb's review of research on resiliency led her to conclude that when children work and contribute to a social network, they feel good about themselves and develop a personal sense of ownership and commitment. Amy learns an important lesson through her parents' insistence on reaching out: When we extend ourselves to others, we feel good too.

I don't believe that "random acts of kindness" are the same as responsibility. When we do something randomly, it's whimsical. As a result, if we're relaxed and happy, it's a kind day and we're exceptionally nice to others. At another time, we excuse ourselves from politeness because of boredom or unhappiness. We can't exempt children from responsibility because they're not in the mood. Yet, parents often note that "She won't do something unless she's really motivated." Helping others is an attitude that rarely develops without parental insistence. It's accompanied by showing respect for adults, siblings, friends, and pets. The best way to instill this attitude is to compliment children for caring behaviors and to redirect them immediately when they are self-centered or ignore others' needs.

If children are disabled or otherwise at-risk, it may be difficult to see how they can help others when they appear so needy themselves. As a result, a child with health problems may grow into a demanding adult, feeling entitled to attention without giving much in return. Parents may not ask their teen with a learning disability to help a younger brother or sister with schoolwork, quietly sending the message that they doubt the teen's competence. Everyone has something to offer others. Children gain in pride and self-confidence when they're viewed as able to give.

Kathy was a thirteen-year-old student with Down Syndrome enrolled in my self-contained Special Education class. Walking to the room each morning from her small, "special" bus, other "Regular Education" students unkindly called her *Retard* or *Dummy*. Tossing these names at her as they moved quickly to class meant nothing to them. Indeed, they seemed to forget the taunts as soon as they made them. A student I chastised once told me with certainty, "Don't worry, Miss. The retarded don't understand anything. She has no idea what I'm saying." That student should have lingered to see the tears well in her eyes or her face remain bright red for minutes. He had never witnessed the headaches that plagued her constantly. Kathy and her classmates understood all too well what "special" meant.

The school had a tutoring system where fourth and fifth grade students with fully completed assignments were allowed to instruct younger children for an hour each Friday. Some of the tutors worked in my classroom, helping students with reading or math assignments. I never assigned Kathy a tutor, because as one of the oldest in my class she would have felt badly receiving instruction from someone her own age or younger.

Observing our visitors, one Friday an excited Kathy asked me if she could be a tutor in another room. Since her skills were approximately at second grade level, this would be a problem. My colleagues were busy and I couldn't ask them to take on another student, although Kathy's behaviors were quite good. After a weekend of thought but no solutions, I decided to turn it over to her.

"What age do you want to tutor?"

"Little kids. Big ones are mean." So much for her not understanding anything.

"What would you do when you tutor?"

"Read and play. Like I do with my cousins." Clearly I should have just asked her instead of worrying all weekend.

Kathy spent the next two weeks practicing *Curious George* and *Madeleine*. She read daily to me and her classmates and visited the Kindergarten room during after-lunch play. She was thrilled when the teacher appointed Kathy's cousin Cyndi as her assistant, to help her organize the children and direct the reading session. Kathy would read a few books to them each week and then be their "big sister" during playtime.

With a smooth transition into Fridays, she glowed in her new status. One week even the Principal dropped in to watch her. Delighted, later he reported the details of finding her seated on the floor with her small charges propped against her body or climbing across her lap. She read the practiced stories with character and emotion, interspersing "Can you believe that?" and "Listen to what happened then!"

Newly placed in a foster home, young Angel stood behind Kathy's shoulders and hugged her neck during the entire reading. Instead of joining others in play, she silently caressed Kathy's hand against her own face. Kathy took Angel's hand in her own and kept her by her side as she talked to the other young children.

"Jake, don't hit him. That's nasty."

"Carrie, you gotta share the truck with Lou."

"Don't cry, Lonnie. He didn't mean it."

As required for all tutors, Kathy completed her own weekly work in order to earn her position. Where she had previously been slipshod at times, she was now compulsive about finishing her assignments. Throughout the day, she approached me with, "Is it O.K., Miss? Can I practice for Friday now?" Her mother became a home audience, coaching Kathy in reading expression and reminding her of the social behaviors to use in the Kinder room. Not surprisingly, Kathy stopped complaining of headaches, looking surprised and shrugging when we asked about them.

The holidays arrived and Kathy was invited to the children's party. She surprised them by reading *The Grinch who Stole Christmas* as a special treat. It was fun to hear her finally use the word *special* in such a positive way. She carried a bag of crayons and markers tied with bows into individual bundles for each of her children. Smiling broadly, she commented "I'm just like Santa."

But the best was last. At the spring final awards assembly, tutors individually went up the brief steps to the stage to receive their certificate and shake hands with the Principal. Each class cheered and yelled for their tutors. Then Kathy's name was called. As she walked to the steps there was a start that turned into brief applause, and sadly even some quickly hushed jeers and catcalls from individual students.

From the stage, a startled Kathy turned to the audience as her entire Kinder class stood and cheered. Prodded into action, other teachers and their students rose. Kathy stood uncertainly by the Principal as the applause became deafening. This time, the tears in her eyes and her bright red face told a different story.

Reflecting on how Kathy's success served both her and the Kindergartners, I wished I had thought to require helpfulness sooner in my students. She asked to become purposeful. Through her motivation we were able to work out the logistics that too commonly cancel the best of intentions. Her self-confidence and willingness to work harder at school increased as the young children needed her.

Helpfulness cuts across age spans. In *Another Country*, a book about understanding the elderly, Mary Pipher notes that a purpose in life keeps the elderly from depression and withdrawal. Regardless of age, responsibility for others is a wonderful reason for living. As Kathy's headaches disappeared, so do the aches and pains of retirees who understand that someone has greater needs. Even after my mother's early strokes, she continued to care for my father as he suffered for seven years with Parkinson's Disease. Cooking three huge meals each day, doing laundry, and even waxing tables, caused her to rise early each morning to take charge of making his world comfortable. When he died, her own physical health deteriorated immediately. Rejecting the family's insistence that she "get help" for my father may have extended her well-being

Responsibilities for Children

At home children can

- ❏ help with younger brothers and sisters (food, play, safety)
- ❏ follow parental requests without nagging
- ❏ with adult reminders, refrain from whining and complaining
- ❏ pick up and put toys away
- ❏ keep the kitchen neat, cleaning up after themselves
- ❏ feed, play with, and walk pets
- ❏ put soiled clothes in hamper and hang up clothes
- ❏ care for toys and objects (no climbing on furniture or throwing toys)
- ❏ go to bed at scheduled time without complaining
- ❏ help with meal preparation and clean-up
- ❏ take out trash

To prepare for school, children can

- ❏ wake up independently (by alarm clock) and without parental prompts or nags
- ❏ select clothes and get dressed
- ❏ tell parents in advance what items are needed for school
- ❏ take necessary items to school (books, homework)
- ❏ make their own lunch
- ❏ complete homework independently in a quiet, organized place (desk in room)
- ❏ follow homework rules (no TV, telephone, or other distractions)

Responsibilities for Children (cont.)

When involved in school and community activities, children should

- ❑ tell parents in advance about scheduled events

- ❑ practice without reminders from parents (music, plays, sports)

- ❑ make a commitment to participate in an activity for a designated period of time, lessening their ability to quit if not selected for a favored role or position

- ❑ say positive things to other team members

- ❑ organize and be sure necessary clothing and uniforms are ready for performances or games

To develop personal hygiene habits, children can

- ❑ without reminders, bathe daily at specified time

- ❑ wash hair frequently

- ❑ brush and floss teeth daily

- ❑ bathe after sports or intense play

- ❑ with guidance, collect and wash soiled clothes

during those difficult times. Old or young, few things help us more than helping someone else.

Household Responsibilities

If children learn to serve others when young, it's likely they'll continue as adults. Because the family is the earliest social system, parents can develop a positive attitude by their expectations for family members to support each other. What children master at home they carry with them into larger society. But as Kathy found out from her peers, people may not be naturally kind. It's the role of the parent to socialize the child.

A friend once commented about her son, "Now that he's nice, gets along with his sister, and even cleans his room, he's leaving home. I feel like we did all the work, he's finally where we want him to be, and we're turning him over for everyone else to enjoy!" I watched his parents do so many things well in raising him over the years. As the big brother, he brought diapers and talked to the new baby. As a teen, he babysat and didn't seem to mind helping his sister with her math homework. He's a good cook today because he always had a role in dinner preparation. He'll benefit for a lifetime from their good parenting.

The charts list a number of age-appropriate responsibilities for children and teens. The lists include a routine number of tasks adults perform routinely without complaint. Children's responsibilities should begin with toddlers as young as ages two or three. Chores increase in difficulty as they become older. For example, the younger child helps feed the pets and the older one walks them daily. Even a toddler can "work" along with parents in the yard. Regardless of age, each evening all children can put up their things and collect soiled clothes. It's important for parents to require completion of both home and school responsibilities.

Household chores tend to fall into categories. *General orderliness* includes day-by-day requirements for children to put away clothes, wash dishes as they're used, and keep toys and personal items from cluttering family living areas. Even basic tasks like hanging up towels and keeping the bathroom clean are important since, if undone, they irritate other family members by showing a disregard for shared space. Parents may be tempted to pick up clothes and toys because it's easier or faster. It's important that they not automatically keep the house in order for their children, who'll learn orderliness best by putting things away and picking up after themselves. A good way to reinforce these skills is through one reminder to clean up, followed by an expectant stance, waiting for the child to follow through. No television, play with friends, or even dinner until doing as the parent asks. Rules with immediate consequences have the best effect.

Specific cleaning and care tasks involve jobs that are not ongoing but need to be completed at certain times, such as taking out the trash, walking pets, and meal preparation. In addition to holding a job outside the home, teens are more than capable of babysitting, lawn care, laundry and ironing. As mundane as it may be, few chores cause as many arguments as doing laundry: Is it scattered about the child's room, stepped on daily? Should parents be expected to wash and iron a teens' clothing because the young person is "too busy?"

To parents, these lists may seem too ideal. But these competencies develop over time, with parents giving each child responsibility from the earliest of ages. Immediate positive and negative consequences reward or punish the child, indicating parental expectations. A good rule of thumb is progression by age. All children, including toddlers, can put dirty clothes away in designated hampers or baskets each evening. By age 10, children are capable of washing, drying and folding their own clothes. With parental guidance and practice, children can easily learn to sort clothes by color, add detergents, and set the dryer. Parents may need to remind them that laundry is finished when the clothes are on hangers or away in drawers. Many times children try to leave clean clothes in the dryer or on their bed.

By age 12, children can safely iron all their own things. Again, parents provide initial demonstrations and supervision so that the pre-adolescent masters the skill quickly. If parents step in and continue to do the laundry or ironing because the young person "can't do it right," they establish a pattern of helplessness, excusing the child from trying. Unfortunately, it's human nature to give these chores back to us with any acceptable excuse!

It is important to schedule specific cleaning and care tasks for certain times of the week that fit into family schedules. Instead of waiting for laundry or trash to pile up, the child does the chore at a pre-determined time. Marty may choose to do her laundry Saturday mornings as she watches television. When she's invited to a friend's house for Friday night, her parents agree that she can do it when she comes home. If she has input into when she's to complete the chore and parents hold her to the responsibility, it will be hard for her to say she's busy.

Personal hygiene is another critical area of responsibility. From preschool, children need to bathe themselves daily, wash hair frequently, and brush their teeth. It's important for them to understand that sports and play involve getting dirty, but it's their responsibility to clean up immediately afterwards. Designated play or sports clothes show them that it's

Responsibilities for Teens

At home, teens can

- ❏ follow all household rules without reminders
- ❏ avoid rudeness and arguments with parents and siblings
- ❏ do all their own laundry and ironing
- ❏ without complaining, share the bathroom and telephone
- ❏ follow rules for curfew
- ❏ have a personal budget for savings and spending
- ❏ contribute financially to personal expenses
- ❏ demonstrate good manners and have polite, interactive conversations
- ❏ go to bed at scheduled time without complaining
- ❏ help with meal preparation and clean-up
- ❏ keep their own room and living areas neat
- ❏ be helpful to younger brothers and sisters daily, baby-sitting when needed

To participate fully in school, teens can

- ❏ set an alarm clock and get ready independently
- ❏ take necessary books and completed assignments to school without reminders
- ❏ complete homework independently in a quiet place
- ❏ avoid distractions such as telephone and television until homework is completed
- ❏ treat teachers with respect, following rules and completing assignments
- ❏ work with peers from all economic, ethnic, and racial backgrounds

Responsibilities for Teens (cont.)

Outside the home, teens can

❏ hold a part-time job, demonstrating punctuality, appropriate work behaviors, and extra effort to perform well

❏ demonstrate financial responsibility by purchasing personal items and saving toward future goals

❏ keep parents informed of their social activities, location, and level of adult supervision

❏ take responsibility for others, especially the less fortunate

❏ work actively with peers in organizing and planning activities; carry out individual role responsibly

To prepare for their future, teens can

❏ discuss life goals with parents and educators, considering the best steps to follow

❏ explore college and professional programs

❏ complete college applications independently

❏ plan financially how to reach their personal and professional objectives

To show respect for their own body, teens can

❏ avoid smoking, drinking, and substances

❏ demonstrate sexual responsibility

❏ practice personal hygiene daily, without reminders

❏ eat healthy foods, avoiding fad diets and supplements

fine to relax without concerns about what they're wearing. But when the parent explains the need to take a quick shower or place soccer clothes in the washer, the child learns the process. As their bodies change, teens benefit from reminders about showering immediately after a run or work-out and not leaving sweaty socks or clothes about the house. A quick "Joanie, put your clothes in the washer" is non-confrontational, but gives her direction. If she tries to go off with friends and the clothes are on the bedroom floor, the parent says quietly, "You can go out after you wash your dance squad uniform." Rules and immediate consequences work better than power struggles over who will do her laundry.

Children and teens alike need reminders for good sanitary practices, such as washing hands after toileting, using tissues for runny noses, and not coughing or sneezing on others. While these are personal habits, they impact friends and teachers by spreading illnesses and diseases. The best way to teach personal hygiene is reminding young children, then pausing and waiting to see that they follow through. For example, "Sara, wash your hands before dinner" may be ignored. Parents who send her away from the table and back to the sink show they mean business and no food will be served until she complies. Teens usually become interested in the opposite sex and bathing at about the same time. But they rarely carry tissues even when sick with a cold and may skip routine washing throughout the day. A good-natured tease from a parent about "forgetting" good habits usually works best. "Chris, if you keep talking and chewing at the same time, I'll get to practice my Heimlich technique. It'll be fun to have a guinea pig!" The typical response is rolled eyes, a head shake, and a closed mouth.

Responsibility for schoolwork is critical to young people's future, not only for grades but also to teach organization and independence. Often, parents complain that mornings are the most rushed time of the day. Children may not get out of bed when called and have difficulty finding clothes and school papers that "disappeared" overnight. Since adults need time to get ready for their own job, understandably they become stressed by grouchy or slow-moving children. Evenings and homework are another difficult time, with many parents fighting the television and telephone as enemies. Tired and wanting more fun activities, children procrastinate over assignments and complete them only when parents nag.

To avoid a negative attitude and a later power struggle, again it's important to start training when children are young. By developing an image of themselves as good students, school success becomes a part of children's personal identity. It's critical to get students to the point where they perform well because they want to, because they feel it's important. They're not doing this for Mom and Dad, but for themselves. But just telling them to get organized or do their work rarely is effective. They need to be directed into structured habits. As they take pride in each successful paper and exam, they feel continuously more capable of performing schoolwork independently. For example, to avoid frantic mornings, children can select school clothes and put homework and school supplies in their backpack the night before.

Usually there are two set patterns that result in parents being overly involved in children and teens' homework. The first begins early when adults sit by a child each night to supervise. While the parent is trying to show that schoolwork is important, the young person may view this as shared time. Enjoying the parent's full attention, the child may stop working when the adult walks away to prepare dinner or especially to attend to a brother or sister. A battle begins and increases force over the years as the parent insists the young person is capable of working independently. Seeking even negative parental attention, the child refuses.

It's best to never start this pattern in the first place. When children bring completed assignments for parents to review or ask them to go over facts before an exam, good reinforcement of information occurs. But first, young people should have completed the reading and answered the questions independently. If parents are too available, children rely on them to be teachers or to explain unread information, creating a dependency cycle of not actually completing the assignment, but counting on parental explanations of chapter content. In this way, they never fully read or study all the ideas, relying on parental interpretation. Scores on exams will be lower because of missed information. When usually-present parents are unavailable for homework discussion, children also perform poorly, reinforcing that they "can't do the work." In actuality they haven't fully tried because they've become overly dependent on parental input.

The second pattern that can consume parents' time each evening develops when children have learning problems, lessening their ability to complete homework or do well on exams. They turn to Mom or Dad for assistance. Yet, no parent can be an objective tutor to a son or daughter. Emotions surface easily, stemming from concern about the child's abilities, attitude, and the impact of low performance on college entrance or an eventual career. The parent may not understand why the child isn't doing better, noting that the work is "easy" or the answer is "obvious." Since no parent wants a child to have learning problems, it's easy to blame lack of motivation and effort. Too often exam preparation and homework completion end with a frustrated adult and an angry child. Schoolwork takes on a negative tone and the student feels incapable of successful performance.

If low school performance is creating weak academic self-esteem, parents need to find out *why* the child is performing poorly. Everyone will benefit from a teacher conference, where parents and professionals exchange observations about the child's work. If the student performs lower than peers, the parents might request testing for remedial or Special Education programs in order to take a closer look at spoken language, reading, math, and writing skills. Testing will indicate if learning problems really exist. Parents, teachers, and assessment personnel meet again after the testing to discuss outcomes and to determine the best type of teaching and behavior plans to re-motivate the student toward success in school.

I'm saddened to hear parents say, "Well, at least she won't have to go into Special Ed.," or "He's too smart—he doesn't need extra help." Yet, it's possible to be gifted and have learning problems. Many times students lack basic skills, have poor work habits or a neurological learning disability. It's easy to ignore or deny these problems when children express themselves well and appear quick to learn in many areas. Even students achieving good grades may need extra help if they're working too hard to achieve them, having no life outside school. Some of our best teachers have intensive training in special and remedial techniques and enjoy helping students with new approaches to learning. These professionals gain their reward from watching the dyslexic child learn to read or the unmotivated teen go on to college. But especially with secondary students, their teaching skills may be under-utilized. Parents and children alike want to avoid having anyone know that there's a learning or behavior problem. Yet, without this acknowledgment, the young person can't receive badly needed assistance. While no one wants the stigma of appearing different, parents need to accept the school's offer of special help. The long-term outcomes can move the student from stress to success.

Rarely do children refuse to complete schoolwork or homework because of laziness. They want to succeed in class, have their papers hung up on the wall, and be viewed as smart. But by the time they reach middle school, it's easier not to complete an assignment than to work hard at it and fail. Ernie can say, "I didn't do the math homework—that teacher is really stupid." He can't say, "I feel really stupid because I couldn't do the homework." It's one thing to fail because you chose not to try. It's another to fail because you tried but couldn't do the work. Often, young people hide weak skills behind a "Who cares?" attitude. Indeed, studies of juvenile delinquents continuously point out their high intelligence and low reading levels.

Visiting the Principal of a local high school one afternoon, I was surprised at the row of chairs full of students and parents waiting outside his office.

"These kids are quitting," he noted sadly. "They're here with their parents to sign them out of school. They have no skills, most can barely read, and they don't appreciate anything we've tried. I hope they'll get motivated about something in the work world, but I doubt it."

After our meeting, I stopped outside the office to visit with a beautiful young woman and her tired, stooped mother.

"You're quitting school?"

A shrug and a nod.

"Why?"

Her grammar, profanity, and rough body gestures were in deep contrast to her carefully groomed hair and professional make-up. "Ain't nothin' in this _____ hole for me. School sucks. I'm outta here!"

Quietly, her mother added, "She always hated school. Nothing I can do. Maybe she'll finish someday."

With real anger, "Shut your mouth, Ma! After today, the only thing these teachers gonna see is my backside!" Huffily, she stood and walked away from us to stand in the hallway. Embarrassed, her mother looked away.

The Principal and the mother had given up. The task seemed so overwhelming that I too wondered if we adults could reach everyone or if some young people were just so unmotivated or angry that they were beyond us.

A few weeks later, I had lunch with a good friend, the popular Superintendent of a large local school district.

"I can't stay long today," she commented, looking at her watch. "I have a mother and son coming in at one and it's a really important meeting."

"What's going on?"

"One of our high schoolers thinks he's quitting school. He and his Mom went to the Principal to fill out the papers and the Principal sent them to me. That's my policy, because I don't want to lose our students. Every one is important."

Thinking back to my experience a few weeks ago in another district, I voiced my doubt that she'd be successful.

"Of course we will. He doesn't know it yet, but I won't let him quit. I'll ask him what it will take to get him to stay. Work study, so he can earn some cash? Modified curriculum with special support in areas where he's had a tough time? Night school? Ours won the state award for excellence last year. I'll have a counselor there specifically assigned to check in with his teachers weekly. She'll also meet with the boy and his mother every month to be sure the program is working. If not, we'll change to make school meaningful and to motivate him."

As she rose to rush off, she added, "I'm always sorry if it reaches this point before we intervene. But each of our schools now has "Crisis Intervention Teams" to identify at-risk students early. The time is coming where we'll handle these problems in fourth grade instead of tenth, so there's no danger of losing our kids."

The Superintendent was willing to make any possible modification to save a young person's future, working together with parents and teachers in a "We care" attitude. At the school I had visited earlier, the Principal and mother were "signing out" the young woman, indeed signing away her future. They looked to her to appreciate their earlier efforts and to self-motivate. When adults view the responsibility for failure as the student's problem, we excuse our own accountability. If children, and especially teens, don't find school related to their lives, they divorce education. When we redesign the system to create a meaningful fit with the student's needs, a re-marriage becomes workable. Adults can create the circumstances for school success or failure.

Teaching Responsibility for Others

Many of the age-appropriate responsibilities for teenagers create both a work ethic and an attitude of caring for others' needs. Often, parents and teachers complain that children think only of themselves. We adults may be expecting attitudes such as consideration, sharing, and helpfulness to develop naturally and without adult intervention.

The opposite is generally true. First, it is important to insist on children and teens performing certain tasks competently and without complaining. Adults can do this by praising young people for work carefully done with a positive attitude. If children refuse, adults might comment, "I'm sorry you feel that way. We all have our jobs to do. It makes everyone, including you, feel better if you do them without complaining." At that point, it's best to walk away without further discussion. If the young person still does not do as asked, an immediate consequence is necessary, such as missing a favored activity. *Parents should never give in to a complaining child or teen who is refusing responsibility.*

Over time, the lesson is learned: This *is* my job. Continual parental praise for work done well also creates a positive attitude and makes children proud of their accomplishments. Following household rules ranging from curfew to sharing the telephone and bathroom, young people can become considerate of other family members. Attitude is as critical as acceptance of responsibility.

One of my university students works daily in our office, performing clerical tasks for faculty. She does everything carefully and with real concern. But it's not just how she works, it's her positive outlook.

"Becca, would you mind running something off and collating it for me?"

"No problem!" She's there immediately with a big smile and cheerfulness to spare.

Although her hours are over for the day, I've seen her quietly continue to work because a job isn't finished. Or she'll comment, "I've got to run to class, but I'll come back afterwards and help with that": No extra pay, no one even requesting that she work overtime, just a sense that doing a good job matters.

There's no doubt what her faculty recommendations will say as she applies for eventual jobs. But she's not positive and hard-working because of future references. She has an upbeat attitude toward others because she has one toward herself and her own capabilities.

It's been my delight to observe her practice-teaching with second graders. I would bet anything that she's mimicking her own parents and instructors as she comments,

"Brian, please help Mark carry that."

"Tricia, Ken's practicing that really tough subtraction today. I want you to explain borrowing to him again. You're a great teacher!"

"Who are the best workers in the world? We are!"

Developing a Responsible Attitude

Children aren't born with a desire to work or help others. Indeed, imagine the incredulous parent whose thirteen-year-old asks, "Got any work for me to do around here?" It would seem time for a medical check! But, as Booker T. Washington commented, "Few things help an individual more than to place responsibility upon him and let him know that you trust him."

In addition to the classroom behaviors of sharing and group work that Becca was already teaching her second-graders, school includes many wonderful opportunities for learning responsibility. Beyond fun and social involvement, extracurriculars teach teamwork toward a final goal, such as winning the game, presenting an outstanding artistic performance, or demonstrating finely-honed competitive skills. The ability to be a contributing, respected member of a group is the basis of self-esteem for many at-risk students during a rocky adolescence.

Sadly, a student may feel like a "loser" because of poor academic grades or dissatisfaction with physical appearance. But after school, when climbing onto the stage as first-chair clarinetist, the rest melts away. Or when the debate coach says,

"Glad you're here. We really need your help with this one," the young person feels important. But we mustn't stop with personal esteem: We need to take it to the next level of reaching out to others. So the clarinetist works with two new students, guiding them through a difficult piece. And the debater shares research and strategy with the squad. An *esprit-de-corps* develops around a common purpose or goal such as a competition, with each member contributing and respected.

Many young people feel that events fall together, not appreciating the organization and supportive work from behind-the-scene adults. It's only when in charge of an event that they realize the "devil is in the details." Minor crises occur when no one brings the charcoal for the hamburger roast. Or the costumes aren't finished by dress rehearsal. Or the key to the locker room is missing. Many teen social activities among friends and classmates don't go as planned or are cancelled because of lack of attention to particulars.

An important part of responsibility-taking involves careful planning. Parents and teachers can guide and suggest, but inevitably, the final success must rest on the young person. Adults provide the structure, as children learn that working cooperatively is best. Through ongoing experience, they find that Spanish Club meetings are more fun if everyone gets along. They have to arrange the Spring Break trip to Mexico, with tons of details to organize. It's important to delegate responsibility since no one student can do it all. Together they solve the endless large and small problems: What kind of fund-raisers will finance the trip? How will we get adult chaperones? What types of visas or identification will we need? What transportation is most cost-effective?

Throughout the planning and problem-solving, their impressions about working with others can be impacted for a lifetime. They learn to look beyond peers' surface appearances and accept them at full worth. If groups across the school are divided by race or ethnicity, shared planning and decision-making provide rare opportunities for mutual appreciation instead of prejudice. Many students may have ignored Janie, because she hangs around with "the Mexican kids." But when her uncle in Mexico City recommends hotels and promises to meet the group, she becomes important and prejudice starts to dissolve.

Sandy is in several Special Education classes because of

numerous academic problems. But she has energy to spare and uses her art skills to design posters for Club fundraisers. Usually Tom is so shy that he says nothing. With the teacher's encouragement, members learn that he lived in Monterrey for years and can advise them on what to wear and the customs. They're amazed at how well he speaks Spanish as he tells them the correct pronunciation of common words. He's become a consultant.

Through working together, group members begin to take responsibility for each other. For the first time, Janie is asked to sit with new friends on the bus going home. Informally, students help Sandy spell the words correctly on her posters. And they include Tom in conversations, asking a question and waiting for him to respond. Tolerance and acceptance of others is a precursor for maturity.

Caring for Others

As the school guides groups of children, parents can direct them individually in acts of kindness. After the terrible nuclear power accident at Chernobyl, radioactivity spread across Russia, carrying with it concerns about birth defects, contamination of the food supply, and the health of citizens. Afterward, many children of Chernobyl spent summers in Ireland, living with families who offered love and kindness despite differences in language and customs. Each summer, Irish friends of mine have had two children from Chernobyl stay with their family, putting their own young daughters in charge of helping the Russian children set aside their worries and experience new adventures. "We've had great fun," my friend commented. "They've been no bother. Most of the time, they just play outside with my children. It's amazing how much English they've learned in such a short time. And my own daughters are picking up Russian expressions. We're all so fortunate in this country that it would be selfish not to welcome them."

Closer to home, a family in upstate New York has welcomed at-risk, inner-city children each summer for many years. Living "in the country" for a month, the young visitors experience a totally different life. Of modest means, the family lives in a small house in the suburbs. But to the city children, being away from a daily life of drugs and dangerous influences gives them the opportunity to see alternatives, to set different goals for their own future.

The family's own children also have been impacted dramatically. Put in charge of their guests, they take pride in overseeing a fun time. Some of the city children have spent as many as four summers upstate, establishing a long-term relationship with the family. Frequently, their visits spill over into subsequent letters and phone calls throughout the year. The family's youngest son reports being "blown away" by some of the things their visitors haven't previously experienced.

"They've never gone fishing, or even swimming, in a lake," he reports. "One of the kids liked real fruit in the ice cream so much that we all got some every day! Some of my friends are scared of the city kids at first, but my Mom's always there and pretty soon they get to know them. I'm in charge of being sure everyone understands house rules and has a good time." What a wonderful personal lesson he's learning about care and responsibility.

Other families take in a foreign exchange student, parents and children both learning about customs in another country. Even students from English-speaking countries share remarkable language differences that are fun for the family to analyze. It's wonderful to see a previously egocentric teen become a world citizen, explaining to friends, "Well, in Italy they...," and taking pride in being responsible for a guest's adjustment at home and school. Parents remark how email allows their children to keep up with foreign students after the visit and sometimes even to plan their own follow-up trip to the student's country.

Foster children are a more serious commitment. Often living with a family for years, their behaviors and needs may be extreme because of early abuse and neglect. One of my university students reported how annoyed she and her brother were when their parents decided to take in a foster infant.

"We were really busy with activities and all, and I was just starting middle school. I remember how embarrassed I was explaining to my friends, 'No, my Mom didn't have a baby. We're just keeping this one for awhile.' Now, I'm embarrassed at my attitude. I was really selfish.

"Ironically, I cried the hardest when the baby went back to her mother about a year later. By then she was my sister and I loved to play with her. After that, we made a family decision to continue with foster kids. A few of the older ones have been tough because they act out a lot. But my brother and I learned to teach them the rules. We try to tell them how to act when they're upset so they don't explode. My Dad calls us 'counselors.' We haven't failed yet! The one thing I do know is that when I have my own family I'm going to have foster kids too."

Not every family has the time or flexibility to take on additional children. But they can still model responsibility through helpfulness to neighbors and others more vulnerable. Children might join parents in volunteer work for wonderful organizations such as "Habitat for Humanity" or for local religious and voluntary associations. It's important that young people have their own responsibilities to carry out and duties to perform so that they can develop a sense of competence while serving others. The specific organization is not as important as the sense of involvement and learned helpfulness.

Money and Credit Cards

Another area of developing responsibility involves finances. Debt is the main cause of friction in many homes. Of no surprise, researchers such as Jeanne Brooks-Gunn at Columbia University and Greg Duncan at Northwestern found that poverty is a primary reason for abuse, crime, and violence. Luckily, most of us don't live at near-poverty levels, but we still feel the daily stress of making ends meet. Why don't children seem to appreciate what things cost? Why do so many teens avoid financial responsibility, expecting their parents to support them or bail them out when they over-spend?

The ease of the credit card appears to have caught up with us. Years ago, afraid of "bouncing a check," we stopped spending when the money wasn't in the bank. Today we can buy almost everything on credit, obtain a second mortgage on our home, and even cash in our retirement fund to make major purchases or pay off large debts. When retailers have a profile of our individual lifestyles and encourage us to buy on-line, purchases are a key-stroke away. Instead of enjoying the incredible goods available to us, we worry more about money than ever.

Trinity University offers a wonderful extended summer opportunity for scores of "Upward Bound" high school students to live on our campus and take advanced courses preparing them for college. Participation in this federally-funded program is based on the student coming from a low-income family where neither parent has ever attended college. Our goal is to take at-risk students and show them that they can be academically successful. Counselors help them prepare for SATs, apply to universities, and develop organized study habits while participants are enrolled in challenging courses.

Despite security efforts, the day before students arrive on campus, credit card applications inundate classrooms, dorms, and social areas. CD clubs also leave flyers everywhere, promising a bonus of "free" music for enrollment and getting a friend to join. Every application is easy and promises monthly low interest because companies appreciate student lack of income. For teens who have little money, these cards offer so much and can hook them for a lifetime despite educators' best efforts. The presence of these applications is particularly upsetting because the very purpose of the Upward Bound program is to show the route out of poverty.

Similar applications arrive frequently in everyone's mail. The temptations are there for all of us, but teens are particularly vulnerable. Despite these pressures, parents and educators can teach young people sound financial decisions for a lifetime. It's equally important for children from both affluent and disadvantaged homes to learn careful money management. Rich or poor, it's not the amount of money they have, but the attitude they develop on how to spend and save.

At first I was amused when reading about Princess Diana taking her young sons into McDonald's and requiring them to buy their own food. She had them decide what they wanted, compute the cost, and pay with their own money. With immense credit available to them anywhere, she realized that only early experiences would help them fully appreciate cost and normal spending. So she gave them practice at a level they could understand. Her insight demonstrates that despite financial level, all children can learn from spending their own money on coveted purchases.

Lifetime Spending and Saving Habits

It's critical for young people to learn to spend and save wisely. The charts below include a number of strategies to teach young people how to use money and credit cards. As with most things, children model their financial habits on their

Teaching Children and Teens to Deal with Money and Credit Cards

❑ Personally model good financial planning by avoiding large debts.

❑ Frequently explain how you manage money so children understand the process.

❑ From a young age, have children contribute financially to purchases.

❑ When children want to buy something, discuss whether the purchase is necessary, the reasonableness of the price, and how much they will contribute.

❑ Do not allow children to buy on impulse. Wait and discuss for several days before committing to a major expenditure.

❑ Avoid "window-shopping" as a form of entertainment. Go shopping only with a specific, necessary purchase in mind.

❑ When children work for their allowance (i.e., laundry, uncomplaining homework completion), they learn the importance of earning.

❑ Help young people plan additional ways to earn money.

❑ Do not loan children money. Resentment develops around repayment.

❑ Underscore that finishing college or trade school is the best way to a strong financial future.

❑ Encourage children to talk about their financial goals. Through conversations, list the steps to reach them.

❑ Throughout childhood, de-emphasize shopping and "labels."

❑ Show children how to be comparison shoppers and avoid overpaying for merchandise.

❑ Have children write out their income and expenses. Discuss ways they can live within their budget.

❑ Through conversations, create the expectation that children will be totally self-supportive as adults.

❑ Enforce weekly savings from their allowance at an early age. The child should have a savings account.

Teaching Children and Teens to Deal with Money and Credit Cards (cont.)

❏ Young adults should not have credit cards until they earn their own money and show financial restraint.

❏ Do not co-sign on teen credit cards or loans (i.e., car). If the young person does not repay, you will be held responsible.

❏ Require young people to pay off debts in full each month to avoid interest fees or out-of-control spending.

❏ If a teen abuses a credit card, parents should take it away immediately.

❏ Never "bail out" children or teens when they're in debt. Instead, establish a re-payment plan using only their money.

❏ Teens should hold a job. Part of every paycheck should be deposited in savings.

❏ Teens should pay their own car insurance, and if possible, buy their own car. They should pay for any gas they use in your car.

❏ Don't let teens "hang out" at shopping malls. Behavior problems and excessive materialism can result.

❏ Consider how you will afford their college, but let them earn part of the money or take out loans. Young people treat education more seriously when they have a financial stake.

❏ If young adults live at home, they should contribute to household expenses.

❏ Parents or recommended financial advisors can discuss investment strategies with young adults (i.e., mutual funds).

❏ Parents should discuss the importance of health insurance and a strong retirement plan as young adults begin their first full-time job.

❏ Instruct young adults that they can turn to parents for financial advice, but not for money.

parents'. Is large debt acceptable in the home or do adults pay off credit cards fully each month? Are weekends spent "window shopping" in stores and malls or are purchases planned in advance? Do parents save and invest money for the future or does there never seem to be enough to make ends meet?

Amanda is a single mother of two teenagers. She works hard to stretch her teacher's salary each month with only minimal child support for assistance. While she and her family live modestly, she's pleased about being in control of her finances.

"I set my goals six years ago when I was divorced," she explains. "It took me over a year to pay off all our credit card debts. While we didn't do much else during that time, I explained to Heather and Jeff that we were on our way to getting rid of money worries. After paying off the credit cards, I budgeted for necessities, savings, and college. If the car broke down or we had unexpected costs, I was really tight on money at first. I prioritized investing some money in mutual funds every month. That made me feel better.

"But at seven and ten, the kids weren't thrilled. They still wanted to buy everything they saw. I decided they needed more financial responsibility or none of us would ever be out of debt. I put them on an allowance for work around the house and finishing homework. Jeff did lawns and house-sitting at first, but now he has a job at a video store on weekends. Heather baby-sits constantly. Besides the money she's really gained self-confidence about being in demand! Each has a savings account for half of their money. The rest goes towards clothes, movies, and kid-stuff.

"Jeff's not spending much these days. He's saving for car insurance. When he has enough, I'll buy him a second-hand car. But he'll have to keep it in gas and pay for repairs. He's really excited. Heather was into expensive labels for a long time. So we comparison-shopped when she needed clothes. Since she had to pay for part of them with her own money, she found a few discount stores. Lately she's been saving for horseback-riding lessons through the school, and with her new goal, labels don't seem to mean as much as they used to."

I asked Amanda how she would afford college, since Jeff was only a few years away.

"I'm not too worried. I've been saving and we'll put that

toward tuition. He can work at school to pay for some room, board and spending costs. If he stays in-town and lives at home, he'll just have his expenses, books, and fees to cover. If he goes out-of-town, he can pay for the rest with loans. I've decided to have them in his name, not mine, since he'll be more serious about college that way. I'll introduce him to credit cards gradually. He needs to show me he'll pay them off on a monthly basis before I'll let him have one. He's a good kid, but we can all get carried away."

From personal experience, Amanda integrated the best of financial practices into her own home. She modeled getting out of debt, explaining to her children what she was doing and why sacrifice was necessary. She never just gave them money, but presented ways they could earn it. Since they needed to contribute financially to purchases at a young age, they understood cost and the importance of work. Amanda combined her roles as parent and teacher. She knows her children will be in financial trouble if she doesn't show them the process of earning, saving, and spending. She understands that Jeff is a normal teenager and will be too tempted with a credit card in his pocket. So, as in her classroom, she's presenting one lesson at a time. By encouraging financial responsibility through earning and saving, she allows the children more latitude in deciding how to spend their own money. But she requires them to earn the money before making a purchase, avoiding giving them advances or personal loans. She helps them with items beyond their reach, such as Jeff's car. Yet, she requires his full participation through paying car insurance and covering ongoing repairs and expenses, giving real meaning to "No such thing as a free ride!"

I like her attitude about college. Despite her own financial limitations, she saves monthly. Yet, as an educator she knows that Jeff and Heather will get the most out of schooling if they have to work and take out loans. She doesn't view her role as one of either "bailing out" or fully supporting her children, but instead as guiding them to a lifetime of healthy spending habits.

Children and teens need financial plans in order to understand the power of saving. Whether their goal is to buy a bicycle or car, in addition to a bank account and comparative shopping, the best lesson involves waiting until they have the money instead of spending impulsively. Parents can help young people avoid impulse-buying by talking them through the stages of earning the money, refusing to give in to natural desires to make the child happy with the purchase. I have counseled twenty-year olds who "can't stop themselves" from buying.

One young woman owed eighteen thousand dollars on her credit card and discussed feeling suicidal because there was no other way she could see getting out of debt. Intelligent and attractive, with her whole life ahead, I was moved by the poignancy of her plea for self-control masked by feelings of helplessness. A teen with a learning disability confided similar depression because he felt he could never achieve his parents' standard of wealth and wasn't sure he wanted to live as "a failure."

Both of these young people believe strongly that purchases and objects are necessary for a happy life. In subsequent sessions, their parents were horrified to learn the extent of their children's dependency on money, that they were considering taking their own lives through helplessness over their situation. Despite loving families, they still had mistaken values.

Suggestions on the chart incorporate the role of the parent as a financial model, guide, and advisor. By developing goals and insisting on savings, parents empower children to take control of purchases. Through adult de-emphasis on labels and window-shopping and expecting financial participation, children become more reasonable about what they need and can afford. When parents exact a repayment plan instead of bailing young people out of financial mistakes, they discourage impulsiveness with future purchases. Expecting teens to hold a part-time job gives them responsibility for earnings as well as a sense of pride in their ability to enter the adult world. They also take better care of possessions they have personally earned.

Credit cards are a convenience, not an entitlement. Teens should earn the right to use them through a history of responsible spending. Before permitting young people to use a card, parents might discuss the types of purchases that are acceptable and emphasize that expenditures must be repaid in full by the end of the month, avoiding interest. The first time teens over-spend, they should lose the credit card until they fully repay the money owed. Firmness with strong consequences indicates that parents mean business and that self-control is critical in establishing good spending habits.

A Future Based on the Past

These are wonderful, but difficult times. An intense excitement permeates the new millennium. With a sound economy, never-ending promises of developing technology, and fascinating job possibilities for young people, opportunities are extraordinary.

Yet, it has become easier to fly far distances than to walk across the street to a neighbor's house, more common to search the web than carry a meal to a sick friend. Chat rooms with strangers increasingly replace personal conversations. In an age of distance and detachment, it is critically important for adults to model closeness and attachment. With a sense of responsibility for their behaviors, children will turn to adults instead of guns to solve their problems. When parents are willing to teach and support them, all children can learn that they are accountable and trustworthy. From caring for others to handling financial issues responsibly, children become capable and gain in self-esteem. The more we expect of children, the greater they'll work to meet those expectations.

Lessons Learned

A child's appearance may hide what's really going on inside.

When children have to take responsibility, they will.

It's better for young people to work for something than to receive it without effort.

Helping someone else makes us forget our own problems.

Children will do as little or as much as adults require.

"Me First" children become "Me First" teens.

It's not always popular to be a good parent or teacher.

Often there are more abused parents than abused children.

Required acts of kindness can have a greater impact than random acts of kindness.

Part of childhood is learning responsibility for our bodies, our actions, and our words.

Rules and immediate consequences work better than power struggles over chores.

Homework is based on an unwritten contract between the student and teacher.

Giving in to a child who refuses responsibility can set a lifetime pattern.

Our own helpfulness to others is a wonderful model for our children.

Loaning young or adult children money is asking for trouble.

Children learn financial responsibility through earning and saving.

The more children accomplish, the more they feel like winners.

Chapter 6

Expecting and Getting More from Your Children and Teen

It's funny how life lives up to all our expectations...

Mary Black

She sat, straight but tired, eyes and mouth creased permanently downward as if to dispel any question of mood. How well he remembered that mouth, not only for its incessant frown, but for the tirade it spewed endlessly. Little had changed in these thirty-plus years.

"...It's not fair! I'm old and I'm crumbling. No one cares. I gave my best for the children, those selfish little fools. I hope they all rot in hell!"

She hasn't recognized me yet. I suppose I'm one of those third-grade fools.

"I spent my life trying to teach reading and penmanship. But to lazy children, unreachable. No matter how hard I tried to get through. They were like little piglets in a pen, wallowing in their own illiteracy."

He remembered the pen differently. He could never hold it in the same direction as his friends, or use it to space words out as clearly. His best efforts appeared as gibberish, especially when she glared piercingly over his shoulder.

"Just write it backwards, Lefty!" she growled, as she "taught" handwriting. "Watch me and do it backwards." As if she made complete sense. She always called him "Lefty," mockingly, as if his perceived disability were also his identity. Try as he would, his letters wavered and crumbled in defeat, their size diminished with his efforts. No wonder she didn't place his name today.

Nor had she seen him in his childhood room at night, drawing detailed, elaborate pictures with the tiniest of pencil strokes. He was fascinated by the smallness of things, the natural intricacies that make life flourish. His eyes and hands cooperated so well outside of her presence.

The failures on spelling tests! She accused me of cheating by making letters look alike, challenging her to guess if I could really spell the word. After a time, she failed me on everything. Said that if she couldn't read it easily, it was wrong. This many years later, I remember that test on cell structure I'd felt so good about. The zero made me sick.

"...You know, there are so many losers in this world. I think I had them all in my classroom. Do you think any of those kids I taught care about me? Twenty-three years of obnoxious third graders. Better to live in a snake pit. They came to school with slovenly habits. I hated their messiness, their lackadaisical attitude. They needed the discipline they never got at home."

No, he hadn't been the only one she'd tortured. He smiled as he remembered her witch's Halloween costume. She even added two-inch black fingernails and a tall hat. The class whispered that these were her real clothes, that she was a natural and ate children for dessert every night. As she lamented their laziness, they mused over the content of her witches' brew.

"Eyeballs, hair, body parts! Kids' brains and tongues. Other tasty organs! Mmm...." They would roll their eyes and rub their stomachs gleefully.

But he was the one she had singled out for constant public ridicule. Like the time she took away his chair for an entire day. She made him stand behind his desk in the middle of the classroom, legs and body aching over the hours. She said maybe he'd learn to write more neatly if he weren't sitting so carelessly in his chair. As the day had progressed, classmates toiled, heads close to desk, fearing they might be next. His fingers cramped badly around his pen, trying to write in strokes that wouldn't form. By afternoon, she tore up still another science test and tossed it angrily in the trash. All his work for nothing.

In fury, his mother charged into the school the next day.

The Principal's meek admission that "There had been some other problems" did nothing to soften the teacher's blows. After that, he gave up on his writing and even on his drawing at night. He knew he'd never get it anyway.... He just couldn't let himself care.

Her droning voice loudened sharply, snapping him out of his reverie.

"Can you believe what those idiots did to me? I busted my butt for years, and they kept changing my school. Three times. Then the Board said there'd been too many complaints and fired me. They up and fired me! No Union fight. My representative just told me to take early retirement before I lost benefits. No one ever understood what I gave those kids. I gave them standards. All they ever gave me was gas."

It was not for her that his heart ached today, but for all those children she had bruised.

Michael was "slow," she told us. Guess that's why he's on Wall Street. And Kathleen better "make something of herself" with her "plain" looks. God, she's beautiful! Happily, our kids take after her. Joe had a "jock's brain." Maybe that's why he's twice-decorated infantry. Ronnie had "a big mouth like his brother." All the better when you're in civil rights. Would it change anything if she knew she'd been wrong about us? If she knew her "piglets" were happier than she is today?

"You're one of the few people who've ever listened to me, Doc," she reflected bitterly. "Everybody else said it was migraines, that I just needed to relax. You're pretty fancy with those hands, cutting out a brain tumor that small. You saved my life."

"Not quite yet," he observed. "To make it, you'll need to be on strict antibiotics to follow up that chemo regimen." Her claw-like fingers snatched the small paper from his outstretched hand.

"My handwriting's pretty illegible," he added quietly. "I only hope they can read this at the pharmacy."

Children Reaching Their Potential

Children need to know that we believe in them. They rise or fall to the level of our expectations. One of the worst mistakes professionals and parents can make is to assume that their personal observations of a child's current functioning level indicate a lack of future potential. Researchers such as Burger describe how all children, particularly younger ones, have the ability to overcome problems and become happy, contributing adults. Despite impediments along the way, they usually turn out just fine, especially if we support and nurture them.

But adult attitude is everything. The embittered teacher in the story valued handwriting over a child's feelings and competence. She saw losers in her class instead of winners and predicted that third-graders would be inept adults. Labeling children as "slow" or "plain" or a "big mouth" told them how they should see themselves, setting each up for failure. Since she felt that their families were similarly hopeless, there was little anyone could do to meet her expectations. While she was eventually forced to retire, it saddens me to consider how many children believed her condemnations, giving up drawing fanciful pictures in their rooms at night or the wonderful dreams that are such a critical part of childhood.

Young people look to adults as reflectors, as mirrors of their daily performance. When a parent or teacher says, "C'mon, this is easy," children who struggle feel foolish, knowing that they've let the adult down and demonstrated that they can't even succeed with easy work. During his childhood, the surgeon in the story had begun to believe he was incompetent. He was reflecting the teacher's view. Spending any length of time with her or similarly-critical others might have caused him to put aside his pleasure in science and give up his dreams, wasting a fine potential and impacting his future happiness.

When a parent or teacher says, "This is hard, but I know you can do it," young people expect to have to work, but are delighted when they perform well. Their success is magnified by the fact that an important adult said it was *hard.* When others believe in children, in turn children believe in themselves. Our expectations can create their reality.

The following year, "Lefty's" fourth-grade teacher would have a daunting job: First to dispel the negative identity that even impacted his name, and then to create a sense of trust enabling him to take risks in her class and re-engage a love of academics. And if she were not aware of the scars from his previous year, she might never realize the depth of his self-doubt unless he felt safe enough to confide in her. Plato's comment, "All learning has an emotional base" underscores how we need to accept children's feelings as real, to discuss rather than dismiss them, and to provide situations for regaining self-confidence. Children heighten their own expectations when they know adults believe in them.

While feelings can interfere with learning, they also hold the keys to academic, and personal, success. If children already view themselves as lacking ability, they may try to hide these self-perceptions, hoping to fool others. In his book *Faking It*, Christopher Lee describes a childhood of trying to hide his learning disability. He lied to friends about his spoken language difficulties, telling them he had picked up his father's "Boston accent." He accepted punishments for misbehavior rather than admit he could not decipher words from the blackboard. Christopher endured taunts for not being able to read a menu or even his own birthday cards. With the promise of an athletic scholarship, only excellence in swimming supported his self-esteem and willingness to try college. Through almost-daily support from Rosemary Jackson, his learning disabilities therapist, he not only graduated but also had enough confidence to write a book publicly revealing the disability he had tried to hide for a lifetime. Currently helping others with special needs, he feels bolstered enough by his accomplishments to no longer have to "fake it."

When parents and teachers work together, they help children reach their potential. The academic or social activity rarely matters. Just the acknowledgment of the child's being a competent, worthwhile person in almost any arena can result in miraculous changes in motivation. We see this in the pride in a four-year old whose successful singing of the "ABC" song is met by adult applause, the fifth-grader chosen to be group leader for the day, and the teen who makes the squad or team. Hugs and praise for any accomplishment insure that young people take larger strides toward the next one.

Stereotypes

There are many subtle adult expectations that actually undermine children's futures by encouraging them not to try their best. I was reminded of this late one Monday evening when the phone rang in my home.

"Mrs. Waldron?"

"Yes."

"This is Janie Lawrence, Clark's mother. He's a seventh grader at Padgett Middle School."

Alerted to a potential problem in one of my student teacher's classrooms, my mind did a quick review of the children whose names I should recognize, those with ongoing behavioral or academic problems. No, Clark's name wasn't familiar.

"I'm sorry, Mrs. Lawrence. I don't believe I've met him."

Her anger erupted. "Well, maybe all of you at the school and university should get to know him a little better!"

"What's going on?"

"It's what *isn't* going on that bothers me. It started weeks ago. Miss Barnes, your student teacher, caught Clark and Phillip Ainsley handing in identical math homework a few days in a row. She asked if one had copied from the other's paper and they denied it. She let Clark off the hook, but called Phillip's mother, complaining about Phillip giving homework to Clark. Mrs. Ainsley called me. We were surprised that I hadn't heard anything from the school. When I asked Clark about it, he just laughed. He said Phillip is terrible in math. My son was the one who loaned out the homework. I believe him because he's good in math and always does that homework first. It's easy for him.

"But Clark's been getting a mouth on him lately. He thinks it's cool to insult us and his friends, that he's smarter than everyone else. Just says what he thinks and doesn't care who he hurts. Well, this Saturday he went to the school dance with a bunch of kids. His mouth ran again and Clark called Phillip a 'loser' or something. They got into it and started a fist-fight with everybody looking on."

"What happened?"

"Again, nothing. To Clark, that is. Miss Barnes was there. She got some kids to break up the fight. This morning she reported Phillip to the office and he was suspended. I heard that the kids told her Clark started the fight, but she never even reported him. He came home today just delighted with himself. He was positively gloating and feeling like a big man."

I was baffled by my own student's behavior. "I'm really sorry, Mrs. Lawrence. Shelly Barnes is a wonderful teacher. It doesn't make any sense to me why she would punish one student and let another completely off the hook."

A deep sigh. "We're African-American. Phillip's white. Your Miss Barnes doesn't think my son can be the better math student. Or control his own behavior. She expects him to do poorly in class and misbehave. She's working harder with Phillip, the child she feels has potential. She doesn't think she can change Clark because he's black. So she's giving up on him.

"Clark's father and I want to see him in graduate school some day, not prison. We can't discipline him if the school doesn't tell us what's going on, or if he gets away with things when he should be punished. Today Clark came home laughing at your student teacher and the system. What lessons do you think he learned at school?"

At our conference with Shelly Barnes early the next morning, I asked Mrs. Lawrence to repeat her exact comments of the evening before. The beginning teacher was horrified. A flexible and easy-going young woman, she winced painfully at her own immediate assumption that the white student was better at math. Quietly, she admitted that she had not seen the fight start as she chaperoned the Saturday night dance.

At a point of tears, "I'm so embarrassed. I don't think I'm a prejudiced person, but I hate that I automatically stereotyped the students. I've never even considered what I expect from Clark, and maybe that's part of the problem. If I don't expect anything, he'll never perform. All I can say is that I'm terribly sorry. And thank you."

Keeping our conference with Mrs. Lawrence in confidence, the Assistant Principal had the opportunity to "review the circumstances." At Shelly Barnes' recommendation, he suspended Clark for fighting.

After Clark's return to school, Shelly began to work more closely with him in math class, initially intending to monitor his behavior. When his academic giftedness became apparent, she nominated him for the school's "Math Counts" team. A few competitions later, his peers elected him Captain. On his own, Clark initiated after-school cram sessions where he prepared team members for future events. Over the year, his mother reported a new group of friends and a new set of manners. The change from negative to positive expectations seems to have created a lasting effect. As it will on the future students of Shelly Barnes.

When she encouraged Clark to join the "Math Counts" team, she changed his life. Not only did he work harder to fine-tune his already strong math skills, but through his accomplishments, he felt better about himself. As a member of a group with a goal, his previous criticisms of peers turned into support. Indeed, Clark and others will later look back and remember awards and accomplishments as some of the greatest moments in their childhood.

Avoiding Self-Fulfilling Prophecies

When we think of prejudice, it's usually about *purposefully* denying rights. Yet, few teachers would ever try to be unfair or prejudicial to their students. As nurturing adults, it makes no sense that they'd hold young people back by undercutting their future. Yet, as Shelly realized, while some responses are automatic and unintentional, they can be as powerful as a decisive slap. When we give up on children, they give up on themselves. If they receive no reinforcement for the things they do well, too often they turn to the negative as Clark did, needing to bolster esteem. Without checks on behavior, he and other children are at at-risk of never being fully challenged, of turning to aggression for attention.

Mrs. Lawrence wasn't about to watch her son sink, but she was helpless unless she could work with the school. She chose the unusual road of demanding a severe punishment for her own child's behavior, forcing a beginning teacher to demonstrate higher levels of fairness in her expectations. Only then did Clark find a better way to use his natural intelligence through working with peers toward a common goal.

Other stereotypes occur when adults anticipate children's inability to overcome difficult family circumstances. If children are raised in single-parent homes, by a grandparent or sibling, often we expect them to fail more often than those in two-parent families. However, in her review of research, Maxine Weinreb reports that when considerations of race and socioeconomic level are excluded, children from non-traditional families perform as well in school as children from traditional nuclear families.

Studies show us that even children who witness violence cope when there is a sensitive caregiver available for support. And when grandparents and siblings raise children, they create an extended family that compensates for parental absence. Indeed, at times conflicts arise between divorced parents because both want to attend children's school conferences or activities. Yet, those outside the family may automatically assume there's a lack of parental involvement and expect less of these children from "broken homes." Warmth and guidance by adults and caregivers are far more important than the actual structure of the family.

We must be careful not to psychologically segregate children when they live in less typical situations. For example, some parents have to work evenings and weekends. Most would much rather be at home, but are bound by inflexible hours in a job they need. To help out, neighbors often drive the child to activities and performances when the parent's schedule prohibits participation. Usually, the parent is very appreciative, willing to repay the kindness. It's really sad when a child sits at home alone and depressed, unable to attend an important event because of lack of transportation. Everyone loses.

As writer George Eliot commented, "What do we live for if it is not to make life less difficult for each other?" Instead of creating a self-fulfilling prophecy where children in non-traditional families aren't successful, we can help them academically and socially. Often, all it takes is adult advice, redirection, or help with logistics. Asking, "What would I do if my own child were in this situation?" usually gives us the answer we need for helping another's child reach a wonderful potential.

Asking Others for Help

Equally important, when our work schedule or family demands keep us from meeting our own children's needs, *we may have to ask others for help*. With hurried lifestyles, we can become pressured by the need to be everywhere at once. Rather than a teen being left out of an after-school activity or a child missing a birthday party, we need to become inventive with arrangements by calling on friends and neighbors. Turning to others is not a sign of being a bad parent, just an acknowledgment that we can't always do everything by ourselves. In many families, spouses share driving and attending games and performances. Yet, because of divorce or a spouse who travels or works late, some parents are forced to take on most child-rearing responsibilities alone.

Healthy development requires placing children's needs ahead of parents' schedules. School and community activities are critical for learning new skills, discovering hobbies, and exploring future careers while having fun with friends. Children resent missing social activities because of parents' personal and professional schedules. I recall a legislator's comments about her daughter's initial reaction when she told her that she might run for Congress. Very upset, the daughter asked, "But who'll drive me to cheerleading?!!"

But some circumstances rule out carpooling or attending a child's event. Usually, our need for help is temporary, such as during basketball season or on a weekend where we can't free ourselves to accommodate the child's schedule. At other times, emergencies or unanticipated situations force us to call on others to help with family needs. During these times, people really understand.

Some years ago, I badly injured my knee in a water-skiing accident. Between surgery and recuperation, I would be unable to drive for almost three months, the entire summer vacation. As I lay on the sofa, I worried terribly about my children having to cancel all their summer activities. When I called the Jewish Community Center to withdraw both boys from their day camp, they wouldn't let me.

"Don't worry about it! We'll ask some parents in your neighborhood to pick them up and bring them home. No problem." To my sons' delight, a month of swimming and sports were now back in the picture.

But my twelve-year-old son would still miss his long-anticipated science program, weeks of driving out early to explore snake habitats. And sadly, the nine-year-old couldn't attend the month-long theater workshop he'd looked forward to all year. Yet, the JCC's willingness to find a ride for my sons made me think long and hard.

Many colleagues and friends had asked, "What can I do?"

Not wanting to be a bother, I'd answered, "Thanks, there's really nothing. We'll have to sit this summer out." But we *didn't* really have to...

I realized there was actually a lot they could do. So I swallowed my pride and made a few phone calls. Within an hour, two university Physics professors volunteered to alternate the weeks of hour-long drives to the nature van. We all learned that snakes are morning creatures as my colleagues picked James up at 5:30 A.M. each day. These are lifetime friends.

A lovely receptionist at the Community Theater called a few parents I'd never met. They drove Matt to rehearsals and performances all month, occasionally even sending cookies or a casserole home with him for dinner. I'll never forget his arrival home the first day of the workshop, when he startled me with a blue made-up face and a very realistic "wound" on his wrist. He was thrilled.

Planning the last two weeks was easiest. Instead of cancelling the visit to family in New York, the boys proudly flew off by themselves, were met by relatives, and later totally spoiled by grandparents. Returning very relaxed and with beach tans, they announced it had been their best trip ever.

We all learned a lot that summer. My children found out that during difficult times, not only friends and family, but even people they didn't know were there to support them. They saw that adults care about them and their happiness. But I probably learned more than they did: *Sometimes we just have to ask for help.*

When Winning Becomes Everything

Yet, there's an opposite side to children participating in activities, one that can be quite negative. What happens when competition and winning become everything? When families lose focus on values incorporating cooperation and helpfulness?

Several years ago, three high school seniors attended morning football practice and decided to skip school that day. While parents were away at work, they partied at one of the homes. With the drunkest driving the car back to school, they returned stumbling and laughing to the football field at 3:30, to the delight of cheering teammates. Minutes later, the same onlookers shouted angrily and in disbelief as the Head Coach threw the three first-string players off the team permanently. Then he walked them into the building for their automatic school suspension.

"You can't kick off the quarterback and receiver! And Tony's a defensive end! We're supposed to win Division this year!"

"C'mon, Coach! They just had a few beers!"

"Don't turn 'em in!!!"

The story hit the news the next day, with adult listeners even calling radio talk-shows.

"They're kids. Teenagers drink. Get real! You can't punish the whole team because of what a few guys did."

"Make them run some laps and miss a few practices, Coach. Give us a break. Boys'll be boys."

A similar response on the evening news. Most adults interviewed called the expulsion from the team "a gross over-reaction" and "just plain stupid," with the Division title almost in hand. When viewers learned that two of the players were being considered for football scholarships at very competitive schools, the voices grew louder.

"Has the storm abated?" I asked the unyielding Head Coach a few days later.

He just smiled. "On the news, you don't hear the responses I've received, the ones that really matter. Every parent of a team member and every teacher at the school who contacted me supported the decision.

"They say they don't want the boys back on the team. Not because they're bad kids, but because they did something really stupid. They need consequences now, big ones, or they'll be screwing up when they're thirty. They skipped school, drove drunk, and felt they were too important to be punished. If we let this go, we're sending the wrong message to the rest of the team. The way we react now is more important than the championship." That day he dispelled another stereotype, one of coaches caring only about winning games. He re-defined what winning really meant in the lives of his team members.

"But one of the parents is already threatening to sue because his son could lose a football scholarship. He told me that this is Tony's chance to 'be a kid,' that I shouldn't be so uptight over it since all the boys drink. I'm sorry he expects so little of his own son. I guess Tony'll grow up to meet his Dad's expectations."

The Coach's last comment made me think about parents like Clark's mother, who tell their children they can have a wonderful future, but they have to work to get there. What a comparison with Tony's father, who sends the message that goals can be reached when adults bail out young people after irresponsible decisions. When we hold children to consequences, we let them know they're capable and we expect them to behave responsibly. If they choose to use poor judgment, they'll suffer the cost. A lack of high expectations and immediate outcomes will make them believe that they can continue the same behaviors into adulthood.

But there's another message here, one about the importance of winning. When talk shows even raised the question of whether the coach should have thrown the players off the team, they sent a powerful message about the value of competition. Was winning the Division title more important than giving these young men a lesson in consequences? Or did adults really say that when individuals are superior performers in an entertainment area such as sports, they should be exempt from responsible social and personal behaviors? Happily, the coach's wisdom prevailed and was supported by most parents and the school district, showing that those personally involved with young people cared more about winning lives than games.

Healthy Competition

Competition involves the courage to take risks publicly. Choosing to compete announces that you can perform at least as well as others, perhaps even better. Onlookers judge every move, bringing on nervous stomachs during track meets or choir concerts. But this anxiety also encourages top performance. New world records wouldn't exist unless competitors pushed beyond previous time or endurance. Within these highly pressured environments, scientists develop new medicines and find amazing cures. Indeed, teaching children how to compete enhances their future in business, entertainment, and public careers. There also appears to be a human drive toward competitiveness. It's natural to gauge improvement in our own performance and compare it to how well others do.

Reaching toward a specific goal provides the motivation to develop new skills and discover potential. Often, teens are the most highly competitive as they explore talents and future options. They perform not only for themselves and parents, but especially for peers they feel are constantly judging them and assessing their worth. In front of this critical audience, the stakes are really high. Is the young person praised or ridiculed? Accepted as part of the group, or casually, but painfully, excluded? Teens learn quickly that not everyone can be quarterback or cheerleading captain. Twenty and thirty years later, adults still reflect back with pleasure or sadness on their high school experience. For many it was the most publicly competitive arena in their life.

But competition is no longer positive when it brings on too much pressure. Many young people identify too closely with their skill levels and view themselves as "losers" if they don't perform as well as peers. They may confuse success or failure in competition with their own success or failure as a person. They groan in response to parental platitudes such as "No one wins every time." In a competitive world, winning can be everything from a very early age.

The chart suggests some ways that parents can encourage healthy competition as an important, and positive, part of life. As always, younger is better. It's difficult to convince the teen that winning doesn't matter if it's been emphasized throughout childhood. Indeed, many young adults may appear outwardly to be pressuring themselves to win, while in reality they're trying to fulfill the quiet parental expectation that's always been there.

Young children learn to play games, but adults teach them competition. Instead of starting too early with skill-building in a talent or sport, it helps when parents create an enjoyable, rather than pressured, environment. From the Osmonds to the "Dixie Chicks," many talented musicians have started this way. Their love of music and singing began as a shared experience within the family, and only later included the broader community. In an un-pressured home, fun activities create a lifetime of pleasure. Since most parents don't expect their children to become professional performers anyway, winning or being the best isn't always necessary. Actually, learning a new skill or developing a talent can be better than winning. Many times, childhood activities are the beginning of a lifetime hobby or interest.

Some children aren't competitive. While they may enjoy watching others, they want to relax without pressure. When parents and siblings are strongly competitive, these children don't fit the family mold and may come to see themselves as

Encouraging Healthy Competition

- ❏ Allow young children to play freely without being competitive.
- ❏ Decide if children really want to compete. Some children are naturally less competitive and are unhappy when forced to participate.
- ❏ If possible, encourage brothers and sisters to develop skills and hobbies in different areas so they don't become competitive with each other.
- ❏ Have children participate in activities or sports that they truly enjoy.
- ❏ Sample different types of activities to discover children's talents.
- ❏ Place children in competitive activities where their skills are at least equally as good as "peers." Avoid the child being the "worst" on the team, drawing ridicule.
- ❏ Work with adults in charge of activities to de-emphasize stress on children.
- ❏ Emphasize the process of competition, not just who wins.
- ❏ Children are more successful with a full night's sleep, a meal, and a positive attitude.
- ❏ Be sure that children attend all practices or rehearsals, demonstrating that competition requires work and skill-building.
- ❏ Reduce your own anxiety level. Children sense when their winning is very important to you and will feel they have let you down if they don't succeed.
- ❏ Try not to "hype-up" children before competing. They may already feel tremendous pressure to win.
- ❏ Attend games and performances, cheering for children, but never yelling criticisms.
- ❏ After the event, plan an activity the child enjoys, emphasizing fun.
- ❏ Avoid reviewing children's performance mistakes afterwards. Even on their "off-days," compliment them on something they did well.
- ❏ Do not allow children to blame themselves or someone else (referee, another participant) for a loss.
- ❏ Help children maintain a balance of competitive and non-competitive activities.

a disappointment. Yet, many have high goals for themselves and perform very well in a number of areas. It's important not to force them to compete, to allow them to freely explore who they are and to develop naturally.

Instead of playing on a soccer team, there's nothing wrong with children who prefer riding a bicycle after school. After a busy day, they may need some quiet time away from adult structure. But if your child wants to be alone constantly or just plays video games and watches television every day, you might set up times for play with others. Some quiet is good for all of us. Yet too much time alone discourages friendships. Balance is best, with the child's temperament and interests leading the way.

Competition without Pressure

When I taught high school English, I noticed that some of my students weren't involved in sports or other activities. Mostly from less-affluent homes in a generally wealthy district, they were quietly excluded from social cliques. Bright and never a discipline problem, they just didn't seem to enjoy competition or care much about their performance in and out of school. Many of them were under-achievers, not realizing their academic or leadership potential.

They were my "fringe kids." Concerned about their becoming at-risk, I invited them to "hang out" in my room after school. It gave them a place to go and me the chance to get to know them informally. They dropped in freely, often bringing others, students not even in my classes. And one afternoon came the chess board.

"Hey, that's a good idea! I'll bring another tomorrow. Anybody else got one?"

"I don't know how to play. Can somebody show me?"

"Me too! Who here can teach us?"

"I've played a little. It's not hard."

The school Chess Club was born that day. In addition to occasional visitors who came to try their luck, the steady membership grew to twenty-one. I was amazed at how faithfully students appeared, voicing annoyance when a doctor's appointment or absence kept them away. No attendance requirements, no officers, and nothing written to even declare it a formal organization. Whereas my room had previously been filled with their loud talk and laughter, it became hushed except for the occasional "I didn't see that one!" or "Show me that move again."

I was taken with the good-naturedness of it all. Because chess can be so competitive, I wondered if the students wouldn't gradually develop hard feelings, become overly-pressured to win, or simply lose interest. They never did. They viewed themselves as a team and helped the novices develop skills by showing them improved planning strategies and endgames. Indeed, a few were natural instructors and stayed late every day to teach and encourage the beginners. They casually suggested who should play whom, taking the lead in lining up students of equal skill levels.

When an odd number of students appeared on any given afternoon, I played a game or two. In the relaxed and friendly atmosphere, even quiet Danny teased as he asked with a smile, "Miss, do you really want to move your knight there?" I was amazed at how quickly we novices caught on! Over the months, I noticed how many of the players began to socialize during lunch and leave together after practices.

That spring brought the big surprise. One Monday morning, a large group of excited and noisy members met me as I unlocked the door to my room.

"Miss, we need you tomorrow night!"

"Can you go with us downtown?"

"My Dad wants to come too. He says he can take some of us."

It was my first clue that they had been up to something. On their own they had won the YMCA regional chess championship!

In disbelief, I looked at their grinning faces. "C'mon! How come I didn't know about this?"

Laughter. Barb explained, "At first some of us just went down to a few tournaments on Saturdays. Then we found out about the big event this weekend and called everybody. We decided to win it and surprise you." Just like that.

"Danny even won Novice Division," Mark, his instructor, bragged proudly as his pupil grinned. "When they added up games taken across divisions, we smashed 'em!" To hoots and cheers, "We're the best!" I thought so too.

All twenty-one members and most parents appeared proudly at the YMCA awards ceremony the next night.

Countless students from towns and cities across upstate New York joined us to collect their ribbons and certificates. As we entered the packed auditorium, the Director took me aside and commented quietly, "Your students told you that you'd have to make an acceptance speech, didn't they?" My expression told him they had omitted this small detail.

After the individual awards and during a loud and noisy ovation, I joined the entire club on stage for the championship. My students applauded and cheered as the Director presented the huge trophy for the school showcase.

"It's yours for the year," he reminded. "You'll have even more competition next year," with a knowing look at the serious audience. Turning to me, "Now, please share with us the coaching wisdom that brought your students to the stage tonight. What did you do to create winners?"

"Well, I didn't create winners. They were winners all along..." I continued on, briefly explaining the genesis of our club to a dissatisfied, largely disbelieving audience.

I finished with, "The students supported and instructed each other every day. Some of them hadn't even played before, but their friends in the club taught them how. They never took the game overly seriously, and decided to compete on their own. But when they wanted to win, they were ready."

Shaking his head, the Director announced to the audience, "Looks like she's going to keep her coaching secrets to herself! Let's see if we can figure them out by next year."

The following morning, the Principal read each team member's name during announcements and proudly invited the entire school to look at the newest award in the trophy case. Over congratulatory sodas and cake in my room that afternoon, players re-hashed Saturday's competition.

"What will you do about next year?" I wondered aloud. "Some of those teams seemed pretty blood-thirsty last night."

"Yeah. We talked about that," Chris said. "We'll have to decide if we want to enter again. It's been a lot of fun playing without all that pressure."

"We proved we could do it," Danny added insightfully. "That was the important thing."

Eventually, the group decided *not* to compete the following year. They laughed about their casual attitude, and drifted on, some joining other activities for the first time. I quietly returned the trophy to the YMCA the next spring. None of the members seemed to notice it was gone.

Encouraging Achievement

How I loved that Chess Club. In one academic year, I watched my "fringe kids" embrace school life and feel competent through their outstanding performance. When they became winners, they viewed themselves as winners. But early on, they looked at competition differently than most. They didn't join a typically competitive team, where they had to try out for membership. (Too many of us have observed the hallway tears of girls whose names don't appear on the cheerleading or dance team list.) Without formal membership, anyone could participate. Since there were no criteria for being in my room, students didn't even need to play chess. It amazed me that they all did. Clearly, they were looking for a common ground, an activity to give them a reason for gathering each day.

These students just wanted to have fun. They enjoyed the daily social process before outside competition was even an issue. So they taught and helped each other. They took pleasure in novices as well as advanced players. Indeed, the easy emergence of "instructors" could have created a pecking order. But it didn't. They worked together, stayed late, and took pride in their burgeoning students' accomplishments.

These young people can teach us some valuable lessons. Non-competitive children rise when they choose their own level of involvement, waiting until they feel competent in their skills. With de-emphasis on pressure to win, they learn the most through free exploration and intellectual interest. No one need be the "worst" on a team. It's far better to have different levels of competition with many children winning. In the chess club, divisions blurred. Novices and advanced players competed equally with others at similar levels, acknowledging that at one time, everyone was a beginner.

Despite the non-threatening environment, the students practiced daily. Typically, success comes easily and without much effort for many bright children. Yet the sense that they may *not* be the best can motivate even the most skilled players to try harder. Practices are an important part of the *process* of competition. They help children improve their performance while showing that winning takes work.

But the most important factor was that these students decided when they were ready to compete. They worked together and learned how to be team players. They watched their own skills improve gradually, giving them confidence in their performance. Yet, there was no individual ego involvement, just pride at their own level of mastery. They were doing this for themselves, without adult instruction or intervention.

Winners All

When children decide to compete, there are additional, "quiet" things parents can do to encourage top achievement. A good night's sleep helps all of us, especially when we need to perform. From taking an exam to participating in Academic Decathlon, the school play, or a baseball game, children do best when rested. Many local parents were justifiably upset when a high school scheduled the Junior Prom for the Friday night before PSAT exams, tests critical for National Merit scholarships. Clearly, a very late night and lack of sleep would lower students' scores. Rejecting the alternative of missing an important social event, students assured adults, "We won't stay out too late." Promises later forgotten. Scores were very disappointing. Prioritizing academic needs, the following year parents and school administrators planned the schedule of social events together.

Parental attitude is also important, both before and after the event. When adults are anxious or try to "hype-up" young people before competitions, they send the message that children will disappoint them if they don't win. To show that adults care, attending events is important. But cheers are better than jeers. Parents who yell criticisms publicly embarrass their children. If the coach is overly negative, it's time to find another team. Believing what adults say, children are rarely motivated by "put-down" comments. No one feels worse than the child who misses the goal or forgets the line in the script. Even when children have an "off-day," adults can always find something to compliment, to spur young people on so they'll feel successful and want to try again.

I coached a soccer team of five-to-seven year olds, some so small that their athletic socks covered their entire legs. A few of the older and more competitive ran full-steam toward the goal, practically mowing down opponents. The younger majority watched the ball pass by with fascination. Jamie often sat down, absorbed in re-tying her shoelaces as teammates screamed for her to block the ball flying by.

I was torn between not wanting to pressure young children and watching team morale dip as we continued to lose. Then a parent suggested the 'Ata boy!, 'Ata girl! approach, an addition the children came to love. Each Tuesday night, I cut blue ribbons and taped them to large gold seals, the type that appear on award certificates. With black markers, I wrote on the seal 'Ata boy! or 'Ata girl! Win or lose, after Wednesday's game, the entire team formed a large circle and cheered as each player was called up for an award. Sometimes searching mightily, I looked for anything competitive each child had done during the game.

"Jamie, you didn't sit down once! And in the last minutes, you really chased that ball!"

"Tim, you were a shocker! Where'd you get the non-stop energy today?"

Each child stood for applause while the rest shouted "'Ata boy!" or "'Ata girl!" as I pinned on the ribbons.

Players who scored or blocked goals received extra awards, one for each crucial play. Parents stood outside the team circle, cheering and taking pictures. As they left, younger children chatted on about what they had done well, while the more competitive asked each other, "How many ribbons did you get?" We lost two more games, but the morale seemed better. A few of the players even checked with me each week to be sure I'd brought the ribbons.

And then it began to work. A victory, and the team went crazy. Laughing, hugging each other, and jumping. They were joyous as Tim yelled, "I bet you don't have enough ribbons for all of us today, Coach!" Even before the ceremony, the older players congratulated the younger, arms around shoulders as they bent down to tell them what they did well. Supporting each other, we were finally a team.

We won the next four games straight, and when we lost the fifth, players consoled one another with real compassion.

"Hey, it's not your fault. They were tough."

"Don't worry. We'll take 'em next time."

And they cheered each player as I pinned on the individual ribbons.

We ended that season with more wins than losses. No, we didn't take championship trophies home, but we gained something better: a respect for working together, trying our hardest, and doing our best.

Years later, I chatted with Jamie, now a beautiful nineteen year-old college student and a scholarship volleyball player.

"Want to hear something funny?" she asked. "I've still got a bunch of those *'Ata Girl* ribbons pinned on the bulletin board in my bedroom! When I was a little kid, they made me feel so good about myself. You know, I've loved sports ever since."

I was proud of the way the team won, but also of their attitude when they lost. Instead of blaming the referee (or coach!), another team member, or themselves, they reacted to what each had done well during the game. Parents planned pizza parties to give a social atmosphere to the competitions and to downplay a disappointing game.

It's difficult to strike the balance between de-emphasizing pressure while supporting competition. Jamie was one of the youngest on the team, not yet focusing on the game or understanding peers' needs to win. But with praise, she felt appreciated and became an active player. Compliments often create confidence, encouraging children to explore their potential and then set goals.

As Woody Allen commented, "If you're not failing now and again, it's a sign you're playing it safe." When children have a balance of competitive and non-competitive activities, they develop a healthier perspective, tending to be less pressured about life in general. When they feel good about themselves in one arena, they're more willing to step into another.

But what about those who never join teams or compete, withdrawing into apathy or anger? How can we help young people reach their potential if they don't want to try? Some appear overwhelmed by life and remove themselves from others as much as possible. And as they pull away, they take their parents with them. Certainly, Laura's story reveals this message all too well.

Lonely Child, Lonely Parent

Glancing tensely at the locked front door, Laura moved quickly into Greg's clothes-strewn room for the third time this week. Her worried haste seemed foolish since she knew he was already dragging his backpack grudgingly toward second-period English. But she couldn't shake her worst expectation that he would bound suddenly through the doorway shouting, "What are you *doing* in my room?!!"

Nothing seemed changed since Wednesday, except for drapes more tightly pulled than ever and a few extra Coke cans to welcome ants. Quietly, heart in stomach, she studied the top of his dresser where she had found the poem.

Surprising for Greg, usually so private, to leave it out so carelessly.

Laura inhaled and sorted through the keys and billfolds, her eyes searching thoroughly for clues she hoped never to find.

A new sketch? The skull's eyes were shaded hollows, the cheeks pronounced, sharp blades. Blackened crossbones entwined like ropes that drifted off the paper. She didn't remember seeing it the other day, but she may have been too upset. Now she studied it more carefully, haste forgotten until the dog barked downstairs. She stuffed the picture in her pocket.

Quiet followed and she reached searchingly under the mattress, fingers exploring for immediate stashes. A similar inspection of the top closet shelf found nothing new. With a sigh, she turned to leave.

But the eyes riveted on her back filled her with familiar dread and she rotated to stare at the huge image. Blood pouring from the fang-like incisors of a helmeted rock star with a child trying to escape from his mouth. Why did Greg keep that stupid poster in his room? His father dismissed it as *normal male grotesqueness*. She called it *sick*.

And at that moment, it all flooded over her. The blood. The child dangling from the mouth. The poem. And, above all, the secrecy. He was sick. And needed help. Laura's feelings engulfed her to near-nausea. Where to go? Without money for psychologists, what to do? As she trudged back downstairs, she felt a deep stillness take over. No time for her emotions now. This was about Greg.

Her deep inner silence continued that evening despite the nervous chatter in the parent-filled audience at Brannon High School. Wary, she looked about the metal cafeteria chairs, recognizing no one. Her husband had begged off, claiming an early meeting tomorrow. But she sensed that he too had become isolated, alienated from these mothers with sprayed hair who bragged non-stop about their children's accomplishments.

"Kaitlyn took first in public speaking. We think she's bound for law school." Proudly, "Maybe that's why she argues so much at home!"

"J.T. was first in the Division for backstroke. The coach is looking for a scholarship for next year."

"Mrs. Renwick's a pill in Calculus. That's all Chris talks about at home."

How she would love to hear even a complaint about a teacher from non-verbal Greg, who was always eerily quiet and sulking in his room. Their attempts at conversation were met with quick sarcasm, questions receiving shrugs for answers.

She snickered as she heard a pin-striped husband comment to a friend that his daughter's phone bill was out-classing the national debt. Their phone never rang. Greg had no friends and she realized tonight how much she and Mark had withdrawn with him, more in confusion than anger. Perhaps they were embarrassed by his lack of accomplishment, of even caring. They had nothing to share with another family. Instead of notices about upcoming games or school concerts, they received reports about missing homework. Meetings with teachers had ended gradually. No use anymore. Greg had given up and so had they.

"Let's get started!" The Principal's voice rose solemnly above the din of conversation. A hush.

"It's good to have the support of friends and colleagues when we're confused and uncertain. First, Kyle's suicide from a bullet. Then Eric's overdose. Hard as I try, I can't explain it. These were neat kids, never a behavior problem and always respectful. Now they're gone.

"The grief counselors have called the meeting tonight to respond to your questions. The school psychologist wants to talk about the symptoms of depression. We're here for you. Two deaths are two too many. Let's stem this tide."

Laura strained to hear the endless, grating questions from parents.

"Weren't there any clues?"

"Why didn't the teachers notice?"

"Isn't a parent helpless if a kid really wants to do it?"

Observing from her cold stillness, she realized they were all equally ignorant. Frustrated. Despite their earlier boastfulness, they were as overwhelmed as she with fear that their child would be next.

The psychologist rose to discuss warning signs. He could have been discussing Greg.

"Apathetic. No real friends. Uninvolved in school activities. Beyond private, really secretive. Lack of care about appearance. Lowered grades because of missing assignments."

The stillness left her. She found herself sweating in the cold cafeteria.

When he finished the litany of symptoms, the psychologist asked, "Is anyone here worried about a teen? If so, we need to talk to you. The other parents are here for support. No matter how alone you feel, you're not."

Laura saw her arm rise slowly.

"Yes."

Her surprisingly loud, detached voice filled the cafeteria. "I'm sure it's nothing. Except my son's the artistic type, very sensitive. He draws and even writes poetry."

She pulled the folded skull and crossbones sketch from her pocket and held it up, rotating directions. She heard the gasp of those around her.

"Sometimes he gets down, but that's kids. I found a pretty weird poem, but at least it let him get his feelings out."

"Did you bring it?"

A slight nod. For some reason she had stuck it in her purse.

"You don't have to read it to everyone. But our staff will talk to you about it later if you want to share it then."

The parents nearest her studied the floor.

Without invitation, Laura began. Her own voice distant in her ears, she read with disturbing calmness.

A gun, a knife,
How much is it worth,
This young man's life?

My heart, my soul
Weep on forever,
Death's newest toll.

Graveside bells ring,
Yet, why for me
Does no one sing?

Whoever this prayer hears
Is hopelessly late
To avoid shedding tears.

She heard the voice stop and felt herself gently re-fold the poem and return it to her purse. The silence was deadening as she closed her eyes.

Her body drooped wearily. She felt their presence before she saw them, professionals and parents, some still walking toward her as she looked up. A mother she didn't even know hugged her as tears coursed down both their faces.

The Cycle of Isolation

There were no more suicides at the high school. By finally turning to others, Laura may have saved Greg's life. Researcher Joseph Burger observed, "Hope can be restored if the young person drowning in despair is lifted up by a community of caring peers and adults." Greg's poem shouted his sense of alienation, his status as a *Lonely Child*. Laura was only able to help him when she ended her own self-imposed exclusion and rejoined the adult community. At times, young people are at such a vulnerable point that the parent cannot be effective alone.

There are many lonely children and parents caught in this cycle of isolation. It often begins in the neighborhood and at school when young people judge each other on surface criteria, such as appearance, social sophistication, and skill in a status arena such as sports. From an early age, peers consider certain children odd or eccentric if they don't follow fads and fit in with constantly changing social norms. Without even getting to know them, they stigmatize others perceived as less physically attractive or unfashionably dressed, those with a quiet personality, or ones who don't display talent in a popular area such as sports.

Peers ignore the *Lonely Child's* opinions, sometimes looking at each other with meaningful glances as if the young person were oblivious to their derision. Indeed, some excluded children misinterpret this social feedback and they try harder to belong. Many have a dependent personality that seeks more than normal approval from others, making them particularly susceptible to being ridiculed or ignored. At first, despite the hurt, they come back for more because they want so badly to be part of the group. Not knowing how to act acceptably in peers' eyes, they over-extend themselves, further alienating others by demonstrating behaviors that are even more different or "strange." Some may act as if they don't care what others think, but usually this is a façade to shield themselves from the blows that have become particularly painful. Gradually they stop trying. Like Greg in his bedroom, eventually these young people detach from others rather than face additional rejection. Some further disassociate themselves by becoming disruptive and aggressive to hide their pain.

We all need attention, affection, and approval. Indeed, even in dangerous prison environments, inmates consider solitary confinement as a terrible punishment. So when innocent children are isolated for reasons they don't understand, they feel helpless. They experience the power that others have over their lives. Eventually, this helplessness turns to anger and depression. It's of no surprise that children like Greg act-in by hurting themselves or act-out by hurting others. When suicide or shootings occur, very often the profile is that of a loner: *If others don't accept me, I can believe what they say and hurt myself or I can get revenge by hurting them.*

As Mother Teresa remarked, "Loneliness and the feeling of being unwanted is the most terrible poverty." And when it is their child who is experiencing such rejection, too often the parents isolate themselves as well. *Lonely Parents* are embarrassed by their son's or daughter's lack of social involvement. Their early hopes for laughter and watching their child on the stage or playing field have been dashed. Indeed, the only playing they see daily may be the young person isolated in a bedroom with video games. Through feelings of guilt and a sense of failure, parents of these "outcast" children cut off their own involvement with the school and other adults at the very time they need the most support and advice.

Like Greg's father, some deny the problem. They deal with their own sense of helplessness by claiming that grotesque posters, secrecy, and isolation are a natural part of young people's world today. Even when children cry out by leaving drawings or writings for adults to find, parents survive their own fears with "It's probably nothing." If the child is fascinated by guns, it's easier to complain about violence on television that to accept its entry into our own home. Wanting to avoid family confrontations and expensive therapy, adults may wait for children to out-grow this "stage." And it's very difficult to discuss the young person's problems with a parent of a popular child who wouldn't understand or might think that there was something wrong with the entire family.

Sadly, without the input of other adults, *Lonely Parents* follow their children's lead in removing themselves from social interactions. They are increasingly less likely to seek help as they become enmeshed in this cycle of isolation. Why go to a PTA meeting if kids at the school haven't been friendly to your child? Why be in Laura's situation of listening to others brag about their children when you have nothing to add about your own? Children's anger and depression can't be quarantined. Like a virus, they infect a household freely. *Lonely Children* create *Lonely Parents*.

Helping Lonely Children Make Friends

Greg's mother took the biggest step when she turned to the school for help. In the following days, she met with his counselor and teachers to discuss his lack of friends and his decline into personal crisis. The district recommended a therapist to help understand the causes of his alienation and how to become re-engaged socially. Greg would not attend sessions. But his personal reaction to isolation had become so extreme that parents and professionals could not give in to his stubborn refusal. It was critical to change his situation immediately.

Angry and embarrassed, the following week he sat at a school meeting with his mother and father, the counselor, and a teacher/coach who volunteered to monitor his progress. After an hour of adults describing how worried they were about him, Greg agreed grudgingly to some changes. He would meet several times with the therapist if no one else at the school knew. He decided to work out with the football and basketball teams and see if he liked it. At home, he would eat dinner with his family and limit video games to an hour a night.

While Greg's willingness to become more involved surprised his mother, his anger and sullen attitude continued for many months. Except for dinner, he still had nothing to do with his parents. He resisted their efforts at conversation and was non-responsive to their attempts to include him in family activities. Despite his obvious efforts to continue distancing himself, this time they did not give in. Because loneliness had become his life's pattern, they understood that it would take him a long time to re-attach, even to his family.

But his parents felt encouraged by his involvement with sports. They attended games even when Greg was unlikely to play, demonstrating support for him and the team. Laura joined the fund-raising committee for new football uniforms. Greg didn't seem too embarrassed when his father shouted loudest at basketball games. Gradually Greg became a quiet part of the athletes' social group. Indeed, some evenings after practice, he joined players at a local hang-out, eating hamburgers and talking sports. Imagine his parents' delight when he announced for the first time that he might not be home for dinner because he'd be eating with some friends!

Eventually, he joined his parents as they watched videotapes and ate at a restaurant each Sunday night. They backed away from advice and criticism, making conversations non-threatening. At Greg's own suggestion, driving class was next. Excited by his growing independence, he agreed to get a job in summer to pay for car insurance. Emerging from his crisis of loneliness, Greg is now ready to plan his future. His parents expect more from him these days, and happily he expects more from himself.

In part, Greg will gain confidence through working to earn car insurance money. It's important for parents to oversee the number of hours teens work, helping them create a balance that includes time for homework and studying. Together, they should discuss what the young person *needs* to buy, focusing on necessary items, while avoiding the frivolous. For example, earning money for college is important, while up-grading stereo equipment is a lower priority. Students can avoid *job stress* by first establishing their financial needs and then balancing the number of work hours necessary to achieve them.

Ways Parents Can Help the Lonely Child Relate to Others

❏ Through conversations, help children decide who they are or want to be, defining an identity with which they're comfortable.

❏ Discuss the things about which peers seem to disapprove or make fun (i.e., appearance, verbal interactions, difficulty in a sport or activity).

❏ Which of these areas should the child ignore because he/she does not want to change?

❏ Are there some things the child can do willingly to fit in with peers and make friends?

❏ Help the child make favorable changes (i.e., a new sport or activity where he/she is more talented; different style of clothing; change in school behaviors).

❏ Involve the school counselor, and when possible, therapists who can support the young person's interactions with others. Explain the problem to teachers, asking them to informally include the child in group activities and to encourage extracurriculars.

❏ Steer children away from peers who may ridicule them or those who encourage unacceptable behaviors. Help children select non-threatening peers to invite home.

❏ Initiate more family-involved activities around areas of common interest. Have a shared dinner hour every evening. Don't take "No" for an answer if the child does not want to participate. Pleasantly insist. Restrict video games, violence in TV and music.

❏ Help children take control of their lives by trying a new hobby or area of interest.

❏ Do not accept children's statements about preferring to be alone. Without arguing or disputing what they have to say, sit in children's rooms and visit with them frequently, chatting about non-threatening topics.

❏ Interact in an upbeat way, using optimism and humor.

❏ Create self-reliance by encouraging teens to apply for a job and earn money toward an important objective.

❏ Give them opportunities to make daily decisions and set future goals.

When involved in school activities or bringing home hours of homework each night, a summer and weekend work schedule is best.

The chart includes a number of suggestions parents can use in helping an isolated child interact successfully with peers. Since isolation can debilitate a family, it's important to take it seriously and help children break the mold as young as possible. Often, *Lonely Children* and their parents have lost control over their own identities and become dependent on the way others view them. Their esteem and confidence have eroded as they feel daily rejection.

Children without goals or a sense of personal direction drift toward an empty future. Depressed about their low status, they expect little of themselves because they feel judged as failures or losers. Instead of allowing the child to reach Greg's extreme, it's easier to intervene at the first signs of withdrawal. By working with the child to change the situation, the parent also avoids being drawn in and becoming similarly depressed and isolated.

My students tell me that they feel the worst when they disappoint their parents. When important adults tell them they're competent and expect great things, it's difficult to upset them by letting them down. By helping set realistic expectations, adults can incorporate this natural sense of young people wanting to make their parents proud. The most important time to do this is when the child first enters a period of self-doubt.

"Brenda, you've been pretty quiet lately. Looks like you need to get more involved. What school activities do you think you'd enjoy the most?"

"Don't know. I don't really care right now, anyway."

"Well, you tried out for the Dance Team and that didn't work. But you might be great in one of the school plays. You can be really funny, you know. And you have a great singing voice. You might actually have a better time in Drama class."

"I don't know anybody there. Besides, if I'm ever on stage, they'll say I look stupid."

"Do you think you'll look stupid?"

"Yes!"

"Why?"

"Because my hair is curly and ugly. And I'm fat. Everybody says so. All the time."

"If you liked your hair better and were thinner, would you try Drama?"

"I never thought about it. I might. But I can't just change the way I look, can I? I'm stuck...."

This conversation is the first of many. The selection of a school activity is certainly less important than the way Brenda perceives herself, but it demonstrates her concern about her appearance and the ridicule that she endures. While only one or two others may have commented about her hair and weight, Brenda is very sensitive. Because she's dependent on others liking her, she can't ignore these taunts easily. They cut her like a knife and she generalizes to believe that everyone sees her this way, so she must be ugly. Her formal rejection from membership on the Dance Team reinforced that her unattractiveness is now a public perception. So she stops trying to make friends and withdraws.

It's important for Brenda to decide if she wants to change herself to fit in better. In this instance, she does. With her mother's help, she can find a stylist to design a new hairstyle, one with flair. Then the harder part: She and Mom can go on a healthy diet and "work-out" plan together. By avoiding junk food and joining a local fitness club, they can have a shared activity to bring them closer together as Brenda improves her physical and personal self-image. Contact lenses and a new clothing style in a smaller size will give her confidence to ignore other's inappropriate comments and to join a school activity.

During conversations with her mother, it will be equally important for Brenda to also recognize when the group is wrong and she should not go along with them. Her dependency on approval makes her more vulnerable to try things that can hurt her, such as drinking, sex, and drugs. Her mother can openly share her values, encouraging Brenda to invite home classmates that have the same moral and ethical standards as her family. There are also out-of-school opportunities for Brenda to make friends. She can sing in the church choir or join a youth volunteer group. Each of these activities also provides additional opportunities for the adults in her life to make new friends.

Lonely Parents Can Reach Out to Others

Brenda's pattern of isolation was just beginning, while Greg's was already deeply entrenched. In both instances, the parents had to reach out first. Once rejection sets in, it's normal not to want to risk further heartache. So we can't expect children to keep trying without help. Besides, adults deserve happiness too, needing friends, social activities, and times to just relax and laugh with others.

The chart includes suggestions for ways *Lonely Parents* can relate to others. When Laura met with Greg's teachers and counselor, she lessened a terrible weight on her own shoulders by enlisting their daily support for his re-engagement into school. Sometimes, it only takes one of these meetings to explain children's special interests and needs so that educators can decide how to best incorporate them in school activities. When a caring coach or teacher becomes the daily advocate for the child, the parent is able to concentrate on personal re-involvement in the neighborhood and community.

When parents resist their own withdrawal and become actively involved, they provide a wonderful model for their child. Attending school conferences, volunteering in the classroom or becoming a judge or fundraiser introduces them to other parents who also want the best for their sons and daughters. Sitting with other adults by the community pool or at a soccer game affords opportunities to personally make new friends. Even picking children up from after-school activities helps adults experience the child's world while giving them a chance to meet caregivers, coaches, and teachers.

It's important to not delay attending events until the child is selected quarterback or soloist. Students on the bench and those drawing stage curtains are just as important and loved by their parents as the ones who are front and center. The goal is to have children participate in any manner, not to compete for the most coveted role. Children understand this by parental attendance and pleasure in seeing them as part of the group.

But adults should pursue their own interests as well. If a parent not working outside the home has become isolated within the family and subsequently depressed, it's a good idea to get a job. Research doesn't show that children are harmed by parents' working, especially when the adults continue to prioritize time with their families. Actually, when parents

Ways Lonely Parents Can Relate to Others

❑   Attend all open houses and teacher conferences.

❑   Volunteer in elementary classrooms, asking your child and the teacher where you can be the most help.

❑   Join parent groups around specific school activities in your teen's interest area.

❑   Meet your neighbors, especially those with children. Take your children to the neighborhood playground or pool. Visit with parents as children play.

❑   If you work away from home, seek out healthy after-school activities for children. Community groups such as the YMCA offer sports, arts, and tutoring at elementary schools. Teens need to be involved in at least one activity daily or have a job.

❑   "Latch-key" children are by themselves for hours in an unsupervised environment, naturally becoming lonely. Do not allow children or teens to come home alone to an empty house. Instead, involve them in activities or after-school care.

❑   Pursue additional personal and family activities outside the school. Join a group of adults and children with shared interests and values.

❑   Understand that you are not alone. Unfortunately, many children are excluded by peers from individual events and daily interactions.

❑   Meet with your child's teachers and counselor and express your concerns. Discuss ways you can work together to include the child in school activities.

❑   Decide how to use the child's special interests as motivation to become re-involved in school.

❑   Select a teacher or counselor who will be the campus advocate for your child. This person can meet with the student informally and check weekly with teachers about student progress.

come home from work with interesting stories to tell, it adds to their ability to show children how to interact in the real world.

Personal involvement in religious groups and volunteer associations allows adults to help others while showing their children how to extend themselves outside the home. Involving young people in these activities can also set a lifetime pattern of helpfulness. And when adults enroll in university or community-based classes, children learn through observation that education is a lifetime occupation. Parents should never feel guilty about taking this time to do something they enjoy. Everyone benefits.

When he wanted to add two bedrooms to our small home, my father needed to learn a number of sophisticated carpentry skills. Because of an overly full schedule of work and family, he hesitated to register for community education courses. Encouraged by need, he finally enrolled and experienced several wonderful outcomes. Not only did he discover how to install insulation and lay hardwood floors, he met a number of men who were also attempting major home projects. He looked forward to Tuesday nights, both for information and adult company. For many months after the classes ended, my father and several other "students" enthusiastically worked evenings and weekends as a team to renovate each other's homes. With tremendous pride, they produced beautiful carpentry none of them would have been able to create alone. Perhaps most importantly, through this shared interest they developed friendships that lasted for years.

This type of adult involvement outside the home is even more significant for those who have become isolated or withdrawn because of family concerns. Parents can't set goals for children if they don't have any for themselves. When first reaching out, they take a risk. But when isolated parents re-enter the adult world through participating in shared activities, they set the stage for their children to follow suit. As with my father, some may not feel isolated, but simply too busy to be involved in the community. Because they feel guilty taking time away from family, they don't make time for themselves. But when adults re-shape priorities and become involved, they're personally happier and able to share more with their families. They show their children how enjoyable friendships and social occasions can be. Adults have to lead the way.

Realized Expectations

Yet, sometimes life's brutality minimizes our expectations for success. Indeed, when the odds seem stacked too high against a young person, it may seem realistic to set lower goals or none at all. What a loss that would have been for Harry.

As he was wheeled into my graduate course on child and adolescent development, I took a very deep breath. Strapped into a chair with his arms jerking in frequent spastic motions, Harry was unable to walk, write, or even feed himself. His full-time male assistant was also his only friend, teasing him good-naturedly about everything, including the disability. Cerebral Palsy had totally restricted Harry's body for twenty-two years.

But his mind was brilliant. And kind. We learned this as his painfully slow speech unravelled observations and insights new to all of us. Perhaps because his physical limitations restricted him from other diversions, he took more time to watch and think about social and political issues. He also had a deeply compassionate understanding of people.

One afternoon, as the class analyzed the causes of child abuse and neglect, Harry commented, "Most parents don't intentionally ignore or hurt their children. They're given a child with problems, one who overwhelms them twenty-four hours a day, one like me. What if they can't handle a difficult child, and the professionals don't know what to do? Would any of us like to be in their place? Parents often act out against children because they're overwhelmed. We can't excuse their behavior, but we should give them more support before they reach this point."

When we studied teenagers' impulsive behaviors, he noted, "Few of them do stupid things on purpose, like drink and drive. And it's not just kids who take chances. We all do. We feel bullet-proof. Invulnerable. We don't think that consequences will really happen to us. In our hearts we don't expect to get caught. Maybe as a species, humans have low self-esteem and we believe we're not important enough for others to be constantly watching. So we try to sneak things by."

The semester progressed. His appearance lost its strangeness. In our eyes, his moving arms became gestures to prompt agonizingly drawn-out words. We expected his insights to be clever. Anticipating a new observation, students looked at each other with a smile when Harry said, "Question!" They were rarely disappointed. He philosophized as he asked. And he loved an argument.

So none of us was surprised when a student brought in a column Harry had "written" for the local newspaper. A bit embarrassed, Harry admitted that he would be sharing his observations on people, politics, and social issues in future weekly columns.

"I'm really excited. Finally, people want to hear what I have to say. Because I take so long, only my family and teachers ever listened to me before. Most people ask 'How are you?' and keep on walking. I've even heard a few call me a *vegetable* as if I can't understand or explain.

"Here at the university, it's been different. You ask my opinions and don't care if I'm disabled. So I speak up or you'll think my mind's lifeless like my body."

"But how'd you get to write the column, Harry?"

"I heard they were looking for an editorial writer at the local newspaper. Without mentioning my physical problems, I set up an interview with the assistant editor. He looked surprised when he saw me. He asked a little about my disability, but mainly wanted to know my political and social opinions. *He treated me like a normal person!* The next week, his boss interviewed me and asked me to write the column."

Exhausted by so much speaking, Harry sank lower into his chair. Even his head moved downward.

Silence, as we thought about what he'd said. Another lesson for us all. The class applauded, at first quietly and then progressively louder, with cheers.

Head lifted with painful effort, his eyes filled with emotion.

Resilience in the Toughest of Circumstances

As Julius Erving noted, "Goals determine what you're going to be." Harry's stability and courage carried him toward his desire to demonstrate that he was smart and capable. His joy at finally being treated as a normal person told the sad tale of his earlier experiences. It also showed how others' expectations can encourage or impede success.

Why do some people make it despite the most difficult of circumstances? They succeed because even terrible problems can be offset by supportive experiences. And when there are *many difficulties*, the young person requires support from *many adults*. Harry's disability seemed overwhelming. Yet, he had grown up with parents and teachers who valued and nurtured him. While he missed having close friends, the adults in his life listened to him, making him feel intelligent and capable.

Harry's family wasn't wealthy, so they educated themselves in available resources. When he was younger, they turned to special education teachers and the Cerebral Palsy Center. As Harry reached adulthood, they hired an assistant for transportation and companionship. If the family lived in poverty and didn't understand how to obtain school and community assistance, Harry's life could have been very different.

In exploring *why* some children overcome the seeming impossible, researchers Werner and Smith found that widespread adult assistance and positive expectations can form a protective buffer to prevent life's situations from becoming overwhelming. They also learned that young people's ability to resist adversity changes frequently, according to what's going on in their life at any given moment. *Children are more resilient during certain times and in supportive situations.*

Harry went directly from college to graduate school, academic environments that required him to think and achieve. He was in the perfect intellectual setting to reach his goal of expressing his ideas and opinions. Surrounded by peers, advisors, and professors who expected him to be smart, he pursued his dreams. Within the limitations of severe physical disabilities, it was ironic that his future lay in communication. If Harry's elementary and secondary school teachers hadn't encouraged him academically, he might have spent his adulthood sitting at home watching others live out their dreams. His thoughts might have mirrored poet John Greenleaf Whittier's words:

> *For of all sad words of tongue or pen,*
> *The saddest are these: 'It might have been!'*

Young people internalize adult expectations. They can cope with the most difficult of situations when others believe in them and push obstacles aside. But it's important to reflect on messages that may label children, telling them what their personal expectations should be, and in effect, excluding them from certain choices.

Within the family, is there *the jock? The student? The prettier sister?* Do we view a neighbor's multi-racial child as less likely to be successful? Or a student such as Harry as hopeless because severe disabilities block the real person and potential inside?

Sometimes adults themselves give up when their family's situation seems too daunting. Loss of a job, a divorce, or exclusion of the child by peers can overwhelm expectations that things will work out. Children watch us cope and model on our responses to the best and worst of situations. During difficult times, turning to others for support creates a sense that we can make things work out.

The Talmud tells us, "The burden is equal to the horse's strength." Young people may appear more like foals than horses, small under the weight of life's issues. But they too can be surprisingly strong, moving beyond tremendous adversity when we teach them how.

Lessons Learned

A child doesn't have to win to be "a winner."

Children never fail to surprise us with what they can do when they try.

Let children know you believe in them.

Children rise or fall to the level of our expectations.

As adults see children, children see themselves.

If children don't expect to be successful, they won't be.

The first success leads to the second.

Adult warmth and guidance are more important than the structure of the family.

A "broken home" is bad only if it produces a broken child.

Children's needs take priority over adult schedules.

Sometimes we just have to ask for help.

When winning is everything to parents, it's everything to children.

If the coach is overly negative, it's time to find a new coach.

When they make a mistake, children are their own worst critics.

Practice shows children it takes work to achieve goals.

A team that supports each member is hard to beat.

Lonely children can create lonely parents.

Parents who take time for themselves bring home more happiness.

Chapter 7

Come-Back Kids:
Rebounding from Family Crisis

It's not whether you fall down.
It's whether you get back up.

Vince Lombardi

How strange life was....Just a few months ago she had been home in the Valley, still feeling the glow from her Quinceañera. Now Mama was showing the photos to everyone here at the *Warren House.* It seemed like someone else was in that album, especially looking at the long dark hair flowing over her shoulders and white dress.

The diagnosis had been such a shock. Claudia thought it was just the flu or exhaustion from all the planning and people. Children didn't get cancer, just adults when they were old. Another doctor took more blood and said it was true. He told her and Mama to go to the city *immediately* for her treatment.

She barely had time to say good-bye to Ramiro, or Paola and Tina. They had all looked so scared that she decided she better be the brave one. Especially around Mama, who couldn't even stay in the room when the nurse drew blood. Claudia just told Mama that she was used to it, that it wasn't so bad. By now, that was almost the truth.

But it was Christmas next week. She had left so quickly that she didn't have presents for anyone. And the doctor said yesterday that she needed to stay here through the holidays. She shrugged. She wouldn't need to buy presents after all.

She wondered if Ramiro would get her something anyway. He was so quiet that she didn't know how he felt about all this sickness stuff. At first, she had talked to him every day. But when he said he was coming to see her, she stopped calling. Her hair was almost gone now and he couldn't see her this way, with sparse, thin strands. He loved her hair. She loved her hair. Why did this have to happen?

Claudia watched the group of carolers arrive. They laughed and chatted, pushed and shoved, playfully moving into position. Highschoolers. One girl was so beautiful with her bright red hair and green eyes. But Ramiro liked dark eyes and hair. He told her that all the time.

What about the little one, with the doll-like face? She was so tiny she might break from Ramiro's bear-hug...Would he ever hug Claudia again?

She watched the carolers' expressions with curiosity. They seemed happy to be there, singing loudly, if not always on key. They meant well, she decided, although she doubted if they could ever understand how she felt. How lucky they were not to be sick.

Hard to be alone at Christmas. Pretending to brush a stupid strand of hair from her eyes, she looked away, observing the room through a mist. The sofas for visitors had been pushed to the side of the large living area today, making room for the choir. A little boy with a huge bandage across his neck stood looking up at the hundreds of tiny lights volunteers wrapped around the tall tree yesterday. Closer to the kitchen, countertops overflowed with *pan dulces* and hot chocolate. Immobilized in her crib by the machines that forced her breathing, a toddler with huge dark eyes stared solemnly at the sounds and movements of the entertainers.

Claudia smiled wistfully as a tiny girl on her mother's lap swayed her body to the music. Would she ever have children? She and Ramiro had already resolved differences over her wanting daughters and his wanting sons. They'd decided to have at least two of each, *chiquitos* to love. Mama said she was too young to talk like that, but Ramiro and she knew...

But now? She couldn't even let him look at her this way, with only a few long wisps of hair remaining. Why would God do this to her? A terrible joke, to promise so much and then take it away.

A movement from the hallway. Two older children raced to her around the crowd in the large room. She could even hear the girl giggling behind her hospital mask. They handed her a beautiful box covered by layers of silver and gold foil. Without looking up, she could feel herself getting more attention than the carolers. As the children begged her to hurry, Claudia opened the box tentatively as if to save the paper, really needing to savor the moment.

She lifted the black velvet out gingerly, stroking it with tenderness. The card only said *Claudia— I understand. With love, Ramiro*. She put the beret on her head carefully at first, then tilting it to a jaunty angle. As the children applauded, she smiled.

Faith in the Future

Although very young himself, Ramiro gave Claudia the best gift imaginable—a sense that he was there for her. The ravages of leukemia and loss of hair from chemotherapy caused Claudia to give up hope, to doubt that she could look forward to any real future. Her belief that she had to be the "brave one" for her mother and friends told them she could make it alone, that she was strong beyond expectation. Because of embarrassment over her appearance, she even cut herself off from Ramiro, becoming further isolated. During it all, she sank into hopelessness and depression, with no promise for the future.

In their long-term studies of children in the most desperate of situations, researchers Werner and Smith found that *optimism and faith in the future were critical to the ability to survive adversity and to eventually lead happy adult lives*. These young people were able to discover a strong sense of self and develop goals for the future when they had the support of others around them. During adverse times, family and friends were of greater help than mental health professionals. Because of his important place in Claudia's life, Ramiro provided immeasurable love and support. Indeed, he gave her hope when all else was gone.

Most often, parents and school personnel intervene with youth in crisis. Yet, there is no one person or organization best able to help young people through overwhelming times. As in Claudia's situation, many teens turn to each other.

Others develop a strong religious affiliation, a faith in a divine plan, or a sense that God will take care of them. They may carry this belief into adulthood, gaining sustenance from the conviction that they aren't alone. Members of the religious community can provide an extended family that holds out a hand during the most difficult of times. In other instances, substitute parents and friends provide consistency and caring when life seems to be falling apart. *The key to success is not only to help children make it through the stressful period, but to create a sense that the future will be better than the present.*

Young people have a tremendous ability to survive the worst of situations. But they need help. Unfortunately, if a "way out" is not at hand, they may adopt aggressive and destructive behaviors allowing them to fight back against overwhelming odds without ever winning. I experienced this first-hand some years ago.

On a trip to New York City, I rode the subway downtown after a day-long university conference. At four o'clock, families were leaving museums and filing into train cars, hoping to beat rush-hour crowds. Seats were full of sleepy children, their parents holding gift-shop bags and chatting about the evening meal.

The doors opened at a stop and six young teens raced into the car, shoving each other and laughing loudly. Clearly following a pre-ordained plan, these boys placed hands deeply in their pockets and spread out quickly among the seated families.

Shocking profanities filled the air as they forced their bodies within inches of individual passengers. After mocking her shrunken appearance, one boy spit in an older woman's face! Travelling alone, she cried out in shock and lowered her head into her trembling hands, sobbing. No one was able to protect her, as the youth continued from one person to the next, screaming hostilities and insults at adults and children alike.

Arms tightly fixing sons' and daughters' bodies to their own, parents focused their eyes on the floor, avoiding confrontation. One teen shouted that the group had guns to kill all of us. Taking them seriously, we cowered in our seats. As the sounds of shrieking children erupted, the boys laughed hysterically. They shouted obscenities and placed their faces inches away from individual passengers, defying each of us to confront them. One youth pushed his hand violently against a father holding a crying toddler, daring him to fight. Face taut with anger, the man lowered his head onto his weeping daughter's shoulder. Like oppressive humidity, our fear permeated the air.

An eternity passed in those minutes. Finally, the doors flew open at the next stop. Leaving store bags on seats, parents grabbed children and yanked them onto the platform outside. A teenage traveller put his arm around the older woman, still in shock, and guided her quickly along. Smiling broadly at their conquest and shouting abuse, the six youth remained aboard the subway for their next victims. The doors closed and the train pressed on.

Frozen, none of us moved until jolted by the howls of crying children. Racing to the platform conductor, several adults heatedly reported the assaults and threats, asking him to call authorities to remove the teens from the train car before they terrorized others.

He shook his head.

"Don't bother yourself. This stuff goes on all the time. These kids know they'll be dead at 20, anyway. This is their way of trying to take the rest of us with them."

As we watched in disbelief, he walked away.

Healthy vs. Unhealthy Resilience

Likely, the six teens did view themselves as "short-termers." Without any sense that their future would be better, they grabbed at today. They channeled anger at their out-of-control lives into destructive, survival behaviors. Their personal outrage undercut any sense of empathy or compassion for others. They developed their own style of unhealthy resilience through learning self-protection in a dangerous world. Their strategy was clear: Attack before being attacked.

As often happens in gangs, members lack any positive adult role models. They identify with powerful, anti-social peers who embrace hatred and aggression because of their own unmet needs. Regardless of the neglect or abuse they may have received as children, because of fear or through emotional bonding, they rarely act out toward the punitive adults in their lives.

Instead, these alienated young people transfer their anger onto those who represent everything outside their reach—

affluence, power, and happiness in a system that has evaded them personally. The short-term vicious pleasure the teens experienced on the subway gave them a sense of control over the hopelessness they felt about their lives and future. By terrorizing adults, they alienated the very people who could help them the most. But by the end of that day, clearly none of us wanted to ever see them again.

In his research, Joseph Burger explored the important distinction between healthy and unhealthy resilience. Angry youth who don't see a way out of their overwhelming life situations develop powerful negative behaviors for self-protection. They will survive despite the cost personally or to others. He explains that children behave badly when they feel powerless and humiliated. Some may withdraw into helplessness, while others become strong-willed and obstinate. These young people fight back with amazing bravado and courage, resulting in further punishment and alienation from adults.

When they rage "successfully," their behaviors become more deeply ingrained and are less likely to change. This negative resilience is counterproductive. It doesn't heal wounds, but serves as a band-aid to hide deeper problems. By poisoning human relationships irreparably, angry young people destroy any hope of developing healthy life patterns.

But not all children react so violently. Some act inwardly by blaming themselves for weakness in overcoming their problems, or they withdraw in sadness at life's unfairness. Eventually, they give up, unable to see their life as ever being different or better than it is today. Youth who carry this internalized sense of sadness may be as angry and depressed as ones who use a weapon to get back at others.

Claudia and the teens on the subway have all experienced a terrible adversity, such as illness, poverty, the perceived abandonment by a parent through divorce or death, abuse by a trusted adult, or a lack of support in home or school. Ironically, many strongly feel the loss of things they have never had: a positive family, money, a sense of direction. Their hurt and upset are even worse if they've temporarily experienced positive situations, only to have them taken away. At school and on television, when they observe others who are affluent, healthy, and from two-parent families, they ask, "Why me? Why should I have these problems when others don't?" So Claudia feels jealous of the teens in the choir and the youth on the train terrorize families that appear to have everything.

When children's problems are overpowering, adults also may feel a sense of helplessness and fear. Understandably, no one wants to be around aggressive and dangerous young people. And when children act-in their anger and depression, they give off a false sense of bravado, indicating they can handle the problem without others. So adults don't feel needed. But they are.

Developing Healthy Resilience in Children and Teens

Above all, during times of crisis, children require adults who listen. Young children and teens tend to believe that what they experience today is what they'll feel forever. Only by discussing their deepest concerns do they realize that they can make their life happier, that this low point need not continue. *Knowing that things will get better helps all of us have faith in the future.*

Whether hostile or withdrawn, children experiencing severe problems need adults. When the extent of the problem goes beyond their ability to cope, they respond defensively and almost always demonstrate unhealthy behaviors. Thirteen-year-old Terri was shocked by her parents' divorce. Involved in her own school and social circle, she became overwhelmed when her father moved out suddenly. Her mother's tears and sense of helplessness upset Terri further, as she felt that the adults in her life had lost control and she had no one to help her.

Within weeks of her father's departure, Terri began to complain frequently about aches and illnesses. Yet, the family doctor couldn't find anything wrong with her. She missed days at school, remaining home to assure herself that her mother wasn't going away, too. She wept easily and had trouble sleeping. For the first time, she developed an angry attitude, challenging her mother constantly.

It was critical for Terri's parents to intervene immediately, not allowing her to continue these self-destructive patterns. While it can take months, or even years, to cope with extreme loss, there's no time to wait. Positive or negative behaviors begin with the problem. When adults guide children into adapting, they show them ways of lessening grief and despair.

Supporting Children through Difficult Times

❑ Be sure that there are one or more strong adults available for conversations and support.

❑ Allow children to demonstrate the full range of emotions (tears, anger outbursts).

❑ Understand that young people need to be alone at times.

❑ Listen to what children say without giving in to your own emotions.

❑ Avoid criticizing children for being upset.

❑ Do not allow children to take blame for family problems.

❑ Help children understand that bad things do happen outside of everyone's control.

❑ Intervene immediately if you see aggression, frequent withdrawal from others, or any self-destructive behaviors.

❑ If children act-out against others, remind them of social, compassionate behaviors.

❑ Encourage friendships with peers with positive behaviors.

❑ Yet, put children in supervised situations where they can help others who are also experiencing life's problems.

❑ Begin hobbies and activities that build their self-esteem.

❑ Continue to be firm in your discipline. While understanding that the young person is upset, never allow rudeness or disregard for family rules.

❑ Discuss the future. Plan short-term and long-term goals and establish steps to reach them.

❑ Have children meet with a counselor to overcome feelings of anger or loss.

❑ Remember to have fun. Share family activities that everyone will enjoy.

The chart includes a number of suggestions for helping children like Terri make it through overwhelming problems. Once again, the presence of one or more strong adults is the most important component for success. Involved in their own upset, Terri's parents may feel too overwhelmed to be her sole support, so they'll need to ask family and friends for their help. Certainly, teachers and counselors at school want to be aware of Terri's situation so that they can boost her self-esteem and have her become more involved with friends and school activities.

Terri needs to be allowed time to go through a full range of emotions as she expresses her anger and upset. Her hypochondria is based on anxiety. She craves conversations with her father, assurances that she'll see him frequently and that he'll remain part of her life. Meanwhile, her mother needs to underscore that she won't go away, that she'll be there for her daughter. Terri must be able to express her anger at her parents, followed by opportunities for them to reassure her that the divorce isn't her fault and that they'll both continue to love her and remain a part of her life.

Terri's father has a critical role. It's important for him to call frequently and spend time with her. By his consistently being there, she'll realize that she hasn't lost him and that he loves her. Terri will gradually understand that she doesn't have to be "sick" to get her parents' attention, that she deserves it just because she's their daughter.

Talking provides children a sense of release from heavy emotions. But as adults reflect on what young people tell them, it's important not to interject personal feelings. Although she may be furious at her ex-husband, Terri's mother can't say bad things about him if she really wants to help her daughter. Otherwise, Terri may be afraid of losing her mother by expressing her own anger about the divorce or by acknowledging that she still loves and needs her father. The mother needs to focus on Terri's loss, keeping her own anger for later discussion with friends or a counselor.

When parents are overcome by their own situations, temporarily they may have to put aside their own emotions to arrange for others to talk with their child. Family members, friends, and professionals can play a tremendously important role as listeners. In an open, non-judgmental environment, children can express their anxieties and anger more freely and work through resentment and upset in a healthy way.

If allowed to develop explosive tempers and act out their anger, young people quickly join the ranks of the teens on the subway. Adults help most when they stop these self-destructive actions immediately. If these behaviors snow-ball out-of-hand, adults become less able to stop them because of a fear of retribution. Terri's mother can't accept her daughter's negative attitude or it may become permanent. By correcting Terri, telling her that her personal verbal attacks are out-of-line, and suggesting appropriate behavior, she establishes social expectations that are important even during times of crisis. *We must never be so understanding of children's behavior that we allow it to become unacceptable.*

More than ever, Terri needs to be with upbeat, positive friends. When Claudia became depressed over losing her hair during chemotherapy, she withdrew, isolating herself completely. If young people are alone or with negative peers, they lose faith that the future will be better, cutting themselves off from opportunities to take control of their lives. If Claudia could help with some of the younger chronically ill children, she would have a purpose for renewed optimism. She needs an ongoing connection with people and life's fulfilling activities.

For both Claudia and Terri, setting goals and plans with adults will be so helpful in an improved attitude and ability to cope. Looking ahead instead of behind, planning the future instead of regretting the past, tells us that life is about hope and courage. In writer Albert Camus' words, the child realizes that "In the depth of winter, I finally learned that there was in me an invincible summer."

Recognizing Children's Accomplishments

Part of helping children understand that the future will be better involves immersing them in new involvements and activities and then recognizing their efforts. Showing them that they're special gives a sense that life still can be fun even when things don't go our way. As their esteem grows, they gain a renewed excitement about moving on past today's problems.

To do this, it's important to get to know your child. When does he have the most fun? When does she try harder?

Ways to Recognize Children's and Teens' Accomplishments

❑   Observe children and teens to see what they do well.

❑   Provide opportunities for exploring new activities and hobbies at home and school.

❑   Praise children and teens for trying new things. Be specific in pointing out skills that they're developing.

❑   Attend their events. They'll always look to see if you're there.

❑   Be unconditional in your positive attitude. Don't withhold praise until they do things perfectly.

❑   Openly discuss things at home or school that are difficult for them to do. If they can't meet your expectations, change the expectations.

❑   Focus on areas where they can be successful.

❑   Don't encourage children or teens to set impossible goals for themselves. In the long run, they'll only be disappointed.

❑   A special meal or family activity can be a wonderful way to celebrate a successful effort or outcome.

❑   Let the school know if your child or teen receives a community award.

❑   Don't compare siblings' accomplishments. Find something in each child or teen that's unique.

❑   If an accomplishment is overlooked by others, show how much you appreciate the effort by doing something special.

❑   When success is part of a team outcome, praise the entire group. Children don't always need to stand out individually.

❑   Thank teachers, coaches, and other parents who have helped your child be successful.

Enthusiastic motivation from the beginning usually means children expect to be successful. Without pressure, through additional opportunities at school, community, or hobbies at home, they learn to explore. Parents who are unconditionally positive and who praise specific skill development openly display their pleasure in children's accomplishments.

"Mark, you're making those hoops today!" or "Kristi, I can't believe all those cartwheels!" are better compliments than "You're a champion at basketball (or gymnastics)!" When adults remark on specific efforts, they recognize that individual, critical skills tend to develop over time. Mark and Kristi know that they're not really champions yet, so they'll disregard global comments as insincere. But they'll be very pleased at parents and teachers noticing their progress in practicing a really difficult skill.

And they'll always look to the stands or audience during events. Say what we will to them, if we're not at our children's performances, the real message is clear. When there's a divorce or when an adult travels a good deal, parents may decide to divide attendance according to their comfort level. But the child's needs should always come first. All parents feel badly if their child scores his first touchdown and they're not at the game!

The chart includes a number of ways to recognize all children's accomplishments and efforts. Every child deserves the opportunity to explore a talent or skill, to find new challenges. Many of these activities won't develop into careers, but they will provide the child with a sense of being capable and skilled, in other words: *A Winner.* When recognized publicly for their accomplishments, children dare to take risks in the future.

During a lecture, a middle school Principal wisely advised my students: "If you can't get what you want, change what you want." Sometimes children want something terribly, but it's outside their reach. Adults can't keep encouraging them toward an unachievable goal or the long-term outcome will be more overpowering than the short-term disappointment.

At a clinic, I overheard an eleven-year-old child with spina bifida tell her mother plaintively how much she wanted to be a dancer. Yet, doctors said the child would never walk, but remain permanently in a wheelchair. At that moment, clearly the mother was filled with heartache, wanting more than any-thing for her daughter to dance or even take a single step. Still, she found the strength to look realistically at this beau-tiful child with a disability.

Gently, "Sounds like you want to try some new things. Regular dancing would be tough for you, but I just read about an acting company that has some members in wheelchairs. Should we check that out?" The girl was delighted. No false promises, but a realization that, like everyone else, she has ways to have fun and show off her accomplishments.

South African Terence Parkin never heard the roars from the crowd when he won the silver medal in the 200-meter breast stroke event in the Sydney Olympics. But at the end of the race, as he turned to look at his time and then the standing, cheer-ing multitudes, his grin spread as he waved back. A lifetime of deafness did not diminish his pleasure, but perhaps even enhanced it, as others acknowledged his amazing journey.

That's what it's all about. And, with little thanks, many people outside the family cheer and recognize children daily. Because they care, teachers, coaches, and other parents are there to spur on a child they may not even know. Hours after a work day and on weekends, they put an arm around a shoulder or call a discouraged team "Winners." When looking back on adolescence, so many people reflect on the school activities that gave them public recognition: "I loved Drama" or "Basketball kept me going to school every day." But adults need recognition too. It's important to thank the adults who spend time giving children a chance to shine.

At home, in big and small ways, we need to recognize chil-dren so that they'll try harder the next time. Parents are in the best position to organize small celebrations. Dessert first the night Kathy passed her math exam. Extra hugs when Tom got himself up and ready for school that morning. More often than on a stage or field, real accomplishments occur in the everyday things children try for the first time or exert that bit of extra effort.

While Olympic swimmer Terence Parkin's competitors heard a quick shot to start their race, he had to learn to respond as quickly to a flashing light or he'd never win. But in a lifetime of competitions, these lights are in different loca-tions at different pools, and are worked by different people.

Anticipating and mastering a seemingly simple task can make all the difference. And when others acknowledge your efforts and your positive, non-complaining attitude, you try harder.

A neighbor visited with me recently as I worked in my front yard. Our conversation was interrupted by her nineteen-year-old daughter's charge across the street, yelling "Mom, sing it to me!"

Startled, but with a broad grin, her delighted mother loudly serenaded us all with a child's song:

I'm proud of you, I'm proud of you,
I hope that you're as proud of you as I am proud of you...

Laughing gleefully, she and the daughter sang a few more verses, a wonderfully unexpected event as the two of them stepped high and chanted the words for the neighborhood to hear. Then, she hugged her mother tightly.

To me, she explained smilingly, "I made Dean's List! When we were little, my Mom sang that song to us whenever we did something special. We just haven't let her stop. We love it!" A youthful bound back across the street.

Shaking her head, her mother commented, "I don't even remember where I first heard that song years ago. Maybe it was on *Mr. Rogers' Neighborhood*. But the words are great. My kids hear not only that *I'm* proud of each accomplishment, but that I want *them* to be proud as well. That way, they'll be successful not just for me, but for themselves."

She recalled her daughter's concerns about how well she would do during her first semester of college.

"Just a few months ago, she was worried about whether she could make it academically. Now she knows what we've know all along, that she's smart and capable."

When Parents' Own Optimism is Lost

But despite the daily things we try and the full heart we put into being there for our children, sometimes life packs such difficult punches that we question our ability to make it through the hard times. More than ever, it becomes more important to remember that we're not alone.

Driving home from work on December 21, 1988, Eileen Monetti's thoughts were full of the Christmas cookies she

would bake that night and her last-minute holiday prepara-
tions. This was a special day, with her son Rick flying back
from his study abroad semester in London. Eileen hoped fifteen-year-old Kara was feeling better. She had stayed home
sick that day, probably just run-down from her whirlwind of
school activities. As she turned the corner and saw the number of cars parked in front of her house, Eileen smiled, thinking that Kara's friends had stopped by to speed her recovery.

They were indeed there to support her, but for a different
reason. Just hours before, as she watched television, Kara
learned that her brother's plane had disappeared on radar.
Later, the entire family watched CNN in horror, with tapes of
the fiery plane exploding over the town of Lokerbie, Scotland,
killing 11 bystanders. With 259 passengers, 35 of them
Syracuse University students studying in London, the scene
was chaos. Outcomes unknown, no families had yet been
notified and telephone lines were full. In disbelief, for days the
Monettis and other passengers' families received their facts
painfully slowly from the television.

Originating in Frankfurt, citizens of 21 countries were on
the flight, including 189 Americans. Completing final exams
and papers, Rick and the other 34 Syracuse students had
remained in London later than some of their classmates.
Their peers had left days earlier, sparing their lives.

Endless frustration and disappointment stretched over
weeks, as Eileen and Bob Monetti tried to obtain information
about their son. They were furious at a system that excluded
them from facts during the most difficult time of their lives. At
first, quietly observing press conferences and demands from
families for more information, Eileen's emotions erupted
when she learned that a bomb appeared to be the cause of the
crash. It was reported that someone had phoned in a threat
just 25 minutes before the explosion.

"I was so angry that I had to do *something*," she explains.
"So I gave my first interview to the press." This began the
Monettis change from helpless onlookers to active partici-
pants in a process that would impact many lives.

Syracuse University conducted a poignant memorial service to reach out to the grieving university community. Letters
from professors to parents commemorated the special attachment they felt for their lost students. The university provided

the names and addresses of families so they could get together for support. This move encouraged the Monettis and several others to create a broader list of victims' families in the New York and New Jersey region.

Eileen reflects, "It was a turning point when I received a note from a woman who had lost her daughter in the crash, someone I didn't even know. That letter told me that I wasn't alone."

Tragedy became reality when Rick's body arrived home on January 7, weeks after the crash. Indeed, with the terrible finality of his death, Eileen, Bob, and Kara might have given in to depression and secluded themselves. Yet, after the burial, they became involved in planning a meeting of New Jersey families with Senator Bill Bradley to discuss ways of improving the flow of information concerning the crash. In March, 1989, they arranged for New York and New Jersey families to meet and share information. Police from Lokerbie, Scotland, came to the United States to explain the progress of their search for bodies and personal effects. They described the ongoing criminal investigation and how the Scottish legal system would respond when the terrorists were found.

When a German magazine exposed the lack of security at the Frankfurt Airport and the likelihood that the bomb was easily placed on their loved one's plane, several victims' families understood that more had to be done to protect others from experiencing the same tragedy. On the 103rd day after the crash, more than 100 families rallied at the White House to meet with Senators and Congressional Aides.

A core of this group created the organization "Victims of Pan Am Flight 103," which continues to this day. A non-profit organization, it includes hundreds of members joined by common goals. Working with the authorities and community in Lokerbie in the months immediately following the crash, they smoothed the logistics of returning victims' personal effects to their families. They guided families into group and individual grief therapy with the support of the Lokerbie Fund, using additional monies for education about air disasters. Their broader-reaching goals of improving airline and airport security and examining the United States response to terrorism have impacted all of our lives.

With Bob Monetti as their President, the organization currently works with the Federal Aviation Association and industry groups to improve international security. They have supported the development of techniques to discover small bombs, and were an integral part of the Bush Commission's recommended changes for security regulations, in May, 1990. Their lobbying efforts have been highly successful in areas such as promoting the development of sophisticated Explosive Detection Systems to examine luggage and the use of new technology at airports. To date, Bob and his colleagues speak at professional aviation conferences to heighten awareness of the ongoing need for enhanced security.

Parents Leading the Way

While their long-term efforts have created the largest advocacy group for victims' families and have helped improve airport security for all of us, the personal healing process has been understandably slow and painful for the Monettis. Yet, they provide lessons for all parents in how to personally restore faith and optimism, even during the worst of times.

They had to start where it mattered most—within their own family. Eileen and Bob accepted Kara's need to return to school immediately, to be with her friends and receive their support. Counselors and teachers were the most helpful through ongoing conversations. Kara's re-immersion in school activities gave her a sense of normalcy. Bob and Eileen attended her swim meets and cheered her on, pulling themselves out of their own depression.

Eileen also went back to her job as a high school teacher for adults and Bob to his engineering office. "I kept telling myself, *As long as we keep things as normal as possible, things will go back to normal*," she reflects. But setbacks occurred every few months as a package arrived with more of Rick's belongings. The most painful delivery arrived the day before Mother's Day, moving Eileen from depression to anger.

"I understood that allowing myself to stay this way would be a disaster," she comments.

Eileen knew it was time for the family to move on. The Monettis flew to Scotland six months after the crash and were overwhelmed by the kindness of the villagers. They learned that before their return to families, the personal effects of all victims were laundered with care by local women. What a painful task that must have been! They met Fr. Pat Keegans, a wonderful priest who gave his emotional support selflessly to visitors, often interspersing a delightful sense of humor and perspective. The town of Lockerbie was creating a "Room of Remembrance" in Tudergarth, where the cockpit and many bodies had landed. This, along with the powerful "Wall of Remembrance" at the cemetery in town, honored each of the crash victims.

"I understood from these wonderful people that their loss of 11 villagers and the ongoing need to handle the sudden death of so many strangers had changed their home forever. But instead of focusing on their own loss, they wanted to give support to all of us, people they had never even met."

Back home, as a gray fall approached, Eileen entered grief counseling so that she could regain her emotional strength and better support her family. Bob, too, was making personal decisions. He had become so actively involved in developing the "Victims of Pan Am 103" group that he was spending less and less time in his engineering practice. With the family's full encouragement, he resigned his position and began extensive travels and lobbying as the official representative for the organization.

Suse Lowenstein, a sculptress and mother who lost her 21-year-old son, Alexander, in the Lockerbie bombing, expressed her own pain and helped others understand the impact of the tragedy. She created "Dark Elegy," a series of 100 larger-than-life statues depicting the mothers of the victims as they learned of their children's death. Eileen Monetti is portrayed hugging herself, with eyes and head cast downward. Widely acclaimed, these statues have been displayed on the lawns of a number of universities, including Syracuse, Rutgers, and Fordham.

Years having passed, Eileen and Bob are again deeply involved in their church, where Eileen initiated grief-counseling groups for others needing support. Bob continues his international work in pressing for enhanced airport security equipment and regulations. But their joy lies in Kara. She was married ten days after the 10th anniversary of her brother's death, the ceremony conducted by Fr. Pat Keegans, who was flown to New Jersey by friends who had lost a sister at Lokerbie. Kara's first child is a boy they lovingly call *Ricky*.

Ways for Parents to Support Themselves During Times of Crisis

❑ Do not give up.

❑ Understand that working through grief and major loss takes time.

❑ Turn to family, friends, and neighbors for help with problem-solving.

❑ Do something positive for yourself every day.

❑ Put children's needs first. Adults can't give up and withdraw when there are children in the family who need them.

❑ Attend children's school activities. Share the family's situation with teachers and counselors.

❑ Return to work as quickly as possible after the crisis in order to re-establish a sense of normalcy.

❑ Stay active all day. Avoid excessive sleep.

❑ Don't use alcohol and medications as a relief from problems.

❑ Exercise will help you deal with stress. When depression strikes, it's very helpful to go outside the house, walk, run, or swim.

❑ Return to household routines as quickly as possible (i.e., dinner, homework, and bedtime schedules).

❑ Family members often benefit from individual or group grief counseling.

❑ Avoid making any major decisions (moving to a new house; divorce; changing children's schools).

❑ Talk to others who have experienced similar losses.

❑ Volunteer to help others in need (school tutoring, community or national service groups).

❑ Spend lots of time with your family.

Eileen personally expresses how the Monettis managed to survive tragedy and develop incredible strength to help themselves and others:

"I knew that if I gave into anger and bitterness, the terrorists would have another victim."

Moving On

In *Antigone*, Sophocles writes, "Grief teaches the steadiest minds to waver." There is no grief greater than the loss of a child. Yet, through incredible strength, self-knowledge, and shared love, the Monettis dealt with the worst of tragedies. Going beyond themselves, they also moved to prevent others from suffering unjustly at the hands of terrorists, pouring their own emotions into an international effort to spare other families a similar loss. As unintentional teachers, they showed all parents how to support themselves and their families during crises. Some of their lessons appear in the chart.

The most important lesson is to never give up. Bitterness and anger can pull us away from others. They isolate us from the support all adults must have when life becomes overwhelming. Sometimes we need family and friends to become our eyes and ears temporarily as they help us analyze what is really happening. Years afterwards, former Texas Governor Ann Richards relates how her problem with alcoholism enveloped her so completely that she turned away from friends who tried to help. After a terrible night of public binge drinking, where she staggered home and remembered little, a group of close friends appeared the next morning. Relentlessly bombarded with their upset at her ruined life, she agreed that day to enter a substance abuse program. Years later, during a highly successful career in public office, she continued to underscore how they saved her life.

The Monettis turned to Kara's teachers and counselors for help in supporting her. Despite the hugeness of their own loss, they remembered that they had another child, one who needed them desperately. Too often, during crises such as death, serious illness, and divorce, adults are overwhelmed by their own sense of loss and may fail to fully understand their child's sense of grief. Children come to feel that they've lost their parents in addition to another family member because of the adults' removal into a private healing process. As always, *it's most important to put children's needs first.*

But of course adults need to take care of themselves as well. While anti-depressants and alcohol may appear to provide temporary relief, they separate the parent. An adult who is often asleep or removed from sound judgment can't be there consistently for the family. It's far better to stay active all day, returning to work as soon as possible. Healing often occurs in the midst of daily demands. Exercise as basic as an evening walk helps alleviate stress and avoid depression. Getting out of the house everyday is critical.

Daily routines are also very important. During crises, more than ever, children need bedtimes, family dinners, and supervised homework. School provides a sense of normalcy and structure. Children can't be allowed to stay home or withdraw, even if they claim they don't feel well, have headaches, or stomachaches. Counseling becomes particularly necessary when parents notice a change in children's behaviors, such as withdrawal from the rest of the family or verbal or physical aggression. During crises, brothers and sisters may fight more, demonstrating their own anger and upset. Parents can't allow this to continue, because a close-knit family unit is often the best buffer during the hardest of times. It's far better to discuss the problem openly, listening to each child's worries and upset. Sometimes children don't initiate these conversations because they don't want to further upset their parents. Once again, adults must take the lead.

Sometimes crises can bring on a family's sense of needing immediate change. Tragically, a child dies. The parents are not able to grieve in the same way or to comfort each other. Smaller problems become seemingly overwhelming and divorce becomes a choice. Or there may be a feeling that a family project, such as a new home, will keep everyone busy and bring excitement. But the move may mean children changing schools, taking them from the very structure of friends and activities that can carry them through. During crises, it's best to not make any major decisions or life changes. Coping with loss takes time and these short-term "solutions" can have an even greater negative long-term impact. The Monettis reached out and helped others. Even on a smaller scale, volunteering at a school or shelter, joining a community activity or a group of others in similar circumstances proves that we are needed.

Archbishop Desmond Tutu protested with thousands behind him and spent bleak time in prison rather than give in to South Africa's Apartheid policy. Years later, he still finds no need for vengeance.

"I've always believed blacks and whites can live together as friends," he reflects. His strength and vision took him and a nation far beyond a lifetime's dream.

Ralph Waldo Emerson once commented, "It is the wounded oyster that mends its shell with pearl." The worst of adversity can start something far-reaching in our lives, impacting others beyond what we imagine.

Lessons Learned

If we had more friends, we'd need fewer psychologists.

The best gift is to be there for the people we love.

Optimism and faith in the future can help children overcome the worst of adversities.

Unhealthy resilience helps children survive, but it can poison their future relationships.

In the worst of situations, adults can't allow children to develop self-destructive behaviors.

Helping others gives us a renewed awareness that life will get better.

Believing in children helps them believe in themselves.

Children become "winners" when others see them that way.

Praise makes children try harder.

Recognizing children in small ways can bring about big successes.

Children blossom when we acknowledge their accomplishments publicly.

Teachers and coaches need recognition too.

By healing together, families cope with tragedy.

We grow by appreciating strength in others.

Positive people bring out the best in all of us.

Especially during difficult times, it's important for the family to have fun together.

Great joy can come from bringing happiness to even one person.

Chapter 8

The Best of All Teams:Parents and Teachers Working Together

*When I approach a child, he inspires in me
two sentiments: tenderness for what he is,
and respect for what he may become.*

Louis Pasteur

As teaching intern Pat Thompson and I walked down the hallway of an inner-city elementary school, excited greetings poured from otherwise quiet rooms with classes in full session.

"Hey, Mr. Thompson!"

"Sir!"

"See you in Math!"

Walking by, a small boy tilted his head way back and looked up almost seven feet into my student's kind eyes and white face.

"Are you David Robinson?"

"No, but I wish I were." A direct answer. Quietly, to me, "It's great when kids are color blind."

The tall man reached far down and took the boy's hand, leaving me behind as he ambled along with the child, both engaged in casual conversation. Dwarfed by the intern's size, the thin child looked particularly vulnerable. As they reached the Kindergarten classroom, Pat crouched his body down to make eye contact. He listened intently, speaking only occasionally. They talked for some minutes. By now, Pat's arm touched the boy's shoulder lightly.

"Remember. You come to practice after school today. I'll call your Mom."

"Thanks, Sir." Expressionless and standing by the door, the boy watched Pat walk away.

Shaking his head sadly, Pat returned to my side.

"He told me his father left home for good last night. Now the work begins."

School as a Refuge

In an interaction lasting only minutes, a little boy found acceptance from a kind teacher. Particularly needy and likely feeling rejected by his father, he opened up to another man who gave him full attention. Even in such a brief encounter, the child received the message that he's a deserving person, worthy of approval.

Parents aren't always present, or able, to help. In these instances, as Elie Wiesel noted, we must all be "the watch people for the vulnerable." As Pat observed a boy's need for attention, he left our adult conversation to hold a young hand. He understood which interaction was more important.

I've learned that good teachers do that. Without much pay or many thanks, they focus on their young charges every day. Through instinct and training, they sense when a student needs them and that a few minutes of caring can last a lifetime.

From her work at the Child Witness to Violence Project at Boston Medical Center, psychologist Maxine Weinreb relates a conversation she had with Michelle, a woman physically abused as a child by an alcoholic father who beat both his wife and daughter. While Michelle also had a depressed and unavailable mother and a hearing loss suffered from untreated ear infections, she grew up to be a successful professional with a wonderful sense of humor and a variety of interests. When her own preschooler became overly active, she turned to the Center for help rather than repeat the cycle of violence.

When Dr. Weinreb asked her how she had grown up to be so stable and healthy despite a horrible childhood, Michelle gave much credit to her second-grade teacher. Sensing that something was wrong in the child's life, the teacher had insisted that she stay in her classroom instead of attend a special class, nurtured her with support and care, and spent time with her in frequent after-school conversations. Despite the teacher's questions about whether someone was hurting her, Michelle never would talk about her father. He had threatened to kill her if she told anyone, and she believed him.

She kept this terrible secret to herself for years. Yet, as she went on to new classrooms and life situations, Michelle reflected that the second-grade teacher's love and concern sustained her like "a candle in her heart." Because it's psychologically safe, school is a refuge for many children. In spite of her home, Michelle developed a positive self-image through a meaningful relationship with a teacher.

When the family situation is bad, many aspects of school become really important. In an environment where children are expected and encouraged to be learners and problem solvers, they apply logic to handle life's setbacks and crises. When they form friendships, they find that others will be there for them. Extracurricular activities help them realize their own skills and talents as they gain self-confidence. School places a protective shield around children that removes them from a stressful world and gives them a chance to explore who they really are.

That's why the rash of modern-day school shootings has been so overwhelming. We can only imagine their impact on the Michelles around us, children who witness and feel violence at home and again at school. They have no chance to understand that the world is really a good, exciting place just ready for them to explore. All children and their teachers need to be physically safe as they share this caring-learning relationship.

Charismatic Adults

In their research studying children overcoming adversity, Werner and Smith found that outside the family, most often a caring teacher was the role model with the greatest impact. Happily, few homes are abusive like Michelle's. Instead, many parents feel overwhelmed by time pressures, with a mother and father both working, a single parent stretched for time, or a grandparent raising a second family. Love is not enough to add more hours to the day, so adults turn to the school and especially teachers, to be part of an extended family that raises our children.

At times, all homes can suffer overwhelming setbacks. Is it always necessary to go outside the family? Not if there are enough supports within. Yet, the little boy who spoke to Pat Thompson had a real need at that moment and his family wasn't there. Nor would they be there later as Pat coached him on the basketball team and showed him some fancy shots. Some things that happen to a child are so significant that parents need teachers' support.

Charismatic Adults is the term psychologist Julius Segal gave adults to whom children turn when they have problems and need positive role models. I like the term *charismatic*, because it demonstrates how their positive attitude, sense of optimism, and capability attracts others. Teachers fill this role most naturally, because they share the daily school relationship and become confidantes. Successful and accomplished, they're more available than the superstar hero the child emulates on television. The impact of these teachers can carry the student through the most terrible situations.

While reading the newspaper one morning, I was saddened by the front page story of still another drive-by shooting. But this one was different. Teens from one gang were retaliating for an attack on one of their members by shooting into the front window of the rival leader's home. It was 2 A.M. when bullets poured into the living room of a tiny house in one of the city's poorer neighborhoods. They seriously wounded a six-year-old girl who was asleep on the sofa in her aunt's home. Her cousin, the gang member, escaped the attack. But as the emergency team carried her to an ambulance, in terrible pain, the little girl kept screaming "I want my teacher." Not her mother or even the aunt who took care of her, but her teacher. Only in first grade, this little girl understood instinctively what researchers pore over for years: Teachers really matter. We can count on them.

Of course, in addition to nurturing and supporting children, educators teach critical academic skills. In many states, children's scores on standardized tests are the only measures used to gauge a teacher's success. So if the child who was shot doesn't pass her reading or math tests, her teacher may be viewed as a failure regardless of the impact she's had in this little girl's life.

Teachers need parental support to accomplish their total job. The best place to start is by sending children and teens to school ready to learn. Early bedtime and good meals mean that the child is rested, fed, and physically comfortable. Children also need stimulation. If parents talk to young children, reading comes more easily. When they share values and healthy ways to solve conflict, young people understand that fighting rarely solves problems. As St. Francis Xavier once commented, "Give me the children until they are seven and anyone may have them afterwards."

The Parent's Special Role

Tearfully, Celina received her mother's hug at the classroom door.

"Recuerdas, Mija!"

"Sí, Mamá."

Oh yes, she'd remember the lesson her mother had drilled into her for months now. But this bright new room was so big and noisy and the woman walking quickly toward her looked too young to be a teacher.

"You must be Celina. Welcome to Kinder! I'm Miss Anderson. I'm so glad you're here. Let me show you your desk."

Head bowed downward, Celina didn't respond.

"Hablas inglés?"

Ashamed and with tears about to fall, "No, Señora."

"No es un problema. Hablo un poco de español. Vámonos."

Celina wondered if she would ever learn English. But, looking directly into the teacher's eyes, she grinned broadly. Surprised at the response, Miss Anderson extended a hand and led Celina to her desk.

Never diverted by classmates' chatter or bustling activity, it was from that seat each day that Celina studied her teacher's face intently. She hung onto each of Miss Anderson's words, frowning in vain attempts to understand. Yet, every time the teacher looked at her, the frown turned into a broad smile. Pleased, the teacher smiled back and often came to Celina's desk, placing a kind hand on her shoulder.

Paired with Spanish-speaking Elva, Celina made friends on the playground. By spring, she was chatting away with Elva in two languages.

"Want some galletas?" as she offered her friend cookies during lunch.

And "Where are mis hojas?," to herself, as she searched hurriedly for papers.

But away from the playground, whether walking down the hall to the library or on a field trip to the zoo, she never left her teacher's side. Silent and serious, she hung onto Miss Anderson's pant-leg or skirt, staring intensely when the teacher spoke to her. Puzzled but accepting, Miss Anderson responded with a gentle hand on the bows in Celina's hair.

Celina never again openly displayed the fear that gripped her the first day of school and continued for months. Yet, even now, as an adult recalling her first year in school, she wiped away tears as she shared her story with me.

"I was five years old and really scared. My mother and grandmother had raised me in the Barrio. Everyone spoke Spanish, so I only heard English on television. I was cherished and special. No preschools or daycare, just lots of hugs and friends.

"But the local schools were tough and my mother wanted a way out of the Barrio for me. Just before I started Kindergarten, we moved from our neighborhood to a tiny apartment on the north side of town. We saw my grandmother and friends on weekends, but I was so lonely.

"My mother would lecture me every day in Spanish, 'Mija. When you go to school, there are some things you *must* do. You look at the teacher. All the time. I don't care what the other kids are doing! Understand? The teacher is the most important person. If you watch her and listen, she'll like you and know you want to learn.

"When the teacher looks at you, smile! It doesn't matter if you're unhappy or upset about something. When she looks at you, it means you're special to her. So always smile.'

"My mother got up early each morning and fixed a huge breakfast. She dressed me in clothes she ironed late at night after work. And she fixed my hair with fiesta bows, each day a different style. She told me how pretty I looked and walked me to school. At the door, she always hugged me and reminded me to pay attention and smile."

Now in her thirties, Celina has a doctorate in Bilingual Education. She's a college professor and a consultant who develops language programs for Spanish-speaking children across the country.

"Somehow, in my lectures, I always come back to my mother and my wonderful Kinder teacher. It's as if they really understood what I needed to be successful. They're still a part of everything I do."

"Mom knew that I needed to pay attention to learn English. She also understood that the teacher would respond if I smiled at her. But I don't think Miss Anderson was fooled. She saw a scared little girl who clung to her. So she gave me love and affection. How blessed I've been in my life....

"Although he's fluent in Spanish and English, when my own son started school this year, I said 'Mijo. I don't care what your friends are doing. Remember to look at the teacher. You listen to everything she says. And always smile when she looks at you. A really big smile!'

"You know, it works!"

Parents and Teachers Together

How wise Celina's mother was. Despite her own lack of formal education, she understood how to start her daughter on a life-time road to success. Each day, she fed and dressed her with care, told her she was pretty, walked her to school, and hugged her at the door. So many children from wealthier homes would benefit from this daily attention and affection! It's wonderful to start the day knowing that you're cherished.

Celina's mother told her to listen to the teacher, not only providing a foundation for learning English, but underscoring that the adult was the most important person in the classroom. And what teacher can resist a smile from a child? Research tells us that it's the attitude of the family toward education, not the financial level, that indicates how successful a child will be in school. Indeed, a positive approach can matter more than money. Some other ways parents can support teachers are included in the chart.

In a time of rushed family schedules, many children actually prefer being at school because the structure gives them security. Parents can provide similar consistency through a quiet homework time, an established bedtime, and morning routines. Children are happiest and do best when they go to school un-rushed each day, knowing they're prepared for exams, have lunch money, and a backpack full of clean clothes for physical education. In a structured home, established study and chore times give parents and children a sense of being in control of their lives.

But sometimes things don't go well at school. Children come home angry at a classmate or teacher. Caring so much

Ways Parents Can Support Teachers

❑ Children do best when there's structure at home.

❑ Avoid criticizing the teacher in front of the child. When the child complains, you'll only be hearing one side of the story.

❑ It's best to avoid becoming defensive if teachers contact you about a problem with your child. Teachers call because they care.

❑ To be supportive, teachers and counselors like to know if there's a major positive or negative event going on in children's lives.

❑ If the child is having ongoing problems at home, contacting the teacher will let you work toward solutions together.

❑ It's good to adopt a *We* attitude with teachers.

❑ Parent-teacher conferences are important.

❑ An established meal program lets teachers know when children will eat breakfast or lunch at school.

❑ For safety measures, it's best to write down who will drop off and pick up children.

❑ Attendance is critical. Children shouldn't stay at home unless they're sick.

❑ It's important for children to be at school on time every day.

❑ Teachers should know if children will be attending after-school programs on the campus.

❑ Children should go to school with completed homework and all necessary materials.

❑ Parents might ask for ways they can help in the classroom or during evening activities at school.

❑ Avoid calling teachers at home. It's best to find out when their conference period is scheduled and call them at school.

❑ Thank the teacher—Often!

for their child's happiness, it's too easy for parents to be drawn into disagreements without full information about what *really* happened. When upset over an argument with a peer or a low grade on an exam, children tend to over-generalize their anger. When problems occur, they may expand their resentment over one issue to the entire classroom, and especially to the teacher as the adult in charge.

David, your sixth-grader, reports in disgust, "Joe hit me today. He's a real bully and Mrs. Kane lets him pick on everyone all the time. She's a lousy teacher. I hate her."

Your concerned call to Mrs. Kane the next day tells a different tale.

"Thanks for calling me, Mrs. Hunt. I was going to get in touch with you and Joe's Mom today. I'm not sure what's been going on between David and Joe this week. They're both great kids and never a discipline problem. But they've been calling each other terrible names the last few days. I moved their desks in English class yesterday, but they started pushing and shoving right after school. I stopped them before a fight broke out, because I didn't want them to be suspended. Has David mentioned anything to you? I'd really like to get to the bottom of this before it escalates."

If you'd opened this conversation in anger about David's mistreatment, you'd feel pretty foolish by now, or perhaps even defensive, insisting that it was all Joe's fault. And if you told David the night before that you agreed with him that Mrs. Kane is a poor teacher, it's likely that his behavior would become even worse in school the next day. Children don't have to accept responsibility if parents agree that the problem is the teacher's incompetence. That night, telling David about your conversation with Mrs. Kane would likely bring, "You're not going to believe *her!* Remember, you said yourself that she's been a terrible teacher all year!"

Many times, it's best to leave the teacher out of the discussion completely. Parents understand children's relationships. And when they ask what each of the children did during the confrontation, they help the young person understand the real nature of the problem.

"Mom, I didn't do anything. He came right up and just hit me. I tell you he's a bully!"

"David, even bullies look for a cause. C'mon, now, what's been going on with you two?"

In this way, David can't escape ownership for his actions by blaming someone else. This discussion becomes a lifetime lesson.

When talking to children, it's best to *always support the teacher.* If there's an important issue parents don't fully understand or if they feel a need to intervene, a non-accusatory phone call to the school usually allows adults to solve the problem together. Like anyone, teachers work best with parents who are nice to them.

My neighbor complained often that she had to "really keep after" the teachers and administrators at her children's schools. With four children, it became a full-time job tracking their school progress and contacting school personnel. Overhearing one of her phone calls, I was surprised at how this usually soft-spoken, friendly person became abrupt, even rude, talking to her daughter's teacher.

Afterwards, I asked, "Why were you so upset?"

"Oh, I've learned over the years that you have to be a thorn in the school's side to get results. You should have seen Jenny's homework last night. Too much math practice. She was complaining like crazy. I could see that it was just a lot of busy-work.

"So I called her teacher and asked what her objectives were for the assignment. She hemmed and hawed and finally said that all the students needed more math practice. I'm not sure she had any objectives at all. She'll be more careful in the future.

"I don't tell my kids when I call or they'd be embarrassed. But I know that they get more attention because the school respects parents who care."

Weeks later, returning from a meeting with her son's high school counselor, she was really upset.

"We were just scheduling his classes for next year. The counselor was called outside by the secretary and I picked up Scott's file and started looking through his records. I can't believe what one of his teachers wrote last year!"

"What?" I asked, curious if she were going to sue the school for a negative comment about her son.

Only a head-shake. "She wrote, 'Scott is a great kid, has a wonderful attitude, and is really easy to work with. But his mother is a pain in the neck!'"

To her dismay, I put my head down on the table and roared.

When Children are Ill

Contrary to my neighbor's belief, sometimes quiet support can be the most effective. Teachers appreciate parents whose children have good attendance and are always at school on time. Equally important is keeping a sick child home. Cold and flu season finds many students sneezing on each other and the teacher. My graduate interns are frequently ill, since they're exposed to so many sick children daily. At times, they report calling parents who are in a meeting or have busy jobs and can't pick up their son or daughter. So the child stays at school, miserable and infecting others. Parents aren't trying to neglect children's needs. They just don't have a way out of their own inflexible work schedule.

The best way to handle illness is to have a back-up plan in place. Is there one parent whose schedule is more flexible on certain days? A neighbor or family member who stays at home who can pick up a sick child? If so, it's best to have contact phone numbers and to pay others for their time. While there are agencies that send people to your home to baby-sit sick children for the day, your family will feel more comfortable if you have someone you know and whom your child likes.

Instead of waiting to see how ill the child becomes, it's usually best to go to the family doctor immediately. Claiming it's just "allergies," many children object to doctor's visits. Yet, having a clear diagnosis and preventative medicines for the future will keep them healthier. Likely, they'll be back in school the next day without missing any classes. Parents also help by leaving prescription medicines with the school nurse, both to speed recovery from an illness or for emergencies.

As I entered the middle-school hallway, the loud, terrible sound of out-of-control coughing and wheezing assaulted me. In the main office, a young man sat doubled-over on a chair, his head bent almost to the floor as he gasped loudly for air. Helplessly, the many adults crammed in the small space could only stand and watch.

Visibly upset, the nurse explained, "His inhaler's at home and we don't have any asthma medicine for him. His Dad's out-of-town and we can't reach his mother. We just called for an ambulance. He's getting worse and he's very upset and embarrassed. The stress is only adding to the attack."

As I looked about, the magnitude of the emergency became clearer. While the Principal comforted him, she had to ignore the needs of more than six hundred other students and put aside all administrative concerns of the school. Phones went unanswered as concerned secretaries rushed about, keeping other students, parents, and faculty out of the office. Gossip spread among classmates in the hallway and the student knew he was the topic.

Between coughs, he waved his hand angrily for everyone to leave him alone. But of course they couldn't. I left as the ambulance stretcher arrived. The school nurse was to accompany him to the hospital so he wouldn't feel frightened and alone.

I couldn't help thinking how awful his parents would feel if they could see him so distressed and dangerously ill. Would the asthma attack have been avoided if his medicine were kept at the school? Perhaps not, but likely it wouldn't have been as serious, requiring hospitalization.

Maybe this family lived far away from relatives, or grandparents were unable to help. But there had to be *someone* to call. A note in his record about reliable emergency contacts and procedures could have immeasurably lessened his, and the school's, concerns.

Supporting Children's Daily Needs at School

Other important information for records should include which after-school activities students will be attending regularly and the names of adults who are authorized to take them home. Will the student buy lunch at school? If so, it's good to take advantage of the long-term lunch tickets many schools now offer, so that children don't have to bring money every day.

I'm reminded of the story told by a friend who teaches Kindergarten. One of her students arrived one morning with a note: "Dear Mrs.White. I haven't had time to go grocery shopping, so there wasn't anything to fix for Kimberly's lunch. She doesn't like the school food. Could you fix her a sandwich or find something she'd like to eat? Thanks." Kimberly brought no lunch and no money. Counting to ten in a few directions, the teacher found some peanut butter and jelly in the cafeteria and instructed an unhappy Kimberly to make her own sandwich.

As a result of federal focus, many school cafeterias are serving healthier food these days. When parents are hurried, it's best to have children eat at school or make their own lunch at home the night before. Whether in emergencies such as the student suffering the asthma attack or in daily situations of a child appearing without food, these situations take educators away from their real job of teaching children.

It's also important to let teachers know if there are home factors that are impacting the child. While it's good to be aware of children's accomplishments so teachers can congratulate and recognize them, it's more important to know about issues that can cause a strong emotional reaction. Is there a new stepfather, baby, or a divorce? Is the family planning to move? Has a military parent been sent overseas? Has a grandparent become ill? When students suffer quietly, so does their work. We've all responded to a teacher's empathy. The Japanese saying rings true: *One kind word can warm three winter months.*

The Civility Crisis

There's a virus spreading across America today. We see it in road and air rage, as people become crazed with anger when perceiving they've been wronged or inconvenienced. Out-of-control and feeling justified in lashing out at others, they respond with violence. There's also a much broader social acceptance of rudeness now, from language to physical gestures. More people swear openly, while some become exceedingly confrontational, goading others into an argument.

It's likely a response to hurried, pressured lives, where frustration is just below the surface as we meet tight schedules and become overwhelmed by a lack of social support. Today, we're more alone and physically threatened for our own safety and that of our family. Worries about finances and job security add tremendous anxiety. We can't be late for work, so we take it out on a driver who cuts across our lane of traffic. We're tired ourselves, so we don't give up our bus seat to the elderly. Someone might steal our shopping bag, so we can't make eye contact with anyone as we walk down the street. Another airline flight cancellation angers us enough to yell at the ticket agent.

It's a tougher world these days. So we respond in kind. But the children are watching, both in person and on television. They hear us swear, shout, and complain. They learn not to give up a bus seat and that there are times when it's justified to condemn someone if service is poor. As actor Fred Astaire commented, "The hardest job kids face today is learning good manners without seeing any."

Reports indicate that they spend forty percent less time with their parents than thirty years ago. Many are less disciplined and even openly rude to adults. Often today's children have under-developed social skills. They start preschool earlier and enjoy fewer direct peer interactions if they spend concentrated periods of time watching television and videos. With large classes, teachers don't have the time to dwell on traditional politeness and manners. When parents come home from a busy day, understandably they don't want to spend their time arguing with children. So they avoid disciplining a rude child, in effect reinforcing bad behavior.

Children also learn from sitcoms and videos. During prime time, they're seeing countless shows where people handle confrontation by cheating, lying, and shouting. From Pokémon to MTV, they're observing violence and pain. Even parents who carefully monitor children's viewing have come to accept these negative interactions as a part of the daily media experience.

Laura Bush observed, "Television is no substitute for a parent." A major reason for the civility crisis appears to be children's ability to tune into sex and violence any part of the day. They see murders and attempted rapes more often than helpfulness toward others. When these incidents are in their lives daily, they imitate them. So women are viewed as dumb and sex objects, while men are aggressive and challenging. Without adults to turn off the television and to discuss positive ways of behaving, many children take guns to school or act-out verbally and physically.

Teachers feel strongly about the lack of discipline in their classrooms. Behavior problems have become a primary reason why they quit the profession. Students' not listening in class and basic rudeness would never have been tolerated in traditional schools. Today, they're minor issues in comparison with the students who swear at, verbally abuse, or even physically threaten teachers. When I work with beginning teachers, their greatest concerns are not about teaching content or motivating students, but about maintaining order in their classrooms. Some of their students will be arrogant and disdainful, making teaching difficult and learning impossible.

I recently visited a suburban high school. As I walked along the path toward the entrance, four male students sat on a wall enjoying their lunch hour. But as I approached, their manner changed. One began mocking me openly and threateningly.

"Hey, Miss! You got a pass? A kid at the school? 'Cause we ain't gonna let you in if you don't."

A bit nervous, I kept walking.

"What, you're deaf? We're talking to you. Get over here. Now!"

The four of them laughed and their comments accelerated.

"What, you scared? You better be. Move fast!"

I ignored them and continued toward the door as they shouted after me, delighted with themselves.

That was the problem. For my own safety, I ignored them. While it appeared to be a smart thing for me to do, it told them they could get away with abusing adults.

When I described the upsetting interaction to several teachers, one commented sadly, "Now you know what we live with every day." How depressing.

Stemming the Tide

If I felt we had to put up with these behaviors in our schools, I'd leave Education for an easier profession. But I believe that together, parents and teachers can both handle the civility crisis and create young people who are respectful and polite. The most important way to do this is to have strong rules and guidelines both at home and school. In his book "Mr. Rogers Talks to Parents," Fred Rogers writes:

Call them rules or call them limits, good ones, I believe, have this in common: they serve reasonable purposes; they are practical within a child's capability; they are consistent; and they are an expression of loving concern.

The chart includes a number of ways parents can improve children's behaviors. Household and classroom rules are critical bases for letting young people understand adult expectations. It's important for parents and teachers to react consistently, both when children follow or ignore rules. It's important to explain why we expect certain behaviors and how other people will be impacted by our actions. In order to set a lifetime pattern, we can begin discipline with very young children by telling them "*No!*" and explaining appropriate actions in each specific situation.

Without excusing children's conduct because they're upset or not feeling well, we can set standards. If adults are too understanding, children develop excuses for rudeness. It's better to intervene the minute a young person is out-of-line. Requiring "Please" and "Thank you" isn't old-fashioned. These courtesies remind all of us that we should show appreciation when others go out of their way to be helpful. Requiring children to be polite with everyone underscores basic human respect.

Children shouldn't be nicer to some adults or peers because they like them better or because of status. Snobbishness can start young, or we can nip it in the bud. An elementary school Principal once explained to a large audience of children, "Everyone in this school has a really necessary job. Your teachers are just as important as I am, because they help you learn and grow. If no one worked in the cafeteria, you wouldn't have lunch and you'd be hungry all afternoon. The custodians who clean our classrooms give us pride and a beautiful school. And the bus drivers bring you here and home every day safely. Our jobs are different, but one is not more important than the other. So you have to treat *all* adults with the same respect *all* the time." What a wonderful attitude to impart to children!

And as Celina's mother knew, parents can help their student's performance at school by frequent reminders to listen to the teacher. When their child is punished at school for a behavioral infraction, parents should reinforce the teacher by telling the child how disappointed they are, and as appropriate, by removing a privilege at home. Losing a favorite television show or visit with friends reminds children that parents won't accept out-of-line actions at school. Reflecting on their

Ways Parents Can Improve Children's Behaviors

❑ Set household rules and limits. Immediately enforce them if the child misbehaves. Have consequences for both positive and negative behaviors.

❑ Explain why the child should behave in a certain way (i.e., using "quiet voices" inside the house; not running or interrupting conversations).

❑ In order to set a lifetime pattern, begin discipline with very young children. If they do something wrong, tell them "No," and explain appropriate behavior in that situation.

❑ Intervene the minute children say something rude to you, another adult, or a child.

❑ Never excuse children's behavior because they're "upset" or "not feeling well."

❑ Others rarely enjoy watching children's intrusive behaviors. It's best to stop misbehavior in public places right away.

❑ Teach children to listen and to enter conversations quietly and respectfully.

❑ Direct them to always say "Please" and "Thank you," both to peers and adults.

❑ Tell children to be polite to teachers and school personnel at all times. When there's a discipline problem, support the teacher, not the child.

❑ When the teacher reports a behavioral infraction, remove a privilege at home as well (i.e., favorite TV show, time with friends).

❑ Restrict privileges and allowance when misbehaviors occur at home. Explain to children how they are to behave in similar circumstances in the future.

❑ Don't let children talk you out of punishments through promises they'll behave better in the future.

❑ Use "time-out" in the child's room or in a quiet place if the child is rude or shows negative behaviors.

❑ Err on the side of having many rules and expectations for your children.

❑ Model appropriate behavior. Avoid negative comments or actions toward others, swearing, or uncontrollable anger. When you're upset, discuss your feelings with children and describe how you're managing them.

childhood, many parents remember hoping that their own mother or father wouldn't hear about trouble at school. Almost always, it would result in a second punishment at home. Yet, too often today, the child complains about being treated unfairly and the parent charges up to the school to protest a punishment.

Some years ago, I met with a mother who was concerned about her preschool son. Describing Keith as sensitive and gifted, she couldn't understand why he had been asked to leave one preschool already and now was in jeopardy of being "expelled" from another. While the four-year-old was very active in my office, his movement wasn't the real problem. His mouth was.

He interrupted adult conversation constantly. While I tried to ignore him and continued talking to his mother, she stopped each time to answer him.

Keith's voice elevated almost to a shout so that adults couldn't speak.

To me, "Well, this is a really stupid place. Don't you have games or something around here that're fun for kids? Otherwise, I'm leaving!"

His mother hugged him and said, "You're right. This must be boring for you. Help me tell Dr. Waldron about your teacher and then we'll go."

Now happily on stage, he mimicked an exaggerated female walk, clearly imitating his teacher. His mother grinned proudly.

"All Miss Larsen wants us to do is sit and read. I already know everything she's trying to teach me. When I tell her that I just want to play videogames, she tells me to go sit down.

"I can't stand her. She's just a real b____!," loudly and with a naughty smile.

His mother laughed. "I know I shouldn't let him use that word. But it's true. She really is a b____. They want *him* to leave the school and *she's* the real problem."

Finally quiet, the boy stood nodding with his hand on his mother's arm. The two of them were a team and the teacher was odd-person-out. Watching in disbelief, I didn't have to ask why he'd been expelled from his first preschool.

It was obvious that the mother's attitude and support egged him on. It would be impossible to help them as long as she considered Keith sensitive, when indeed he was terribly rude. After that day, she and I met for several sessions, but I was never able to convince her that the problem was her need to take charge of her son's behavior. During subsequent years, they visited a number of psychologists, but to no avail.

Seeing her socially, I asked how Keith was doing.

"He's a ninth grader this year, with scores off the chart. They tested him again a few years ago and said he's gifted."

Frowning, "Of course they also said he's emotionally disturbed. He still hates the inflexible structure of the school and his teachers don't understand him. The shame of American education is that if you don't fit in the box, they don't want you. We've all tried so hard. I really feel sorriest for Keith."

Frankly, I felt sorrier for his teachers. I could only imagine what this bright, arrogant, and undisciplined teenager was capable of saying and doing these days. The saddest thing was that he was an unhappy child who would carry these feelings of being misunderstood throughout his adulthood. He was prepared to become a difficult colleague, husband, and father. He already demanded more privileges than the world allowed.

Without being overly strict, it's best for adults to err on the side of having a large number of rules and expectations. Through externally-imposed structure, gradually children internalize appropriate behaviors. But it's important to be role models ourselves. Keith's mother used inappropriate language when she described his teacher. He heard it at home and took it to school. In his house, he was on an equal footing with adults, so if she said it, he could too. How much better to have supported his teacher, and if Keith called her a name to stop him immediately with a sharp, "We don't ever call teachers names! Let's talk about why you're upset."

Since children model on adults, it's also important to discuss how you feel when you're upset and how you're handling it.

Driving home, Dad comments to his daughter, "You know, I had a terrible day at work and this traffic makes me crazy. I'm glad I have you for company. Let's talk about something to cheer me up. What good things happened to you at school today?"

Grumbling, "Nothing. I'm tired too, Dad. And I think I failed the Science test." In a raised voice, "I've got hours of homework tonight and I won't even get to watch any TV!"

"You had a bad day too! We need to cheer ourselves up. Right now! Find that music station you like on the radio. And you should pick out a half-hour show to watch tonight. You're pressed for time, so we can tape the rest of them for you."

How much better than yelling at another driver or complaining about the boss or teacher. A simple acknowledgement that things don't always go our way, but we can divert anger into pleasure. Sharing the burden through conversation lets the father become closer to his daughter while she observes mature ways to handle upset. Good solutions, like treating yourself in a small way or working around a problem, help children put daily concerns in perspective by not over-reacting. As a friend once commented, "A real problem is one that can't be solved by time or money." As children learn to handle the smaller issues in life, they're better prepared to handle the larger ones.

Requiring Good Behavior

Recently waiting at a doctor's office, I saw a teenager enter with his grandfather. With few chairs available, they sat separately. I was taken by how frequently each looked up at the other and mouthed quiet messages or pointed out something in a magazine.

"Would you like something to drink?" the grandfather asked, pointing to a juice machine.

"Yeah, that would be great, Sir," as he walked over for the coins.

He came back with two drinks and the change.

"You looked a little thirsty yourself," handing him bottled water. "And, Grandpa, thanks for picking me up at school. Mom was tied up and it means a lot."

"No problem."

When someone vacated a seat close to the teen, he waved and patted the chair. The older man moved and soon the two were involved in a lively conversation. Shoulders touching, they laughed often as the boy shared something that happened at school that day. His name finally called, he walked toward the examining rooms. He turned around quickly.

"Grandpa, it would be OK if you came inside with me too."

Later, as they left the examining room together, the teen's mother arrived. She hugged her son and kissed her father, thanking him for picking the boy up from school after a football accident. Again, with a smile, the grandfather said, "No problem."

As he and his grandson walked outside the building, I commented to the mother how impressed I was with her son's respectful behavior. The bare finger on her left hand and her use of "I" told me she was a single mother.

"Kids are kids, you know," she reflected. "It wasn't always this way, so I've had to work at it. But in my house, rudeness just doesn't fly. He's always loved his grandfather, but I've required him to show it in everyday ways that matter."

Such basic wisdom, as the boy and his grandfather laughed outside during an animated conversation.

When Being There Matters

Sally Bowers is a petite blonde, only 5'2" tall and 114 pounds. She's a Registered Nurse in Anchorage, Alaska, specializing in treatment of cancer patients. Sally is also a National and World Champion Powerlifter. In Bench Press competition, lying flat on her back and holding the barbell at arm's length, she lowers 132 pounds down to her chest and presses it back up again. Standing upright with a 298-pound barbell resting on the back of her muscular shoulders, she squats down and rises back up to her original position. And in the Deadlift competition, she grips a 352-pound barbell from the floor and stands upright.

She began Powerlifting at a local gym with her teenage children, Jason and Jennifer, while her husband, Paul, watched with interest. As her amazing ability became obvious, coaches encouraged her to join the State team, the "Alaska Iron Maidens." Within a few years, she was travelling from South Africa to the Czech Republic, breaking world records and winning international awards. In addition to placing and winning in numerous competitions, she has been the Alaska State Champion, and USA Powerlifting Women's Champion. In 1997, she was the World Champion Women's Best Lifter.

Clearly, Sally is a powerful woman. Between the families she's supported through cancer and the rigorous training for her championships, her life is both full and meaningful. Yet, she prioritizes her children and been an important influence in their lives. One of her proudest moments was in her son's JROTC classroom.

"Jason was 17 and a Junior then," she reflects. "It was 'Parents' Participation Day.' You know, one of those times where you go to all of your children's classes. I went with him to each of his academic subjects, but he really lit up when we went to JROTC. It had sustained him all through high school.

"He introduced me to the teacher and class. The kids were doing their physical fitness exam that day, competing over the number of sit-ups and push-ups they could do in a two-minute period. I guess Jason had told some of them I was into Powerlifting, because they asked me if I'd work out with the girls.

"It wasn't common for parents to be involved here. The Dads looking on decided not to compete. But with a student holding my feet, I started doing sit-ups. Within the first few minutes, a number of the girls stopped in fatigue. I kept on going. Pretty soon everyone quit and was watching me. They started cheering me on. It was really fun!"

In both tests, a few girls reached the *Excellent* category for their age, while the majority performed at the *Satisfactory* or *Good* level. Sally surpassed *Outstanding*, the highest level. She set a new all-time JROTC female record with 42 push-ups and 90 sit-ups in each two-minute interval!

"That day, Jason was posting scores. As he listed me the winner, along with the time and number of sit-ups and push-ups, you could just see his feathers fluffing! He was so proud and glowing. It was really special for him, not just to have me there as part of the JROTC group, but to know that his Mom could jump ahead of girls his age and set a new record for them to beat. And he got to post the score. Other students visited the room throughout the day, saw the new record, and commented to him about it."

Today Jason is a Marine. A graduate of the Aviation Electronics School, he's had many opportunities to develop as a leader. His future in the Military is already underscored by recommendations from Alaska senators and even the Secretary of the Navy.

"Jason has always been a neat young person and a gentleman," Sally comments proudly. "But the Military has made him even wiser."

Despite her titles, medals, and records, Sally Bowers looks back on that day in her son's classroom as a life-time memory.

"It was just a *great* experience."

Parents at School

Most of us will never lift a 352-pound barbell or do 90 sit-ups in two minutes. But we can appreciate that those times when our children recognize us as special are some of the finest in our lives. Despite personal honors and a busy life, Sally put Jason first. Taking time away from work and training, she spent the day at his school. No wonder he's gone on for more education himself. Jason's subsequent Marine leadership and physical training are a tribute to his family and their involvement in his life.

Parents and grandparents need to become part of school activities. Sometimes, they can volunteer to tutor or help sponsor an event. Other times, like Sally, they might share a special skill, making their children proud and other students more aware. If they keep away from school, they appear disinterested. When they're involved, they send powerful messages to their children about love, involvement, and the importance of education.

Adults also can have fun. In an early childhood center in Copenhagen, an elderly man proudly showed me his design of special shoes with a padded metal brace attached. They allowed a young boy born with a birth defect to stand for the first time. As we talked, a two-year old scooted by in a play car. "I molded that seat and shoulder harness for him. He can't walk yet, but he wanted to ride around like the other children."

When I asked him if he were a carpenter by trade, he laughed.

"No, but I do have a grandson with cerebral palsy. A few years ago, I adapted some toys and a wheelchair so he could move about more easily. I hung around the school so much that they began to ask me about modifying equipment for some other kids. Now it's become a hobby and it seems like I'm here all the time!"

What adults can offer are not just hobbies, but gifts, to children, teachers, and themselves. Watching your son grin proudly as he records your accomplishments or helping a young child stand for the first time are what life is all about. In many ways, we're not giving of ourselves, but to ourselves. As Sally Bowers reflects, it's "just a great experience."

Unleashing a Wonderful Potential

I could have overlooked John as he first entered my tenth-grade Honors English class that October. No name. No introduction. Certainly, no smile. Just, "Where do you want me to sit?"

"Hi, you must be John. I'm Mrs. Waldron. Welcome to our crazy class! Actually, there's a lot of fun people here you'll want to get to know."

"Right. Can I sit there?" He moved toward the far back to a seat next to the file cabinets and totally out of class view.

"Nope, that one's for students overwhelmed by hormones on any given day. Jake, please move a desk up here next to you so you can teach John the ropes."

Class finally settled, I introduced John and asked him to tell us where he was from. I noticed a few students smile knowingly. Clearly they had been through this earlier in the day.

"Everywhere and nowhere. Military. My Dad gets transferred a lot."

"Hobbies?"

"None. No time."

"Brothers and sisters? Pets?"

"No. Just me."

Julius Caesar seemed an uproarious comedy after his uptight responses.

Weeks passed and John literally became an unremarkable student. He showed no interest in class discussions, at times sullenly lowering his head to the desk, feigning sleep so I wouldn't call on him. No activities. No friends. Never rude, he just ignored us all.

But he always completed homework, however haphazardly. And his was among the 143 essays I received every Friday. That week I read John's paper with surprise. To date, his writing had been as unremarkable as his class performance. But in this essay on "The Best Place I've Ever Been," he excitedly described his previous three years in Frankfurt, Germany. He detailed how he and friends would "...meet at the *Bahnhof* on weekends and hop the train" to attend Euro soccer matches and German football, watch cars whiz by when they travelled the *Autobahn*, and "with everyone laughing hysterically," use their own form of language to communicate in the city. He added,

"Those were the best and quickest years of my life. Then the usual transfers started to happen. A few of my friends moved on with their families. Finally, my Dad got his papers and we ended up here."

That was how he concluded his paper, with the sad note "We ended up here." No wonder he kept his distance, afraid to re-attach to friends he'd have to leave. Without hope for the future, he could only anticipate another move and more losses.

But besides its telling content, there was something different about this week's paper. John had finally responded with enthusiasm, actually with a writing flair.

As he entered the classroom on Monday, I pulled him aside.

"John, your essay this week was wonderful! Your first *A*! You wrote beautifully—great choice of words. You really pulled me into some of those times in Germany."

A smile. "Thanks."

"Would it embarrass you if I asked you to read that part to the class? I'd like for them to see really good work."

Hesitation. "It's OK, but could you read it?"

I shared several paragraphs with the class, pointing out John's strong use of adjectives and inclusion of interesting German words. He looked down at his desk while receiving some good-natured teasing.

"Hey, John!"

"Will Shakespeare himself!"

Following excerpts from a few other students' papers, we discussed the power of "enthusiastic writing" and then moved on to the day's work.

A thought was hatching. As he left, "Again, great writing, John. I'm looking forward to reading your next essay."

Recently, I had read Rosenthal and Jacobson's study where researchers randomly selected some first graders. They told their teachers that these children were actually very gifted, but "late bloomers." They assured the teachers that with nurturing, the children were ready to reach their wonderful potential. This would be their year to shine.

And they did! With the teachers' enhanced expectations and attention, by spring the selected children out-performed peers who were just as smart. The key was that the teachers expected more, provided extra opportunities for success, and praised children's efforts, encouraging them further.

Here goes, I thought. *Poor John.*

Next Friday's essay came due. John marked a few last-minute changes and passed his on. It was longer than required. When I instructed students to read another's paper and write their reactions to the content, John smiled broadly at Jake's comments:

Shakespeare,
You've done it again! I was even interested. I marked a few places where you're a little stiff. Relax! Otherwise, quit showing us up! —Jake

Always delightful and positive, Jake must have been in on my research project. As was Jenny Ballard, the Journalism teacher I approached that afternoon with "I need your help...."

The following week she asked John to see her after school. Jenny told him that she'd heard of his reputation as a strong writer and needed him on the newspaper staff for the big holiday edition.

She elaborated to me later, "He hedged at first—said he might not have time. But when I explained that he just needed to give it a try with the December newspaper, he agreed. We'll hook him. I just know it."

And they did. After December, she put John in charge of sports writing, clearly an area where he was knowledgeable. He had to attend weekly games and gradually became friends with other students on and off the news staff. As spring continued, "hanging out" after the games, they argued loudly over team members' performance. An excited, "John, why don't you write...!" became common.

When Jenny and he initiated "Things You may have Missed," human interest photos around school events, his father bought him a good camera. John turned out to be a really talented photographer, with wonderful sensitivity. Students began to anticipate the amusing, and at times, poignant scenes he depicted: the lonely student in the wheelchair looking longingly from the sidelines as her classmates played field hockey; the spelling error in the Honor Society's induction announcement; the Principal throwing a temper tantrum at the umpire during a baseball game. John caught it all.

In my classroom, he never lowered his head to his desk again. Smiling more often and quietly friendly now, he was respected. He was inseparable from Jake, who continued to call him "Shakespeare" and goad him on to new projects. And John developed a following of admirers across the school who stopped him in the hallway to whisper clever suggestions about an issue he might cover in a column or a photo he should take.

A number of his candid shots appeared in the Yearbook that spring. The following fall, he was selected unanimously as Editor of the newspaper. John's parents became his greatest supporters. He and his Dad set up a darkroom at home and learned processing together. His Mom approached community businesses and raised a great deal of money for newspaper and Yearbook ads.

He went on to next year's teachers. I missed him. I really did. This plain, vanilla student had blossomed beyond me and taken off brilliantly.

Several years passed and we all moved on. Now a graduate student, one afternoon I walked in snowfall across a frozen sidewalk in front of Syracuse University's Newhouse Communications Building.

"Mrs. Waldron?" A tall, dark-haired student rushed to catch up with me.

No recognition. "Yes?"

Hand outstretched, John re-introduced himself.

"I'm a student here now. My Dad decided we'd had enough moves and he retired. So this is home."

"Great, John! Have you decided on a major?"

He waved a gloved hand at the modernistic structure behind us.

"Journalism, of course."

That snowy afternoon, the smile on his face told it all.

School, Friends, and Family

These many years later, as I read the *New York Times* or *International Herald*, I still look for John's name. But even if I never find it, I'll always marvel at the level of accomplishment and happiness he derived from the school and family who helped him realize his future. Optimism grew from depression through a true village of support.

Instead of being threatened, Jake became an encouraging friend. Teacher Jenny Ballard wouldn't take "No!" for an answer. In a positive way, she forced John to participate in the newspaper and then worked with him to expand obvious talents. Building on the school's efforts, his father encouraged John's photography skills and their time together through a shared hobby. His mother supported him by finding sponsors for school projects. And peers elected him a leader. Once John was recognized, he blossomed. His optimism for the future developed because others publicly acknowledged that he was talented and special.

While it's harder to raise children today, in many ways it's more exciting than ever. Our hurried life style alone can seem overwhelming at times. And when life throws a curve ball, we may wonder about our family's ability to take charge and go on. But then we look at the children like John. With our help, they're brimming with potential, excited about the future, planning for next week while today's still here.

Through sharing life's great and small challenges, adults get in touch with young people. With the support of grandparents, sisters, brothers, and teachers, we're raising a healthy generation of tomorrow's adults. In the meantime, children are discovering special things about themselves, talents in music or science, interpersonal skills that make them caring friends and strong leaders. There's always an involvement, a hobby or activity, that can make children winners. And by requiring their helpfulness with others, we give them both responsibility and perspective.

Their potential isn't dormant, waiting to be discovered. It's there in the daily spirit of childhood, the energy and bounce that we adults envy as children race past or pour out in exciting conversations with friends. And when life gives "lemons," children's lemonade can be even sweeter with the protection and direction of adults who care. As Althea Gibson once commented, "No matter what accomplishments you achieve, somebody helps you." It's good to be that person for a child.

Lessons Learned

A kind act only requires a moment, yet its impact can last a life-time.

After parents and family members, teachers are the most important people in children's worlds.

It's hard to fail if your parents and teachers won't let you.

Children who are cherished learn better.

Structure reassures students by telling them what to expect in an unpredictable world.

When parents support the school, children complain less.

Angry words with a teacher rarely have the desired effect.

When children bring home problems from school, parents hear only one side of the story.

School forms a protective shield around young people.

If the family situation is bad, school may be the child's only refuge.

Children and teachers should never have to worry about physical safety.

Young people look to adults to learn how to behave. When we swear, shout, and complain, they're watching.

Anger and cross words have no place in our homes or class-rooms.

When a child misbehaves, become upset with the behavior but not the child.

Consequences tell children that others are watching their behavior.

Conferences between teachers and parents should be like friends working together to achieve a common goal.

Parents are under-rated. So are teachers.

The classroom is a child's home during the day.

Every time a child learns something new, so does a teacher.

Unleashing children's potential means removing the chains from their creativity and promise.

References

Anthony, E.J. (1974). The syndrome of the psychologically invulnerable child. In *The child and his family*, Vol. 4: *Vulnerable Children*, eds. E.J. Anthony & C. Koupernik, 3-15. New York: Wiley.

Burger, J.V. (1994). Keys to Survival: Highlights in resilience research. *Journal of Emotional and Behavioral Problems*, 3 (2), 6-10.

Elkind, D. (1988). *The hurried child*. Reading, MA: Addison-Wesley.

Gardner, H. (1993). *Multiple intelligences*. New York: Basic Books.

Goleman, D. (1997). E*motional intelligence*. New York: Bantam Books.

Lee, C. (1992). *Faking it*. Portsmouth, NH: Boynton/Cook.

Pipher, M. (2000). *Another country*. New York: Berkley Publishing Group.

Rogers, F. (1994). *Mr. Rogers talks with parents*. New York: Barnes and Noble Distribution.

Segal, J. (1988). Teachers have enormous power in affecting a child's self-esteem. *Brown University Child Behavior and Development Newsletter*, 4: 1-3.

Weinreb, M.L. (January, 1997). Be a resiliency mentor: You may be a lifesaver for a high-risk child. *Young Children*, 14-20.

Werner, E.E., & Smith, R.S. (1982). *Vulnerable but invincible: A longitudinal study of resilient children and youth*. New York: McGraw-Hill.